Praise for

# *Lola's Luck:*
# *My Life Among the California Gypsies*

"A wild and bittersweet adventure into a world none but Machvaia Gypsies know."

—Susan Sarandon

"*Lola's Luck* is a nourishing Romani studies stew freshly cooked up as a romantic self-narrating potboiler. This very private recipe for general consumption is an affable and affordable book-gift from Carol Miller, one of the most widely-cited among contemporary American Romani-studies scholars, and a specialist on California Machvaia customs and ritual behavior."

—David J. Nemeth, *Romani Studies*

# Early praise for

# *The Church of Cheese:*
# *Gypsy Ritual in the American Heyday*

"Carol Miller's book is the first among the very few that deal with one particular Romani American population—the Vlax Roma—because it is written from the rare perspective of the outsider-insider. The author describes in intimate detail the challenges faced by a people whose culture, and indeed whose very existence, has been threatened by the yádo or outside world. This is a book that will be as informative to many young Roma as it will surely be to the ethnographer, and will, one hopes, dispel the 'Esmeralda and Carmen' Gypsy image once and for all."

—Ian Hancock
Director, The Romani Archives and Documentation Center,
The University of Texas at Austin
Represented the Romani people at the United Nations

"When you understand why the title of this charming, informative exploration into the world of American Roma people is so apt, you will also know why Carol Miller is unique among scholars of Gypsy life. *The Church of Cheese* is an extremely compelling read. Take up this book; you will find yourself in the hands of the best possible guide to life among Gypsies in the U.S.A."

—William Kornblum
Chair, Center for Urban Research
Professor of Sociology
Graduate Center, City University of New York

# The Church of Cheese

## Gypsy Ritual in the American Heyday

CAROL MILLER

GEMMA

BOSTON

First published by GemmaMedia in 2010.

GemmaMedia
230 Commerical Street
Boston, MA 02109
www.gemmamedia.com

Printed in the United States of America

13   12   11   10   09      1   2   3   4   5

ISBN: 978-1-934848-61-6

**Library of Congress Cataloging-in-Publication Data**

[to come]

Carol's connection to Gypsy life is remarkable and her understanding of the Gypsy people and their customs is very rare.

I met Carol briefly when I was only twenty-five years old, just before I left my family for an American life. I so wanted that American freedom.

I returned home twenty years later when my mother got ill and found many things changed. The Gypsy way of life, as I knew it, was gone.

Carol and I began a friendship that has lasted over thirty years. No other relationship can match my connection to Carol. She understands and shares my love for both worlds.

Carol is welcome in many Gypsy homes, largely because of her respect for the women. They share what it is like to be a Gypsy and what it is like to be an American.

I know is Carol is a woman of great passion; she would have to be to transform herself for the good of our people. If future Gypsies remember the past, it will be because of her written words and the love she felt for all of us.

Carol is no longer an Outsider; we have adopted her. This is where she dreams best.

To your honor, Carol.

—*Machvanka Anastasia Todorovich, April 21, 2009*

# Contents

# A Song, and a Poem, and an Origin Myth

*O Lord, Make Me a Bird, so I Can Fly, to the top of the Church!*
*And if I Lie, Let Me Die!* (translated from Romani)

In the Sixties, Duda, Lola's daughter-in-law, often sang this song at parties and when we went to Seattle nightclubs to celebrate the Machvaia women's "night out."

\*   \*   \*

### Devils Dancing

*Chasing my warrior spirit away,*
*I am the tree.*
*Do not take my fruit and cut my roots.*
*My father's sky has rained on me.*
*My mother earth has held me.*
*The sun gave me a yellow crown.*
*I stand.*
   *Waterfalls, bushes*
   *Full of gold,*
   *Air of flight,*
   *Come chase the devils tonight.*

Anastasia, Lola's niece through marriage, sent me this poem. She said the dancing devils are the small fears and strange thoughts that race through the mind, unbidden.

\* \* \*

*The reason Gypsies have no church and the Gadzé (non-Gypsies) do, Katy said, is that God made a church of cheese for the Gypsies and a church of stone for the Gadzé. But the Gypsies got hungry and ate theirs. After telling me this, Katy admitted she wasn't entirely sure The Church of Cheese was true. Her mother Lola made a face and insisted it was: "Anyhow, I like to believe that," she said.*

*Bibi said, when she was a girl, the people would joke that long, long ago, when they were very hungry, they had traded their church for a church of cheese.*

Diane Tong's *Gypsy Folktales* (1989:103–4) offers yet another version.

"Once upon a time the Gypsies built a church of stone and the Serbs built a church of cheese.

When both churches were ready, they agreed to exchange them—the Gypsies were to give the Serbs the stone church and the Serbs to give the Gypsies the cheese church and five pence as a makeweight. The Serbs had no money so they owed the Gypsies the five pennies.

The Gypsies immediately began to eat their church, until little by little they had eaten it all up; and that is why they have no church now.

The Serbs still owe the Gypsies the five pennies, and the Gypsies are still asking for them, and that is why the Serbs have to give them alms."

# Introduction

## East Meets West

Who are the people we call Gypsies? Celebrated in song, painting, poem, and story, they represent, to many Westerners, the romance and nostalgia of an imagined nomadic lifestyle, a simpler, more physical and close-to-nature existence. Why should we not be charmed by this presumed way of life? The human race only began to gather into villages ten thousand or so years ago—modern sedentary living is only a blip in human history.

Mention Gypsies, and one stereotype that comes to mind may be the dancing Spanish Gypsy, a raven-haired woman stomping the beat of flamenco, a Carmen Amaya. Equally famous Gypsy performers like 1940's-era French jazz guitarist Django Reinhardt or the popular modern French-based band, the Gipsy Kings, fit neatly with this stereotype of the rhapsodic Romani. But Gypsies have yet to garner a place as a viable ethnic group in America. In the early 1970s, when I was teaching anthropology at a local college, most of my students hadn't the least idea any Gypsies might be found in the States. Intrigued that I actually knew some, they begged me to bring one—like a show and tell—to class."

There is an amorphous, unsubstantial quality to the topic of Gypsies. In an unending diaspora that has embraced five continents, they now share the citizenship of many nations while lacking a particular territory, or a national identity, of their own. The Gypsies I have read about and the ones I have known have lost the creation myths or the myths of origin that might point to a motherland or substantiate an ancient system of belief. Until very recently, the people kept no written records. But we know from genetics (Gresham 2001:1314–1331) (Ioviță, Schurr 2004:267–281) and the linguistic evidence presented by Ian Hancock (2002:6–16), a professor of linguistics and Gypsy origin, that some small founder populations, traveling west and north, left India about a millennium ago. They arrived in Eastern Europe a few hundred years later, certainly by the thirteenth century, and there are, even yet, and despite the horrors of Hitler's pogroms, more Gypsies now living in the Balkans than anywhere else in Europe (Fraser 1992:299).

By the fifteenth century, several traveling families of likely Gypsy origin were noted in Western European records. They claimed to be from Egypt, and, as Christian converts, eligible for food, shelter, and asylum in a "Christian" land. For a time, these travelers were called Egyptians. Eventually, the word contracted to Gypsies. There are many other names for Gypsies, such as zigeuner, bohemian, gitane, most of which have nothing to do with what a Gypsy might historically call herself.

TWO-THIRDS OF THE ROMA now resident in the States are, according to Ian Hancock (1999:2), Vlax Roma. There are also non-Roma, Romanichels (or "English Travelers"), Boyasha (basket or furniture makers), and the Bashalde (translated as musicians). Of course Gypsies, or the people we call Gypsies, have been arriving on American shores since the late sixteenth century. Hancock (2002:27) writes that Columbus brought several. Assigned to the criminal class in Portugal, Spain, England and Scotland, they were forcibly transported to the Colonies with other undesirables, and many Americans today may count, unknowingly, a Gypsy or two among their forebears.

Of course, there are many more types of Gypsies and many, many more kinds in Europe, and elsewhere. The question is, are Gypsies a single people, or many? Today, the peoples known as Gypsies are of such variety that there is literally nothing they all have in common. Very few are still nomadic. Romani, a Sanskrit-based language, is spoken by only about 2.5 million of the putative 8–10 million European Gypsies, and the many extant Roma dialects are only comprehensible to all in terms of basic words for food and family (Kovats:2001:97). Some traveling groups, like the Yenische of Germany and France, have emulated the Gypsy lifestyle for centuries and are usually classified as Gypsies. Indeed, it seems that the label of "Gypsy" has been applied to any group that looks and acts according to whatever expectations non-Gypsies have for a Gypsy. In fact, the scholars Gheorghe and Acton make a persuasive case for the likelihood that the illusion of ethnic unity has, in fact, been created by the existence of a common thread—the racism of non-Gypsies.

LARGELY FROM EUROPEAN RECORDS, we learn that much of Gypsy history was fraught with terror and abuse. The VlaX-speaking Roma, for example, were held in slavery for hundreds of years in the area now known as Romania (however, the term Roma, as Romani speakers describe themselves, does not relate to Romania). Gypsies were among the first victims of the World War II Holocaust. On occasion, Gypsy injustice continues in Eastern Europe today with persecution by racist groups, like skinheads, and legislative decisions designed to penalize and punish travelers.

A legacy of misfortune lives on in the blood and bones of the Gypsy people and, from the first, I had a pretty fair idea that becoming acquainted with their lifestyles, and getting straight answers, wouldn't be easy. The Roma in Seattle described themselves as Kalderasha or Machvaia. Descendants of Vlax-Roma, they had ample reason, historically speaking, for hostility and resentment. The children tried to drive me away with noise and scary stories; the adults tended to paranoia, suspecting the word *anthropologist* was code for CIA or FBI, something foreboding and governmental. Everything I read described Gypsies as masters of prevarication, a secretive minority historically at ostensible war with non-Gypsies. Nevertheless, at the time, having fallen between the cracks of the traditional wifely role, I think I secretly identified with anarchy and rebellion. Also, being a woman who became adult before the Sixties, before the burn-your bra era of Feminism, I was all too familiar with the practice of dissimulation.

I had first encountered Gypsies, when, a few years back, in Portland, Oregon, I signed up to volunteer with a literacy program for adults and was assigned to work with a young Gypsy couple. Two nights a week, escaping the gloom of an impending divorce, I would back cautiously down my long circular driveway, and head across town to the home of Baby Steve and Alice. At first, the teenaged pair met me at the door and seemed quite eager to master the wacky tales of Dr. Seuss. Then, perhaps frustrated and expecting faster, less arduous results, Baby Steve was often gone while Alice was left at home with their daughter, two-year-old Taffy. To describe her little girl, Alice proudly averred, "She's mean and tough," thereby introducing me to the values her Kalderasha family considered appropriate for the female sex.

Initially, Taffy had an older playmate who, I would now guess, was probably on loan in order to be included in the family subsistence check. But once they realized I was not directly affiliated with the welfare office that was sponsoring our elusive study hour, any interest in reading improvement ground to a polite halt. Baby began showing off, racing through the text. Tossing the wavy length of his black pompadour and thrusting his chin contemptuously in the direction of the *Cat in the Hat* in his lap, he told me he had already learned to read from road signs. Alice indicated she could see no pressing reason to read at all, as she never expected to drive, cars being the exclusive domain of the male. "Baby drives me," adding caustically, "when he can." She stubbed out her cigarette. "Anyhow, I get nervous. All the time he drives, I say 'Look out!'" To this enterprising pair, there was apparently no need to read except to pass the required ordeal of the Oregon driver's licensing test.

Baby Steve and Alice never installed a phone—or admitted they had one—so that I might call ahead and ask if they were available. The cross-town drive took most of an hour and, after that first month, the perplexing pair were seldom home and, if they were, they explained their previous absence without the least apology or remorse. "We were at a party," adding the clincher, "Big Smith came to town." Sometimes, daughter Taffy in ribbons and bows, they were leaving as I arrived and suggested, "Come back later. Tomorrow. Or next week." I would often sit at the curb during the elected hour, waiting and mulling over the intriguing nature of the Baby Steve domestic situation. What happened at those parties? How was it possible to live so well and go to so many parties by occasionally selling a used car and collecting an insignificant monthly stipend from Aid For Dependent Children? Our drama came to an abrupt end when I mentioned in passing that I was teaching them gratis. "You're not paid?" With that, I apparently lost all credibility and status.

So I can't say that when I decided to study Gypsies, I didn't know what to expect, or hadn't been warned. I had a pretty fair idea that it wouldn't be easy.

DISTRUST OF THE UNKNOWN GOES BOTH WAYS. Even today, Gypsy groups in America are an exotic and badly understood minority whose notoriety stems primarily from newspaper accounts of Gypsy criminals. During the decades of my off-and-on research, I have encountered surprise and even disbelief that Gypsies might be a worthy research subject on a number of occasions: "Gypsies? Why Gypsies?" Do they think a Gypsy is just a Halloween costume; a clichéd thief with a bad character; or a con artist with a crystal ball; or that artists like the *Gipsy Kings* have assumed their Gypsy identity as a commercial gimmick?

## The Make-do Anthropologist

Why, then, choose the slightly unorthodox topic of Gypsies for my fieldwork? I was disappointed to find that books about Gypsies in the Portland library were, at that time, largely fiction written by Englishmen who had studied travelers rolling past their hedgerows from the upholstered comfort of their sitting rooms. I began to think of the study as a challenge, an exciting mystery to be solved. I realized early on that their hostility was not personal, that it had more to do with their own tragic history and cultural differences designating non-Gypsies as the antithesis of all they held dear. When, after the first few months of teasing and taunting, the community I was determined to breach discovered I wouldn't go away, several Machvaia women took me aside to kindly assure me that, because of my difference by blood and my foreign nature, no matter how hard I tried, or how long, I would *never* be able to understand them. They pointed out that, "God made it this way. Roma with Roma, Americans with Americans."

Nevertheless, I persisted. Maybe I got stuck with Gypsies because, in the Sixties and Seventies anthropology grants were largely federally subsidized and as a marching-for-peace hippie opposed to the long war in Vietnam and a son approaching draft age, I couldn't imagine requesting what I thought of as a turncoat grant from such an uncongenial government. This meant I had to work on my own, funded by myself, incredibly slowly, sporadically, whenever I could, and, eventually, following the Gypsies' lead, by guess and manipulation of whatever living circumstance became available. Over the years, financing my own research has meant working an "American" job part of the time and attempting to do fieldwork the rest, hoping to be present during the ritual moments that mattered—ritual and belief was the focus of my studies. Like so many of my Gypsy friends, I wound up living hand-to-mouth at times, a situation I recklessly welcomed, supposing poverty and being close to the rhythms of my luck—Machvaia luck is something like karma (see Chapter 3)—would hasten my understanding and insight into the Machvaia culture, and it probably did.

My research, six years in Seattle, followed by twenty-five in California, mostly the San Francisco Bay Area, and then more, primarily by phone these past ten years back in Seattle, has lasted longer than expected. But equally significant to its length, no doubt, was my growing identity with the people themselves, the pleasure felt in their company. Describing their foreign world became a scene of unending discovery, and even a kind of feral joy. Like many anthropologists before me, by studying others, I grew in comprehension of life's mysteries and myself.

BUT WHY CHOOSE MACHVAIA ROMA as the subject of my research, particularly as they were a minority in Seattle, just a few young families, never more than five or six. And these families frequently returned to their native California for important social events, the very aspect of their lives I wanted to study? According to their self-defining story, Machvaia considered themselves of exalted rank, relative to the Kalderasha, the majority Roma population in the Seattle area. They seemed more approachable than the Kalderash; they spoke better English. Also, the Machvanki (Machvaia women) treated me like an equal; professional spiritual readers without peer, they looked me directly in the eye and assured me they had careers: "We work, too. Like you." Hearing that Machvanki were expected to provide the entire real income for their large extended families, and maybe because I was recently divorced and had never before been self-supporting, the choice of which group I would study was clear.

## The Heyday

My research findings relate primarily from 1966 to 2000, when I lived with and among the Machvaia. Most of my contacts were with those considered lucky and fortunate—"up", as the people put it—and my data undoubtedly reflects this bias. In any case, I found these families the better resource for my interests, more knowledgeable, more concerned with the permutations of ritual and belief than those scrambling for income and bidding on a better status.

I consider it an incredible gift to have been the record and witness to so much of the gain/loss of cultural adaptation during this past half century. For background context, I have attempted a sketchy historical context reaching back to what one aging Machvanka, Bibi (Auntie), called the olden days. When the people arrived in the States, the number attending any particular Machvaia event was seldom more than one or two guest families. But by the Seventies and Eighties, the "big money" heyday of ritual celebration, the number had grown, on occasion, to many hundreds.

This heyday was a time of noteworthy *communitas*—a time to have fun, to create a bounty of good luck, luck being made by good times. The people didn't always pay their bills, but they managed to sponsor gambling trips to Vegas, three-day weddings, as well as opulent *slavi* (saint days), baptisms, holidays, engagement parties, and fabulous tables and offerings for the Dead Ones. As the cost of living has escalated and more Machvaia must focus on earning a living, however, it has become evident that only a few, not the many, can afford freehanded generosity. The heyday, this particular heyday at least, is done.

## Romani Ritual

I set out to study ritual and belief, but suspect I have done what most anthropologists do, which is to focus on what seemed important to the people themselves and what appeared most distinct and challenging from my own cultural standpoint. In truth, the Machvaia have no categories corresponding to my concepts regarding ritual and belief or, for that matter, religion. Romani has no word for religion and the people assure me they *don't* have a religion, something they associate with "Outsider" priests, pastors, steeples, and churches. At the same time, they profess to being closer to The God, O Del, on the basis of Roma birth and their *vorta* (right) and felicitous conduct. Once I asked a Machvanka of forty years with five young children what she might consider a sin. Raida answered, "Sin? What is that? Maybe the right things to eat. We have no Romani word for sin. Our old people tell us what to do and how to live."

MACHVAIA RITUAL, as what Turner (1986) calls social drama, is performed cooperatively, with ample space for spontaneous invention. I like Felicia Hughes-Freeland's definition of ritual, in *Ritual, Performance, Media,* which borrows suggestions from Schieffelin (1998):

> A ritual is not a text with a pre-established structure of meanings, but something which emerges as participants bring together bits and pieces of knowledge in the performance: it creates reality and selves experientially. What validates the performance is that it is made real by the audience (1998:15).

Half the chapters in this manuscript are not social dramas in Turner's sense, however, but rather the ubiquitous daily rituals of purity, respect, hospitality, and luck designed to benefit family and *vitsa* (named lineage group), and to give form, merit, and meaning to daily social interaction. They are the rituals that only become public on the very public occasion. At least one ritual event, the Serbian *slava*, was obviously borrowed. The topics of several chapters, particularly those concerning luck, death beliefs and grieving customs, and the fervid obsession with cleanliness, apparently originated with the people's ancient Indian forbears and then became retranslated in terms of the people's own historical trajectory. Some effort has been made to compare one Machvaia ritual to that of another

Roma group; more could be done on this by my European colleagues. The occasional ritual consistency between groups is amazing, given the number of non-Roma contacts, the variety of host cultures, the generations, time, and miles of separation, as well as the way that unwritten ritual is passed along from one generation to another. The elders are to instruct the naïve and inexperienced, and, by rule of custom, knowledge of a particular ritual step only becomes available at the relevant ritual moment. Without finding agreement, I have spent many years asking about elusive ritual details—the number of candles at *pomana* for example. Over and over I was informed I would have to ask someone older.

ALTHOUGH I HAVE TRIED to be reasonably objective, I doubt I have written everything about Machvaia ritual in any final sense. Lola claimed her mother Stanya spoke five languages and like so many Machvaia, having had had contact with many cultures and truths, the people tend to regard truth as relative, as whatever seems true to the individual. "True," to the people, is no more than "true for you"; this book contains what seemed true to me.

Because the method of collecting and recording is fundamental to what is seen and reported, between the chapters concerning ritual are brief interlude chapters, moments when I felt the thrill and surprise of culture shock; these provide color and aptly demonstrate my limitations as an Outsider. By including two abbreviated life stories, as well as bits about my friend Lola and her daughter Katy, I have tried to personalize the events described and make Machvaia ritual a bit more comprehensible and compelling.

MACHVAIA PREFER THE TERM "AMERICANS" to the Romani term *Gadžé* (Non-Gypsies). Because USA-born Machvaia are also Americans, throughout the book, to avoid confusion, I have taken the liberty of using the term "Outsiders" for what the Machvaia might call "Americans" or *Gadžé*, capitalizing it to give it the same emphasis as Machvano (Machvaia man) or Machvanka (Machvaia woman). I was often described as the Djuhli (American woman). I still am.

# Chapter 1

# CRAZY FOR LOVE: ROSE'S STORY

*T*HE CHOICE OF PLACE TO MEET IS MINE, the Sun Grove, in 1977, the newest bar on Union Street. At considerable expense, blonde wood and roots have been flown from their Southwest desert home, scrubbed and waxed into burnished bones, then carved into designer chairs and wide-planked floors; a glamorously spare effect magnified by mirror ceilings and mirror walls.

Rose, my latest Gypsy acquaintance, and I agree on a table and, seated, we rest our forearms on a circle of wood where the green of a single fern, like a flower, curls over a patch of moss. I like the effect, the pleasing collusion with nature, the smell and sigh of real leather, the feel of the round icy glasses that hold our wine. But Rose's soft face registers panic, and her round eyes glance uneasily into the corners, searching for something, perhaps for the warm reds, the fringed pillows, the gold plastic fretwork and paintings on velvet, the plushy thick layers of carpet like those I later find in her flat. Or maybe that isn't it at all.

The fact is I had hoped to please her. We have waited so long to meet. For years, Rose was no more than a name scribbled on my kinship charts, parallel to the names of her sisters and her half-sisters: five ciphers that dangled from the line dedicated to Catherine, her mother, the woman I address as Bibi which means Auntie, a Big Woman among the Machvanki. It was Catherine, in fact, who heard that I was living within walking distance of her middle daughter and suggested I look up pretty Rose, that I get her out of the house and take her to Tahoe, to bingo, dancing, to get her blood

1

going and cheer her up: "She's too much alone." That's how I found her, the daughter who is never mentioned in public, outlaw Rose, outcast Rose, who "ran away" from Machvaia rule and married an Outsider.

Such intimacy, Machvanka and Outsider, is considered criminal. If Rose had ventured to attend a Machvaia wedding or a Saint's day, some of the women might have turned their backs in disdain and refused to talk to her. A few of the more nervy might even have called her *curva* (whore) to her face.

Gossip creates and recreates reputations, and rumors relating to Rose often quickly devolve into epics about Rose's legendary parents. Miller, her father, was the most beautiful, it is said, of all the Machvaia men. Like follows like, and the blessing of beauty is expected to manifest beautiful luck. According to Rose's aunt Lola, Miller, a fancy dresser, was smart when "we didn't know nothing." His people, of course, couldn't understand him, but Miller didn't care. Until his late twenties, Miller had great luck, becoming the Baro and "boss" of San Francisco. He and his queenly wife Catherine were popular with Outsiders; the Chief of Police and the Mayor were guests at their house. Only on his say-so could any of the Roma open a fortune telling business in the city.

But after all his worldly success and good luck, Miller went crazy, entirely crazy for love.

When I mention her father, Rose pulls her mink-trimmed sweater tight around her shapely shoulders, and her eyes turn, for reassurance, to the elegant reflection in the mirror opposite of the woman with a dark French Twist hair. "Oh, you've heard about my father," she says, masking unease with a coquettish twinkle. "Yes. Going crazy for love runs in the bloodline. Everyone in my family is afraid that could be our luck. Papa died, you know, in the crazy house."

Rose complains about the abysmally lonely American lifestyle. Her two high-class and wealthy sisters won't talk to her. The poor, no-class half-sisters, Anastasia and Sarah, might—like Rose, they have left the Gypsy rule and run away to an American lifestyle—but no one knows where they ran to. Rose's main security is her mother; she adores her mother. On the days Catherine doesn't have much fortune telling business, the pair meet secretly at Catherine's

2

downtown storefront with the astrological charts in the window. They shop, eat lunch at the Emporium tearoom, keep each other company on their trips to doctors.

Rose says her Italian in-laws are no help whatsoever. They don't consider her part of their family. Unaware of Catherine's royal status, they treat her as shabbily as they might an Old-Country Gypsy, speaking Italian whenever she visits. Rose's Italian husband Giorgio is Catholic. But Rose and Giorgio weren't married in the Catholic church, and his family considers Rose single and unmarried or, worse yet, still married to her previous Rom husband. Even with the family priest on Rose's side—she has won him over with judiciously edited versions of her life story—Giorgio's parents refuse to acknowledge Rose as family.

A Rom husband is often home. But Giorgio is absent. A butcher, he is gone all day, cutting, packaging, selling meat at the counter. Good sons make good husbands, and Rose is proud he shows his aging parents filial respect. But she is not entirely pleased that on weekday nights he feels obliged to join his parents for dinner. "Lonely," Rose complains. Beseeching eyes turn to me for the miracle of a solution. Jeweled hands and L'Air du Temps fragrance float aimlessly in the air.

Asked if she likes Giorgio, Rose allows she does, "well enough." Her first husband, Túlo, was Frensússuria (French Roma or "Strangers" as she called them), embarrassingly ugly, and no "match" for her whatsoever. When she, newly married, went to the celebrations, the Gypsies in New York said she didn't look right with that short dark husband, Túlo. "I don't think of myself as beautiful. The other people say it. I don't. When they saw me with Túlo, they'd say there was no resemblance, '*Chi bezel!*' What a shame!"

Giorgio, on the other hand, is indisputably handsome. Giorgio has a chin with a dimple. But she never gets the chance to show him off in the places that would matter, where the Machvaia Roma might see him. Túlo, her first husband, was unimaginative and not given to affectionate displays. Giorgio is crazy for her. Or maybe just crazy. Mornings, before leaving for work, he kisses her a long American goodbye like the kisses she sees in the afternoon on her program, *Days of Our Lives*.

Pausing to consider the good luck of Giorgio changes her mood and she smiles. "The Italiano Giorgio is my happiness," she assures me, patting my arm.

With him, I have that feeling that I wanted from a husband. When he said I will take care of you, I felt he really meant it. He really cares for me. A lot. Otherwise, he wouldn't have put up with what he did. For an Italian man to get with a Gypsy woman, plus older, no way. His older brother took him by the shirt, and he was going to beat him up. The brother said, 'What are you doing, Giorgio? The Gypsies will kidnap you and take you far away.' But Giorgio didn't listen. The brother's wife said, 'I never saw a man to love a woman so much. The way He looks at you! I wish my husband was that way.' And she was jealous.

On the weekends, Giorgio takes me everywhere. We go to the Italian families and play cards, a whole house of Mafia Italians, well, they look Mafia. [Mafia has positive connotations for Rose.] I walk in there, a little bit embarrassed because I am so much older than Giorgio. And Gypsy. And a little fat. But he makes me feel very good and comfortable. He puts me next to him with all the Mafia men at the table. He calls me Pumpkin: 'Pumpkin, come over here and sit next to me,' he says. And all the wives are by themselves. So who's winning at poker? I am. I do it a lot. Cause I am really lucky, in a lucky streak. Everyone is jealous. Men and women. The men get mad and say not to bring me next time. And Giorgio calls me Pumpkin. His Pumpkin. His winning Pumpkin.

Before Giorgio, I had no luck. I tell you most of my life was out of luck. It started the day I married Túlo. I said, 'No, I don't want to go, Ma'—I was twelve or thirteen. I didn't like to go, but I had to. It felt like jail, the end of the world, like someone is taking me away from my mother and giving me up for adoption. I cried all the way to New York. And they said for me to cheer up because when you see New York, big, it's big . . . And when I saw New York, all the snow, where we had to live, very bad neighborhoods, slums and dirty stores, no-English Chicanos, the cockroaches, the fleas. When you

4

turned the lights on, you could see all the cockroaches running. I never saw cockroaches before. So it was miserable. If I go to a movie now and it has pictures of New York, particularly the poor places, I leave.

The Frensússuria were different, different, so different. They slept in in the morning and got up late; Ma believed good luck only came to those who get up early. Those people slept on the floor, mattresses on the carpet; I was used to beds and sheets. They don't let the women tell fortunes.

The French Gypsy food is different. Kind of Russúria (Russian Roma) which I think they were at one time. They drink tea and eat cream cheese on toast for breakfast. Lots of borsht, cabbage soup with tomato sauce. Even the meat and potatoes were different.

When I think of the years I was at Ma's, men and women were pretty separate— that's the Machvaia way. The women didn't go to bars, couldn't do discodancing while the men were watching, all the women had to be together in the back of the house while the men sat in the front.

In the Frensússuria people, husband and wife, always together. You go shopping with your husband, not the mother-in-law. Never does a man go to parties by himself, like the Machvano. A Frensússuria man always takes his wife or he's embarrassed. If a woman sits alone in the kitchen, they would ask the husband what is wrong, did you have a fight? But it's not like love. They think it's a duty. The husband brings money, buys you clothes, and so you can't complain that you don't care for him. Caring isn't important.

Different, different. Different.

I used to curse my mother so much. Hate! [In New York] I got bitten on my finger sleeping on the floor. In my dream I felt someone hitting me with a nail and I'm screaming. I woke up. It was a big rat, chewing my finger. It took a piece off. Blood all over the blanket, the pillow. They rushed me to the emergency and gave me injections. After that I couldn't sleep at night.

I was brought up nice. When I asked my mother-in-law for sheets, she made fun of me, "Oh, you want to be an

5

American lady." Because Ma was always Americanized, that was how she raised me. Sheets, satin comforters, very expensive towels, washcloths, white carpeting and Persian rugs, different forks for salad and for dinner.

To tell the truth, my life was now poorhouse. In Túlo's tribe, the men worked and the women couldn't, they weren't allowed to tell fortunes. I had to beg for money. I had to go to the church and ask for money. I had to go from door to door.

Strangers. Those Frensússuria people were strangers. I will never understand them! That family lived poor—even when they had a little money.

Why, she wonders, why would anyone choose the hard life, cheap flats in bad neighborhoods, always looking for luck in places it was scarce. To emphasize the intensity of the scene she describes, Rose takes a deep sobbing breath, her bright gold bangle bracelets crossed tight against her chest.

After a while, I had four children and no hot water. I had to heat the water, do all the diapers myself, wash, plus look good, entertain people when they came, serve the tea and coffee. Misery. I couldn't go out with the girls; there was no money for a coke, a lipstick, nail polish, nothing. Anyhow, my mother-in-law was jealous and didn't like me to go out. She said I had *curvitsa iaka* (prostitutes's eyes), and that meant trouble.

Sometimes we had something to eat. Sometimes, we didn't. We stayed in New York, Newark, Detroit, the South— a lot of traveling to find work. Túlo went with the men; his father did the talking. Túlo was never good at business. He didn't know how to talk.

The men of Túlo's tribe, she explains, her elegant little nose wrinkling with the effort, repair metal pots and boilers, contracting jobs as a group, and then splitting the profits. "They make a fire," she said, "and get to work." But her man was ill-favored, awkward, lazy, and couldn't find partners or work.

6

Those other men knew a good customer. They were like Ma.
They knew how to talk to the company president. And they
knew how to listen. Túlo, to this day, will go on and on, talk,
talk and never stop to listen. Túlo didn't care how much time
he wasted. The people used to say, 'Get to the point, Túlo.'

When Kilai (Túlo's brother) tried to help, Túlo didn't
want to learn. Túlo would say, 'How can he help me? I'm
smarter than him.' Túlo was never a business man. He wanted
to dress up, put on dark glasses, and look at the women. That
was his hobby. That's all he knew. He'd borrow. And he
couldn't pay it back.

I never had a good day. Until I left Túlo and got back to
San Francisco and started giving readings. And I met this
person [Giorgio]. You could say I was happy ever since then.
No more begging. Safety. I felt safe. Anything I want I get.
Food. Clothes. No worry about the rent. Plus I am giving
readings and making a few dollars. It's not a steady thing
because I really don't have to. But I'm making a few dollars
and we go to Reno, on vacations, picnics, swimming,
shopping. It is peace of mind I have with the Italiano. I
guess I'm really crazy about Giorgio.

Then, perhaps to deflect the danger of her admitted passion, Rose
flirts with the Asian bartender across the room, catching his eye
with a Mona Lisa half-smile, dropping her lengthy eyelashes, and
shrugging her shoulders in a helpless fashion. I ask Rose how long
she has been with Giorgio. She says she met her Italiano four years
ago, shortly after she left the French Gypsies and husband Túlo, returning to San Francisco and her mother. At the time, San Francisco, which had been her mother's exclusive territory, was short
of readers. That's when Rose began telling fortunes.

I had to be brave because I really didn't know how to do it.
But I got a place at a fair, and the man from Coffee Cantata
saw me and asked if I'd like to work in his place. He took me
upstairs and—boy!—I could see it was going to be good.
Come Fridays and Saturdays, he said, and wear some kind of
costume. The man took a liking to me. He was an attractive

gay man with money galore. I said I was Egyptian and the man just fell in love with me. He laughed when I asked what percentage he wanted. He didn't want a penny.

The minute he put a big Psychic Reader sign up, they were coming and asking for a reading. Sometimes the people had to wait a half an hour to eat. In the meantime, I was the time-filler. Everybody had a reading. And the tips! I charged $20. Oh, I was making money!

I done a lot of things in my life that most women wouldn't dare to do. But it wasn't like I was looking for a good time. There's a difference. I guess maybe when I was telling fortunes I was looking for an older man who would give me money. A customer. But it happened to be a young man that came along and I don't know where he came from. It's not that I expected him. He came one day, and there he was.

One evening when my daughter was with me, Giorgio came upstairs. God bless him. He came upstairs and just looked at me. I thought he was a silly kid. High school, maybe. He kept looking at me, looking at me. I was dressed in my long green velvet, dark green velvet with a square neck—I used to wear that dress all the time. One of my Gypsy dresses. And I had a lot of hair.

So I was sitting there in my green dress, low-cut, on a velvet pillow. Sitting on the floor on those big giant pillows. Had a lot of costume jewelry on. He walked in and I'm sitting there and he's waiting to be seated. There's a little bar where you could have a drink, read a magazine, play a game. I looked up and saw him there and wondered what he was doing. He's a kid, I think, and I tell my daughter, 'I think he wants me but you take him.' So Suzy says, 'You want your reading?' And he says he wants me.

After that, he used to come to the house. He used to tell me he can't sleep at night. I thought, Oh, God, what am I going to do with him? I said, go home now. He said he would. But he parked the car across the street and waited. Night after night. So we are upstairs dancing, having a party.

And he's out there in the car until two in the morning. Oh my God, I got worried. I worried he might get sick.

Then Giorgio's second brother got married and Giorgio wanted me to come to the wedding. I bought a beautiful black dress, long, and a big hat, lacy, and they thought I was some kind of movie star when I walked in. There were lots of people and they all looked like gangsters. Giorgio's father asked me to dance, Italian dancing side by side—not a waltz. Real Italian music. Like *The Godfather* movie. Then Giorgio danced with me. He only danced with me, no one else. And his people knew I was the one he wanted. Oh, you have to see Giorgio. He's gorgeous. Light-complected, jet black hair, tall, real nice figure. And he used to wear a black turtleneck sweater. The real Italian look—I always liked Italians. Gosh! His eyes are so blue, blue . . .

Despite these positive attributes, I can tell that Rose doesn't know quite what to make of Italiano Giorgio, an earnest man, a stick at discos. She worries that he is young; he must be at least fifteen years younger than she is. It's not only that. Every day he is on public display behind the meat case and available, talking to women customers. What will she do, she asks, if he leaves her for a younger, prettier, more Italian woman?

Rose's story ripens into melodrama, capturing the attention of a couple at an adjacent table who, I note, have stopped talking to listen. She complains that her days seem as washed out as this restaurant, and her nights—she gestures enviously—as long as the legs of our young waitress. Depressed, often sick, she thinks it may be cancer. Or love. "How do you know the difference?"

Sometimes, at night, she awakens to the gallop of her heart, "like it is trying to escape my chest." The message of the Machvaia bloodline is impossible to deny and, again, she admits to her terror of the weakness that runs in her family: loving too much, going crazy for love. She had been only four when an usherette at the Fox Movie Theater caught father Miller's bad luck eye. "Platinum blonde," she explains succinctly, her mouth curving again, as it tends to do, in irony, and her pencilled eyebrows arching in a wild dismay.

9

ROSE AND I ARE GETTING ACQUAINTED. I am trying to learn what I can about her and hoping for a future friendship. She is testing the effect of her story-telling gifts by tallying my response and wondering if I can be trusted.

## Giorgio and Suzy

Rose's second-floor flat was just two blocks from my studio apartment and, after our Sun Grove introduction, I began stopping by. Rose would seem impressed whenever I arrived by bicycle and say she was planning to get a bicycle "soon" and join me. But I could tell it was more of a half-wish than a promise.

I tried to call and come by whenever her Italiano was away and she was lonely. On occasion, I'd find her daughter there. Suzy was an attractive girl of maybe nineteen, with a doleful demeanor. We would all go window-shopping on Union Street, Suzy pushing her little boy in a stroller.

I found Rose genuinely kind and agreeable—she wanted to be liked, and liking her was easy. She was also full of complaint; although with the admitted love of her life, she seemed to be waiting for the other shoe to drop, to fear some unknown outcome. Often, during our conversations, I felt we weren't alone, that she was performing for an invisible audience. Her eyes would slide past mine to the window, the wall, and she would gesture expansively, as if auditioning for someone in the back row. Was this part of an act that once earned food for her children? Was she soliciting help from the powerful, although invisible, ancestors? Was she seeking a way to bridge the difference between being raised in an atmosphere of comprehensive fellowship, of being told what to do and believe, and the unfamiliarity of her new, unknown and relatively independent, lifestyle?

THEN DAUGHTER SUZY DISAPPEARED. Abandoning her American husband and child, she ran away with a Machvano. Within the month, she had married the Machvano. The receiving Machvaia family paid Rose the appropriate brideprice amount, the wedding was broadcast to the Machvaia community-at-large, and Suzy went to live with her new in-laws.

Almost simultaneously, Giorgio announced he wanted a separation. Rose said the reason was her continuous crying. But I think it more likely that Giorgio saw how easily Suzy could leave her American family, assume a new identity, and disappear. His mother always said you couldn't trust a Gypsy. "They just up and leave—like that."

Of course there were other reasons that Rose didn't initially mention. She had been away several weeks for Suzy's wedding celebrations and the follow-up, during which, absorbed in her starring role as mother of the bride and finding herself, for the moment, a functioning part of her original community, the Machvaia, she never bothered to phone or write Giorgio. That omission, along with Suzy's escape, probably broke any confidence he might have in a future with Rose.

> Giorgio had a nervous breakdown. He kept saying, 'pressure, pressure.' When I came back from the wedding, he looked like a sick man. The minute I saw him, his face, his eyes weren't right. I said, 'Giorgio, what's the matter?' He said, 'Nothing,' and he turned away. He put his head in his hands. He just knew that I cared for my kids too much. He wanted a lot of attention from me. [long pause] I don't really know what it was.

I often visited Rose's mother Catherine at her *ofisa*. Between appointments, she talked about the days of traveling and I, of course, was delighted to take notes. Concerned about her daughter, Catherine warned me that Rose had threatened suicide.

That is why, the evening I found Rose's apartment door locked, the lights and music on, I called her son and we broke the glass window in the door. But she wasn't lying on her bed, an empty box of sleeping pills in hand. Instead, we found her at a bar around the corner, dressed to the teeth and petulant, angrily drinking herself into oblivion.

I saw little of her during her heavy drinking period. The few times we went out together, she became loud and obstreperous, and I let her get home on her own. Rose defended her drinking:

I'm not smart. I'm not strong. I never learned to take care of myself. I can't get along on my own. Ma wants me to marry a Rom. But I'd rather marry an American, one that wouldn't keep it a secret, one that takes me home with him to eat dinner with his parents and has lots of sisters for me to visit. I've never really been alone before. This is my first time being so alone.

Then Rose called one afternoon and said she wanted to talk about Giorgio.

So what happened? What ruined it? Well, we stayed together for a long time. A pretty long time. [Maybe five years.] Still, I wanted to see the Gypsies. I kind of missed the Gypsy life. Not that much. But I was alone a lot and I'd think about my family. [All her children initially married Americans.] What I might be doing and how I wouldn't be alone. I started liking the idea of going to the Gypsy parties and talking about things. Cause, when we were together, I hardly saw Giorgio. He'd get up at seven in the morning and I wouldn't see him until nine at night. So I was always by myself. I used to argue with him, how long will this go on? So he had pressure, I gave him pressure. Until today, I feel very sorry about that.

You have to wonder how such a thing could happen. That I wanted to go back to my people. I wanted to show my mother, my sisters, all the Machvaia how I could do something good. I didn't want Ma to have to sneak around to see me. I wanted Ma to be proud of what I could do with business. Since I began telling fortunes, she likes to brag. She makes me sound rich, and I'm not.

But what really happened was I thought he was trying to get involved with my daughter. [Rose was often jealous.] Now I know it wasn't true. But like, your daughter is young, she's pretty, she's blonde, she comes into your house too much. [Suzy had lived with her baby and husband right across the street.] She'd walk in, I'd get up from the couch where I was sitting next to Giorgio and move to a chair [which is proper Machvaia etiquette]. He wouldn't like that. He'd say for me to stay next to him. He'd say, 'I want to feel you next to me, Babe.' And I would insist we take her to the park, to the beach, that we go see how she was doing. Giorgio would get mad. He wanted to be alone with me. But I kept thinking about her being so much alone.

I done it. I paid too much attention to my daughter. She spoiled the whole thing. She always wanted me for herself. That's why she wiggled her behind at Giorgio. People—my brother, my customer—said she had an eye for Giorgio. Maybe the problem was that I was happy and she wasn't.

He stopped calling me Pumpkin [after Suzy married]. He never took me to the Italians to show me off, never again. Ma had tickets to Lena Horne and she took us. But I couldn't stand it. I went home at intermission. He wouldn't look at me. Or talk. A stranger. Changed. He was having a nervous breakdown. That's it. Giorgio would have bought me anything, even a house. I know that for sure. And we weren't rich. But I was safe, safety safe. For years I didn't have to worry none about food or money.

Maybe it's my fault. I never could really believe in the good luck of Giorgio.

## *Chapter 2*

# MEETING THE MACHVAIA

In 1966, when I began my study, all the Roma in Seattle, both Machvaia and Kalderasha, spoke Romani, but with dialectical differences. Romani was a Gypsy child's first language and the preferred language in the home. The elders were illiterate, and adults, if they could read, read only under the pressure of earning an income. For the men, this was usually the car section of the newspaper.

Like the French Manouche that Poueyto (2003:19–23) studied, Seattle Roma had no letters, books, writing, or signs that could substitute for something absent or afford an orderly perspective on their history. The Machvaia, the Roma group who became my focus, cared little about the past and lived primarily in the moment—at least more so than I did. Advocating firsthand experience as the measure of truth, they considered each moment unique, an event to be maximized and cherished. They taught me to study the emotional tone of situations, to value the human connection, to be considerate of others, and not intrude or interrupt.

How to meet them? I tried several of the local Gypsy storefronts, pretending to be a prospective client. But when I timidly asked, "Do you tell fortunes?" the women claimed they didn't give readings. The ones with Palm Reader signs said they were "too busy." While suggesting I come back another day, the expressions on their faces made it abundantly clear that when I did, they intended not to be in.

Later, I heard one Kalderasha woman suspected I might be a witch—her baby wouldn't stop crying after I left. To add to my unpopularity, a family "back East" had recently, for reasons unknown, lost all their children to Child Protective Services. In truth, any Outsider was a likely threat, not least because it was illegal to live in storefronts and those Roma who did feared a visit from the Housing Authority. In keeping with the prevailing opinion, as one of the wary women told me later, "You looked CIA. You did! You didn't look to me like a customer."

Arriving in California several years later, I found I still had no gift for impersonating a prospective client. Stops at the Psychic signs along the highway to Los Angeles proved futile; no one would tell my fortune.

But my luck must have been waxing that first year in Seattle. A kindly professor in my department at the University of Washington, Edward Harper, who, as an undergraduate, had studied a Gypsy family in Portland, arranged for an introduction. Katy, the daughter-in-law in the household I approached, tried various ways to brush me off. But, eventually, accustomed to risk, curiosity won out over Katy's better judgment.

YEARS BEFORE, AS PENALTY for running away and in keeping with Machvaia custom, Katy's father had "thrown her away" to the first family who asked for her—the Kalderasha Stevens. Married for eighteen years to Ephram, Katy now lived in a decrepit storefront with snow-white criss-cross curtains. As fortune telling was illegal in Washington State, small pamphlets on the window sill suggested the ruse of a business—Katy hadn't the least idea what kind! Katy's storefront was near Elliot Bay and the downtown taverns, and her clients were usually male, mostly alcoholics and sailors. This was in some contrast to the other Machvanki who advertised in the newspapers, on the radio, and by passing out flyers, and whose clients tended to be women.

Initially, Katy and her mother Lola expected me to vanish, discouraged by the impossible task of studying Gypsies. But I kept hanging around, and they began to instruct me in matters of the gravest importance. Over and over, I was told food must be fresh, fish and meat particularly. Lola wanted me to know, "We're neat," and advocated paying attention to "a clean place, clean food," cautiously removing the saucer into which some of my coffee had spilled, and putting a clean and unused one under my cup.

That summer, after classes, I would head for Katy's First Avenue storefront and, seated on her over-size sofa, be served the courtesy of coffee by her two older daughters. The family's hospitality service usually involved a sweet tea made with fruit, fruit jam, sugar, but I was asked for my preference. Tea, I later learned, was Kalderasha, coffee was Machvansko. Katy was usually on the phone, the younger children playing games or watching television, and I felt like an icon of sorts, pointedly ignored and uneasily out of my element. Nevertheless, it was a lesson in perfect service; the coffee was kept at the scald, the table spotless, my paper napkin continually replaced.

Who could have guessed that, over time, the bulk of my fieldwork would be sponsored by Katy, Katy in transition and on her way back to her *vitsa* (named lineage group) of birth? For by the end of those first plodding years of fieldwork, Katy had switched beverages, tea to coffee, she was moving to a little storefront in the Farmer's Market with her four youngest children, advertising as Mother Mary, Spiritual Reader, attracting a bevy of loyal clients, and inventing the lifestyle of Seattle's first-ever Gypsy bachelorette.

WHO ARE THE MACHVAIA? Language identifies the Gypsies' origin as India. Regarding their early migrations, Angus Fraser (1992:44) writes "there was a diaspora of people with no priestly caste, no recognized standard for their language, no texts enshrining a corpus of beliefs and code of morality, no appointed custodians of ethnic tradition." Of course we don't really know any of this for certain; the conditions of their departure are neither recorded nor remembered.

Currently, Machvaia have no origin myths—other than the cartoonish "Church of Cheese" found in the Introduction—no priests, no kings, no writing, no Robert's *Rules of Order* or written Ramayana. And yet, for centuries, they have persisted as amazingly durable small societies within the larger. The Machvaia resembled what Keyes (1981:13) calls an "ethnic enclave," a minority group with an almost totally separate existence, or so it seemed in the Sixties.

In 1966, my first impression of the *vitsa* Machvaia was that they were "rich," or so they said. The Machvanki (Machvaia women) were quick to inform me they were whizzes at fortunes, the breadwinners for their families; household activities were built around the women's appointments with clients. Most of them lived in houses and, when they entertained, the food and drink on their tables tended to be sumptuous.

The Kalderasha—in Romanian, "caldera" refers to a copper pot or cauldron, and likely relates to the people's ancient metal work trade—also arrived in the States in the early 1900s. Although most of the Kalderash women in Seattle told fortunes, their men had the chief responsibility for income; they bought and sold cars, and they did car body repair—knocking out dents—wherever they could find jobs. Their men kept cash on hand for used-car purchases. They thought in terms of scarcity, were adverse to excess of any kind, and conceived continence and thrift as fostering good luck.

Territory is the basis for the fortune telling business, and territory is held, I was told, on the first come, first served, basis. Most of the local Machvaia families, or their parents, had set up in Seattle at various times during the past century. But the number of Kalderasha had grown and the Northwest had transitioned into Kalderasha territory. Two large families of ten adult children each, the Georges (Ginershti *vitsa*), and the Stevens (Rishtershti *vitsa*) divided the city by halves, south and north respectively, and they were intent on keeping the property rights for themselves and their children.

Machvaia toeholds in the Seattle area existed largely through kin relationships with the Kalderasha, through marriage or godparenthood; the latter is regarded as a sacred kinship. But, for Machvaia, the Northwest remained something of a frontier outpost; they periodically returned to take care of their property holdings in California, and to attend the parties and ritual events given by their relatives. Quite possibly, the last straw regarding the possibility of a more permanent residency was their disinclination, after years in Seattle and as their children reached pubescence, to arrange future marriages with the local Kalderasha. Indeed, I heard one Machvanki say to her husband, "We got to get out of here before Sabrina gets interested in one of them."

At the same time, it has been the general rule, as far back as anyone can remember, that those Roma who have should help those who don't. Indeed, one of the Machvaia families I knew was resident on the admirable basis of sharing. When asked nicely, an elderly

Kalderasha Rom-in-residence had granted Machvano Stévo the privilege of territorial access. Some years later, Stévo became *chivro* (godparent) to one of the Rom's grandchildren, consolidating his territorial claim with enduring ties of kinship.

During my years with the Seattle community, the late Sixties into the early Seventies, the prescribed principles of sharing, love, and generosity seemed often at war with an underlying competitive friction. Some of this was owing to *vitsa* differences of custom and lifestyle, and some to jealousy, particularly of Miller, Katy's younger brother—named for his famous and gorgeous Uncle Miller who once ran San Francisco. Although the custom was for men to spend their time with men, Miller often went fishing with his wife Duda and their children. While most of the other Roma rented, on the advice of his live-in businessman father, Miller owned six houses in Seattle. Miller's home was a large Colonial whose interior decor celebrated his many hunting and fishing trips to Canada. Between the lace curtains and antique oil paintings, the giant horned taxidermied heads of an elk, a caribou, a deer festooned the walls and, over the fireplace, a curving marlin pointed its silvery snout up in the lucky direction.

Good time Miller was full of fun, but the Kalderasha sometimes misunderstood his jokes. On occasion, even his father, Phuro (Old) Bahto, gave offense. Once, several local Kalderash Rom were insulted when Phuro Bahto wearily indicated it was time for his bed. Hospitality, in the Sixties, was ideally unending.

THE RITUALS THAT AMELIORATED, at least temporarily, any rifts in the local social fabric were the parties, three-day *slavi* (saintdays), *pomani* (commemorations for the dead), and holidays (Christmas, New Years, Easter). Then, the good will of hospitality became a giant Band-Aid for the damage of envy.

Health threats and the specter of death were other unifying factors; emergencies like these unified the people. The most harmonious weeks I can remember during those years were when Old Zorka, mother of the George brothers, was hospitalized for weeks with a failing heart. Everyone prayed and sent good thoughts in Zorka's direction. Everyone agreed. Zorka's West Coast relatives flew in and added to the sense of sharing.

Lola bought Zorka, who was on a restricted diet, a medley of food offerings, "so she gets better," including a three-foot long box of chocolates; chocolates were, of course, taboo, but Lola said "it shows that I love her." The two shared a long-ago history. Bahto had been married to Zorka before he married Lola. "He said I had nice legs," Lola explained. "And I do."

*Chapter 3*

# LUCK

*M*achvaia purity and respect were easy topics to learn about. I listened, observed, asked questions, and found articles and books about similar matters in the library. Machvaia luck, on the other hand, lacked examples and proved provocatively complex for years.

To solve the mystery, I sought means of employment similar to what the Machvaia men did. Instead of cars, I sold hand-pulled etchings, cold calling door-to-door in the Financial District of San Francisco. Even so, even though I felt like I was close to the issues involved in making luck, I hadn't the luck of my Gypsy ancestor's— as far as I know!—to support and guide me. And that, according to Katy, was the essence of my problem.

For Machvaia, everything, including knowledge and understanding, depends on bloodline inheritance. Machvaia luck is based on the luck of Machvaia Ancestors. Yet for years, the people's answers to my questions made no mention of the Dead Ones. The people tried valiantly to avoid the offense of vocal mention (See Williams, 2003). They tried to keep the land of the living from juxtaposition with the land of the dead. So I was at some disadvantage in comprehending all that *baX* meant.

## *BaX* (Luck)

Machvaia translate the Romani word *baX* as luck. *BaX*, as Sampson (1926:22) and Gjerdman and Ljungberg (1963) have noted, appears to be related to the Sanskrit word for destiny or fate (bhagya).

Machvaia say *baX* determines the quality of life's main events which, as in Indian belief about karma and bhagya, includes "time of death, length of life, identity of spouse, serious illnesses, number and sex of children, illnesses and deaths of children, lameness and maimedness, level of poverty or prosperity . . . occupation" (Kolenda 1964: 73), and more. Regarding a lower Sweeper caste in northern India, Susan Wadley writes: "While [bhagya] too can be written (like karma), it presents a potentiality of capriciousness and lack of predetermination that contradicts the premises of karma." Also, bhagya derives from "the word "share" or "portion." It's one's share of fortune or misfortune (nirbhagya)" (1983:160). Wadley's "fortune or misfortune" approximates to the Machvaia idea of good or bad luck: *baX* or *bi-baX* (without luck).

At times, Machvaia may seem to use the term for luck in a manner similar to that of the West. But this is illusory, as Machvaia luck, however capricious, is never accidental or by chance, but rather due to factors that are believed must be there.

DURING THESE PAST SEVERAL DECADES, the word "karma" has been added to many Machvaia vocabularies as Outsiders' interest in Eastern religions has grown. In keeping with their belief in divine retribution, Machvaia explained karma as something like "if I am good with you, you will be good with me" or "what goes around comes around." On occasion, finding a place familiar, the people I knew would say they might have been there in another life, suggesting rebirth. But these beliefs seem not formally linked with karma, as they are in Indic texts. Rather than the rebirth of each karma-laden soul through spiritual transmigration, Machvaia assign the experiences of this world to a *baX* that is inherited, primarily, through ancestral bloodlines, that can be altered and transformed through the nature of personal activity and contacts, and that is invariably passed along to descendants. As Hindu karma also relates to present and past actions, a family resemblance of Machvaia beliefs about luck to Hindu beliefs about karma is apparent.

This karmic carry-over can be found in other Roma groups. In her memoir, Ilona Lacková, a Slovakian Romni, recently wrote that "Fate is just." She says her people once believed, and some still believe, that "everyone would get recompensed for what they'd done, whether in this world or some other one, whether in this life or the next one."

## Inherited Luck and Transformations

Western thought, for many decades of the last century, attributed human behavior to culture and experience; according to the science of the time, only animals were hard-wired with instincts. Since then, Western psychological research has been teasing out what is learned and what was genetically given, a subject often described as nurture/nature, or innate/learned. Machvaia, on the other hand, credit fate and the lessons of life, good and bad, primarily to inborn inheritance.

As Marriott and Inden (1977:229), as well as others, have noted, all genera in the South Asian universe are believed to have an inborn code of conduct involving morality, physicality, preference, thoughts, and so on. This Asian code, although given, is certainly not genetic as it encompasses all manner of attributes that could not be so considered. Nor is the inborn Machvaia inheritance genetic, as it also involves various qualities and propensities regarding morality, physicality, preferences, thoughts, the rule of custom, the *romani baX* from forebears, lineage, and *vitsa*, as well as the shared inheritance of all *but thiem* (human beings). This would include what Anne Sutherland (1975:101–2) describes as "*romania*" which subsumes everything Roma: tradition, custom, ideology, morality, belief, ritual, attitude, law, and the nature of the appropriate punishment.

For Machvaia, this inborn code explains why one Machvaia lineage is known for large appetites, another for a tendency to thrift, and another for heart attacks and dying young. A Machvano who was rich, but not popular, was said to "have money luck in the way of the Adams [lineage], but no company luck." Inherited luck explains why Machvaia Roma are well-favored and considered more auspicious than the Kalderasha Roma. Inborn tendencies explain the Machvanka aptitude for fortune telling and reading the future, why the power of the human will, intent, empathy, intuition, and soft hearts are familiar to Machvaia, and not, ordinarily, given much credit by Outsiders. It explains why *gadjensko baX* destines Gadjé/

Outsiders for school and jobs with regular salaries; they become doctors, lawyers, presidents, and run the world. Adult Machvaia, on the other hand, are predestined for trades according to sex and in-born code: fortune telling for females; marketing horses, and now cars, for males. According to the Machvaia ideal, in faithfully fol-lowing custom and inheritance, the given seeds of luck will blossom to a ripe fruition, and their fullness will be found.

At one time, the Roma believed there were American diseases and Gypsy diseases (Sutherland 1975:278). The elderly Gypsies I met who spent their childhoods outdoors, running after the wagon, laid claim to remarkable health; "We didn't get colds. We didn't get any American sickness." In earlier days, the American medical es-tablishment was treated with profound suspicion; to provide sup-port to the ailing, hospitals were flooded with groups of, sometimes, hundreds of Roma. Forty years ago, when I first encountered Mach-vaia, it was considered unlucky to read books or to keep track of money; I was told that "every time a Gypsy counts his money, it gets less." Planning for the future, writing down those plans, buying in-surance, obtaining credit, owning houses, all were considered the inherited luck of the Outsider Gadzé and disaster for Machvaia, a failure of congruency and matching. The American public school system was suspected of undercutting belief in the elders and the virtue of custom; some suspected it might damage their daughters' inborn ability to read the future for future clients. (Interesting to consider: would the focus on rational thought undercut intuitive thought?) In those days, the difference of inherited luck, Ameri-can and Machvaia, was emphasized by, "*Pei Gaženzhi baX* (Back on the American people's luck)," an expression intended to send mis-begotten luck back to the appropriate party.

I haven't heard "*Pei Gaženzhi baX*" for several decades. Mach-vaia inherited code, or luck, is, like the South Asian code, subject to contact, flow, transformations, and adjustment. The *romani baX* of the Machvaia has apparently changed with the passing years and become more like what the people describe as "the American way."

FOR THE HINDU PERSON, a given code is not static. Nor is Mach-vaia inherited luck static. Any activity, particularly those involving food and sex, has an effect. Marriott and Inden (1977:232–3), writing about South Asian categories, call these changes code modifications or enhancements, which is the same as an exchange of particles of substance. Marriott (1976:109–10) adds that

> Indian thought about transactions differs from much of Western sociological and psychological thought in not presuming the separability of actors from actions. By the Indian mode of thought, what goes on between actors are the same connected processes of mixing and separation that go on within actors. Actors' particular natures are thought to be results as well as causes of their particular actions (karma). Varied codes of action or codes for conduct (dharma) are thought to be naturally embodied in actors and otherwise substantialized in the flow of things that pass among actors.

Citing Nicholas and Inden (1970) and David (1973), Marriott (111) continues, "Persons engage in transfers of bodily substance-codes through parentage, through marriage, and through services and other kinds of interpersonal contacts. They transfer coded food substances by way of . . . feasts and other prestations. Persons also cannot help exchanging . . . influences that are thought of as subtler, but still substantial and powerful forms, such as perceived words, ideas, appearance, and so forth." The result is that people are considered composites of what has been taken in, and their substance-code is continually susceptible to, and in the process of, change, unlike "Western popular beliefs in the standard, stable entities and in the normally impermeable, autonomous person." (Marriott:110)

To summarize, the idea in both South Asian and Machvaia societies is that the nature of any contact involves transfers and transformations that may or may not affect the nature of inheritance. Unlike Western sociological and psychological thought, actors are not seen as separable from their actions. Everything is capable of contagion, and relevant to the better, or worsening, condition of life experience. Good and evil are everywhere, and they are often experienced as good luck and bad luck.

## Luck by Association

Good luck is associated with good thoughts, generous gifts, the beautiful, graceful, aesthetically pleasing, the new, the merit of fresh beginnings. Owing to the power of contact, these are the items to keep near, and the activities to pursue. As *baX* is conceived as flowing from one person to another, the intimacy of living and sleeping together combines some of the powers of husband and wife. Eating from the same table has a similar effect. Those who wish you well are lucky, Lola assured me. "Whoever means good for you, that's the way you're going to be good; you better stick with that person."

Petrović, a doctor who studied Serbian Gypsies for many years, writes, "He who has no luck of his own may derive it from someone else" (1940:41). When I asked Lola how an unlucky Machvano might change his luck, she said, "He should sit next to the lucky people." Then she added this practical advice. "He should study them and find out how they do it."

Luck through association is similar to what O'Flaherty describes as "transfer of merit," an old and persistent concept rooted in the Vedic tradition and intrinsic to the theory of karma (1980a:xiii). Merit transfer indicates "the process by which one living creature willingly or accidentally gives to another a non-physical quality of his own, such as a virtue, credit for a religious achievement, a talent, or a power." O'Flaherty also notes that this is "often in exchange for a negative quality given by the recipient" (1980b:3).

Machvaia agree, and, to preserve their luck, they ordinarily prefer to avoid those who look bad, poor and wretched (*tchoRo*), mean (*bengjailo*), lawless and uncooperative (*nai pachivalê*), or without shame awareness (*nai lažhav*). The poor are believed to be desperate and to take great risks for meager gains. Machvaia rank *vitsi* according to wealth, virtue, generosity, and the degree of risk involved in earning a living, fortune telling being largely without risk (since it became legal). Pick-pocketing, on the other hand, is considered high risk and ranked very low. Those who are *tchoRo* cannot be trusted. They are suspected of thievery, bad thoughts, jealousy, curses. Because of contagion, bad luck people can enlist pity, even charity, but they are usually avoided by those with better luck. To protect their luck, the Machvaia, much like their caste-born Hindu forbears, are continually ranking everyone, Roma and non-Roma, and every-thing else as well.

When I first visited Katy, she lived in a shabby storefront on First Avenue. Her customers were largely the down-and-out and hardly anyone with whom she would normally associate. She explained the hazards of fortune telling as follows:

> If there wasn't trouble in the world, no one would come to me. If I help somebody, they don't come anymore. That's why I have to charge money while people have trouble. Because when times are good, they disappear. It's hard to listen to the bad luck and nothing else. Bad luck has the tendency to stick around. Like a bad odor. It's like the customers are leaving it behind and I can't get rid of the bad feeling. Then I clean the house, bathe, put fresh clothes, cook, play the stereo and dance to bring back good times.

## BaXtali Lola

In Seattle, I heard Lola referred to as BaXtali. Machvaia associate the entitlement of BaXtalo (Good Luck Rom) or BaXtali (Good Luck Romni) with beauty, wealth, popularity, health, intelligence, being kind, good, generous, as well as "understandable" to other Machvaia. I could see evidence of almost all the above in Lola. Lola was always insisting I drive to her children's houses or Roma storefronts with presents, bolts of cloth, candy, cakes, doughnuts. Nearly every day, she went downtown to "give them some of my money," a shopping activity she called sharing. Her lively presence—she loved to dance—tended to turn any get-together into a party.

But the Lola I knew was not rich. There were times when there was nothing in her refrigerator except the half-and-half she liked in coffee. Had she been rich, she would have certainly taken me and her seven daughters to Paris for a long weekend: "I hear it's good times," she said. A freehanded spendthrift, the minute she made any money she spent it: "You got to spend it to make it. You know that's my way."

When I asked her children how Lola became BaXtali, they re-ferred to their childhoods in a roomy Sacramento storefront.

"That's where," Pretty Bobby, one of Lola's daughters, confided, "Ma learned to make and spend."

We had a beautiful storefront, two picture windows with a jukebox in one window, a shoeshine stand in the other, a yard in the back with a porch and patio, a big tent for shade with long tables and lots of chairs. When the rich people came over, Father took them out to the tent. All his brothers used to come. All the sisters-in-law. People from San Francisco and Los Angeles. The Adams. The Lees. Big George. Yasha and his brother. Dushano, Long Nose's grandfather. The men sat outside, the women inside. Some of the men played guitars.

Lola and Bahto had two boys and seven girls. During World War II, the older girls entertained servicemen with readings, they danced for them to the swing music playing on the jukebox; the younger girls shined their shoes. Sometimes Lola sang her favorite song that began, "There'll be bluebirds over the white cliffs of Dover, tomorrow, just you wait and see."

Business was good, wonderful. Every day, Ma took a taxi to the stores. Make and spend. She took several hundred for shopping, and came back to more. The girls—that's us—we'd been busy in the storefront.

Lola never gave up on that great good luck. She refused to admit there was anything she couldn't afford. Whatever she wanted, she said she got. "That's why I don't get jealous. I never been jealous. I don't know how it feels."

DR. RICHARD WISEMAN, head of a research unit in the psychology department at the University of Hertfordshire, finds that expectations about the future often have the power of self-fulfilling prophecy. In *The Luck Factor* (2003), he writes, "Lucky people dismiss any unlucky events in their lives as short-lived and transitory (and) maintain their expectations of a bright and happy future" (102).

So it was with Lola. I drove her to all the Seattle celebrations and parties. When we arrived, she made her "Bette Davis" entrance, pausing at the door, one hand on hip, one eyebrow arched in nonchalant abandon, waiting to be noticed. Then she might order drinks all around for the house. Good luck is compounded by giving, giving to yourself whatever you need and want, giving whatever you can when the hat is passed around to help the hard-time Roma in crisis. Generosity is the boundless gift of time and effort; giving advice: giving good times to the treasure of guests: offering the bereaved attentive sympathy: giving whatever has been admired to the admirer: sharing the bounty of good fortune—it can be no more than a smile or a handshake—with those less fortunate. The ideal is a world of good will without lines, limits, or measure: Lola embodied this unlimited ideal. Machvaia consider good luck contagious. Much like Hindu merit, everyone wanted to be near her, to share the benefit. I came to understand that Lola was still a rich and important woman because of the many moments of happiness she had enjoyed, shared, and was still giving away.

Even before they had settled in Sacramento, there were periods that making money was easy—so Lola explained.

> We dressed up pretty, put the tent next to the highway, waved at the people driving to the beach. We'd holler"'Stop! Hey, we're Gypsies! Come on over and get your fortune." If they didn't stop, we'd do a little dance, just to show we could. "Stop!" we'd holler. "We'll show you a good time!" And every night we'd have good money, enough for everyone, more than a hundred to divide.

As the first child in her family to be born in the States, the message of Lola's luck began early. At six-years-old, her new godparents gave her an American name and a red American-style coat and hat to wear; baptism signifies fresh beginnings and the direction of the future. At seventeen, Lola was the only one in her family of marriage to succumb to the influenza of 1918, what Americans called the Spanish Flu and the Machvaia called the American flu, suggesting the nature of her destiny. The mature Lola assured me that like

American women she "had my own mind"—for one thing, she got an American-style divorce when subscribing to the Outside legal system was forbidden. [In fact, no one I asked, even her children, could remember the divorce, and I presume it remained secret to avoid scandal.] At that time, women seldom went anywhere without a Machvaia chaperone or companion. But the intrepid Lola still managed to travel, to shop, to visit, "to see new things" every day— and without supervision! The days I couldn't drive her, she went by bus. Sometimes, being unable to read, she got on the wrong bus but, as she pointed out, the bus always, eventually, brought her back. "They are like that," she assured me.

THE DAY WE MET, the Amerikanka Lola immediately adopted me as her chauffeur: "My Cadillac is in the garage. I need a ride home." Months passed, however, before I realized she saw me as a potential instrument of her good luck. Bad luck items are rapidly discarded and whatever I gave her, she kept: a raincoat that struck me as too conservative for the hippie 1960s; an oil painting of a mother, child, and sewing machine by my sister Joan; a vivid life-size Art Naif Saint, painted on a sturdy board; a pair of earrings I had especially liked.

A series of dreams confirmed her judgment. In one, I was painting her room a shiny, bright pink—new paint, shine, and bright colors are all auspicious and lucky. To fulsomely realize the benefit of the dream, she promptly made herself a bubble-gum pink full-circle Gypsy dress and bought a matching pink feather boa. In a later and equally auspicious dream, Lola said I was pulling hundreds of fish into our boat, a dream she explained as indicating increase and bounty, wealth and good times. I was perplexed about these dream interpretations as, at that time, I was working odd jobs, taking class notes, typing letters for professors, and living frugally with my son on a modest alimony payment. I was so poor that the women invariably picked up the tab on our bi-monthly late-night sorties to Seattle nightclubs. But likely they would have insisted even if I had been more financially able for, as I later learned, giving puts the giver into the more auspicious category and moves both giver and receiver "up," increasing the golden value of the moment.

Eventually, my good luck on Lola's behalf did become more apparent. During the years her family lived in Sacramento, husband Bahto had owned a used-car agency, kept up with his yearly tax payments, and, for legal reasons, insisted that he and Lola secretly marry the American way. My letter to the Office of Social Security validated Lola's once-married identity and, finally, for the first time in her life, she enjoyed the regularity of a monthly income. In the past, whenever her bills exceeded her ability to pay them, Lola got her son on the phone and ordered him to find her a more promising location. Now, having enough for the rent, Lola never moved again.

## Luck, Rank, and Matching

Despite the fact that there are equally handsome, rich, and generous Kalderasha Roma families in America, the Machvaia assured me theirs was "the best vitsa, the most respect." Ian Hancock, a professor of linguistics and a Rom, concurs; "both groups [Machvaia and Kalderasha] regard the Machvaia as the most prestigious" (1999:2). Luck flows from luck, happiness from happiness, and those already well favored can expect further bounties of good luck: "They are luck," or "They know how to do it." That's how the people described the situation when, in 2005, an already wealthy Machvanka in Sausalito cleared a whopping twelve million playing the state Lotto. "Luck goes to luck!" young Janet of San Francisco wistfully explained.

Machvaia concern with ranking is consistent with Hindu grading and ranking; Marriott (1976:114) writes that South Asian genera originating "from homogenous ancestry and from more consistent or harmonic . . . acts of mixture stand higher" (Marriott and Inden 1973, 1974). Matching, keeping the good with the good, associating with others of an equal, or better, rank, is Machvaia ethos, ethic, and *vorta* (right) action. Marriages are arranged on the basis of rank and reputation, marriage of Machvaia to Machvaia being, of course, the preference. Non-Gypsies, the American Outsiders, are also continually ranked. Until recently, fraternizing with Outsiders was a serious matter, a mix of *gadjendji baX* and *romani baX*, and not in the best interests of homogenous bloodlines and good results. The people, nonetheless, seem always to have favored Outsiders, the police, lawyers, government officials, from whom they could gain a measure of political clout and some assurance regarding their business and territorial claims.

*BaX* is associated with the loyalty of friends and relatives, with popularity, with endless rounds of eating and drinking, with that fortuitous state of grace in which one pleases one's self while pleasing everyone else. Great music and joyful dancing is a given. Bringing the divine Saint to His or Her *slava* is a concerted effort that requires intensifying the luck of good times to get more luck.

ON THE MACHVAIA CALENDAR OF EVENTS, saints have annual *slavi* (saint days) and ancestors are celebrated on holidays, rituals of renewal and fresh beginnings that must be matched with community harmony and good will. At the first *slava* I attended in Seattle, a party for Saint Mary, Katy explained, "Everything has to be perfect." But it wasn't, the party failed, owing to domestic issues, community conflict, and a lack of pleasurable esprit. "St. Mary couldn't come. She wanted to. But she couldn't." Katy said. She got some credit for the weeks of preparation, the expense. But Lola admitted she hadn't even felt like dancing.

Saints protect good health and luck; ancestors afford favors and boons. On the afternoon after the morning a Machvanka buried her beloved mother, Eggi, in Sacramento, she headed for Reno where she played the number and date of Eggi's death, and she won five thousand!

## The "Up" and Auspicious

Certain actions are auspicious and move the actor in the "up" and spiritual direction. Those associated with cleanliness, purity, ritual avoidance, and fasting, and those involving respect, etiquette, and hospitality are particularly potent. Birth, baptism, and marriage constitute beginnings and increase luck powers exponentially. Singing, dancing, gambling, giving gifts are activities of merit that are said to create good luck. Serving *sarma* (cabbage rolls) and *gushvada* (strudel), foods associated with *baX*, is mandatory at *slavi* and other celebrations. Odd numbers are required for important ritual acts; odd numbers of people, of plates of food, of days, dates, and candles. In the natural order of things, increase is believed to feed through the entire extended family.

Certain items are pure, damage-resistant, and of an enduring value. These include the holy pictures and icons, the giant saint-day candle, incense, items associated with the ancestors—the magical tape that measures the Dead One, for an example—fresh air, trees (particularly trees with blossoms; indeed Saints may appear in trees), green leaves, fresh fast-running streams (water, fire, and incense have the power of transformation), bottles of whiskey, new and uncut bolts of cloth, beautiful music and dancing, the colors red and green, fresh fruit, fine jewels and gold, the shiny, the abundant, as well as less tangible assets, like wisdom, knowledge, good advice, good wishes, good intentions. These convey refined powers and are highly ranked on the scale of desirability; any of these make the ideal gift. Dreams of green snakes, the bright, the new, dancing waves and froth, anything moving in the upwards direction, anything suggesting increase or beginnings—a baby, for an example—indicates oncoming luck.

AT WELCOMES AND FAREWELLS, housewarmings, baptisms, weddings, holidays, the beginning of any new endeavor, and whenever thanking someone for a favor, the wish "*sastimasa, baXtasa*" (to your good health, to your good luck) is standard, and expresses the heartfelt good will, family to family, believed to be essential. At ritual events of renewal, The God, the Saints, the Spirits are requested to bring health and luck, which the people say is everything devoutly to be wished. Prayers will begin as follows: *Del* BaXtali Patradji (Give, Happy Easter), *Del* BaXtalo Nevo Bersh (Give, Happy New Year), *Del* BaXtali Kolunda (Give, Happy Christmas). *BaX* connotes both good luck and happiness.

At baptisms and weddings, the changing status of the new baby and the bride and groom must be matched with new clothes, entire wardrobes that include shoes, socks, and underclothes. Weeks and months are spent on *slavi* preparation, cleaning, scrubbing, painting, polishing, and purchasing new clothes for everyone in the family. The most important purchase is the ten-pound Saint's candle at a church store. New clothes are even more important, both before the burial and after, as entire outfits are given the proxy representing the deceased. The proxy also takes home the offerings, all new, a wall of items for the Dead One that are believed, in some fashion, to follow Him to the Other Side.

WHATEVER IS IN A BEGINNING STAGE has cachet, a purity and power expected to create new luck. Moving maximizes change and new beginnings, moving from neighborhood to neighborhood, state to state, and, a century ago, moving from country to country. Machvaia believe luck can be found on the road (*baX po drom*), the place of discovery. Young couples with small children tend to be especially mobile; they often look for a new business territory and financial independence from their elders.

But, in the Sixties, before the boon of the Social Security check, Lola was no longer young and she still moved, on average, once or twice a year. A new address, new stores to shop, the novelty of new clients and new neighbors meant, she hoped, fresh infusions of good luck.

Lola also changed her name to change her luck. When clients stopped calling her for readings and her October birthday was due within the week, Lola threw away her business flyers and announced, "Ruby. That's my new name. How do you like it? You be Ruth now. Ruth didn't do a thing for me."

## Misfortune and Escape

Machvaia often speak of making luck (*cherés chi baX*), and, on occasion, of keeping luck, looking for luck, or getting rid of bad luck. Most misfortune is attributed to lack of luck. But small and frequent disasters may also be blamed on the ill will of jealous people (invariably Roma), bad intent—intention has power—and witchcraft. A disaster of incomprehensible scale, like the 2005 and 2008 tsunami disasters, is attributed to The God, rather than luck.

Dreams, omens, and premonitions of disaster are respected, particularly when shared. On several occasions after the 1989 earthquake, the local Machvaia left San Francisco in a line of cars. Duda, Lola's daughter-in-law, called me in a panic, insisting I join them: "Hurry, get your things. There's going to be a terrible earthquake. Can't you feel it?" The escapees visited their friends and family in Sacramento, staying in motels, returning in two weeks. I later learned I had missed some wonderful parties.

Good powers are offered the good thought; they are to be sought, venerated, and adored. Evil—an unfriendly ghost, epilepsy, The Devil—may have to be fought, destroyed by fire, cleared away with incense, threatened with defilement, bought off with money that is cursed, or tricked into submission. Those who suffer repeated bad luck become privy to various games and pranks intended to fool and vex bad luck.

But that wasn't Lola. She called these "superstition of people without luck." She recommended avoidance and escape instead— escape is a well-known Machvaia policy. Indeed, moving repeatedly and running out on her bills was a kind of escape. "Or you could light a candle. Pray."

Lola escaped her marriage and, in her forties, divorced her husband. Her daughters often called when I was Lola's guest and I would overhear complaints about no-account husbands and miserable living circumstances. Lola always told her girls to leave, to get a divorce, to come and stay with her; "You'll get sick, living like that." Hanging up, she would sigh and say, "Wasted breath. She won't do that. She can't leave her children."

TO AVOID *BI-BAX*, Lola advocated positive thinking. As like has an affinity to like, Lola created an upbeat climate to attract good luck's favor. To think poor was to be poor and she considered generosity and spending essential to accumulation. Instead of complaining when she ran out of funds, she conjured benign thoughts and used the power of intention. To get what you want, she said, "You just hold it at the back of your mind, lightly, not too hard . . . Believe it, and you will get it."

Complaining about bad luck or talking about misfortune, damages the tenor of the day and lends the words a reality that might make such luck happen again. When I once asked Miller, Lola's son, about the Nazi pogroms and what may have happened to his distant relatives in Serbia, he begged me to be silent. "We don't want to hear about that," he shouted, jumping up from the sofa, waving away the distress with both hands.

## Chapter 4

# FEELING

## Feeling and "Finding Your Luck"

My first years with the Seattle Roma, the pop song "Feelings" was the Roma favorite, played over and over at top volume. At all the parties and public events I went to, "Feelings" relentlessly announced the cultural value of feeling. After fifteen minutes or so of ear-splitting repeats, I would have to go out "for air."

Machvaia use the English word "feeling" for a variety of experience, including the emotional, the intuitive, the empathic, and *zhav* (feeling sorry), which is described as akin to love. Feeling, as intuition, seems largely a matter of cluing into the sensation of the moment and suspending critical thought. This falls into what Marriott, writing about South Asia, calls the category of less tangible, more transformable, subtler, and relatively higher powers. Despite the lack of a Romani term that glosses feeling and intuition—although *gindo* (mind, will, intention) often serves in a pinch—both are employed as elements that, to the pragmatic Westerner, might well be considered psychic, "lying outside the realm of physical science or knowledge," according to Merriam-Webster.

Reading feelings, emotions, and thoughts is what fortune telling clients expect for their money, and what Machvaia expect of each other. Daily living requires sensitivity to others; "putting your mind" with the mind of someone else is a given. The people are also expected to know their own feelings and thoughts. Understanding yourself is considered wisdom and said to make one "understandable" to others.

To Machvaia, a feeling is reason enough to take action: "We started celebrating May 6th because we had the feeling," a Machvanki, Luludji, told me. "You follow the feeling to find your luck," is the way Katy's second husband put it during our discussion about the elusiveness of *baX*. Machvanki advertise as psychics and following intuition is precisely what they do when giving readings. The women, while teaching me to tell fortunes, advised me to say whatever I was thinking or feeling at that moment: "It's easy. Let it out." After our years together, Katy knew me quite well. She knew I might become overly concerned with what I might say. "Don't think too hard and don't worry!" Otherwise, she said, the words wouldn't automatically pop into my mouth.

Once, when I asked how to say "to feel" in the Romani language, I was told *filiz*, a term apparently adapted from the English word and possibly made up on the spot. Later, Anastasia, Lola's niece, explained that what I called feeling was something better not discussed, assuring me this made it more powerful. Machvaia place a considerable faith on the unseen and unspoken, and find the value of words limited. In the past, to show respect, the names of the Dead Ones were ideally not spoken aloud. So it is with the French Manuš, according to Patrick Williams' recent ethnography, the endearingly titled *Gypsy World: The Silence of the Living and the Voices of the Dead.*

## Intuition

At the turn of the previous century when Sampson studied the language of Welsh Gypsies, a conservative dialect, the verb *baXter* had two definitions: "1. to bless, to wish or make happy . . . [as] May God bless thee [and] 2. to wish, to will, to conjure, to effect by an act of volition (especially in magical transformations . . .)" (Sampson 1926:23). Machvaia currently have no verb for *baX*. But they do believe in the power of the wish and the will to affect present and future events.

In regard to her studies of the New York Roma, Gropper concurs, "that a strong belief in something brings about its own fulfillment" (1975:167).

STÉVO WAS A MACHVANO who was never known to be particularly lucky. In the Sixties, when we all lived in Seattle, Stévo's wife had too many small children underfoot to concentrate on reading palms. For income, Stévo bought used cars at a bargain price and sold them for as much as he could get. He didn't know much about a car's mechanics, but, based on years of experience, he had a genius for avoiding lemons. He would sit in the driver's seat, eyes closed, listening to the song of the engine, and make his decision to purchase the car, or not, accordingly.

Each day began with the traditional ritual of cleansing: "I get up, wash my hands and then my face. Then I feel fresh. I feel different." If his children hadn't ripped the newspaper into unreadable shreds, he checked the ads in the automobile section while he drank his coffee. If he wasn't required to run a sick or injured child to the emergency clinic or perform some other urgent fatherly duty, he might ease into the day with the luxury of a second cup. "Then I feel rich. That's the right way to feel when you are going to work."

If his wife hollered at him before breakfast, however, her anger bathed his prospects with bad luck, and he refused to leave the house. "She ruined it." Of course, inactivity wasn't always a viable option. When there wasn't enough for groceries or the rent was due, Stévo was required to change the character of the day and do something he wasn't good at, something he considered low class drudgery, and really hated—which was curbside car body repair. He would *del ando vas* (to give from the hand), making an offering to the ancestors, asking for their help and blessing. Then he would look for his luck *po drom* (on the road).

One time he was kind enough to explain the details of his day to me. "If I get up with a good feeling, like I did this morning, and drive around where I feel a job might be, I do all right. Like I drove north for awhile, and then I came back to town, went to Alki Beach, and got the feeling to go back north. That's where I made fifty dollars, fixing a fender on a Volkswagon. It was a pop-out; I didn't even break the paint! I knew I would find business. I had the feeling. It's an extra-sympathetic feeling. That's how I live."

LUCK, GOOD AND BAD, is empowered by intention. Once, Old Yasha's wife accidentally sat on his lucky hat, juxtaposing a lower body surface onto an upper body object and thereby incurring a taboo. But because he knew she didn't mean to do so, Yasha laughed and put it on his head.

Although the nature of intention is critical, taking positive action is also recommended. Last year, young Gina, who had a business location in Los Angeles, complained about a client who, while demanding quick results, left the resolution of his unreciprocated affection for a fellow employee entirely up to her. "I told him, if you're not going to do anything about it, if you don't talk to her, it's not about to happen. Visualizing is important. But you have to do more."

Gambling, a favorite Machvaia pastime, involves both activity and feeling: "You bet the way you feel," Bibi explained, putting her chips on a roulette number. Following the feeling, feeling/intention/action, is the winning combination. Lola's youngest daughter Zoni, Katy, and I went to Lake Tahoe to gamble. By concentrating together on the same number, we won three games and got so lucky the club closed the table down!

The people regard gambling a perfectly legitimate means to enjoyment and, despite considerable evidence to the contrary, believe gambling has great windfall potential. On occasion, they even get lucky. A decade before the Sausalito Machvanka won twelve million in the State lottery, a Machvano in Las Vegas confirmed this positive line of thought about the rewards of gambling by winning a three hundred thousand dollar jackpot.

Machvaia play their hunches; they attend to feelings. The message in dreams, the feelings in dreams are frequently discussed, credited, interpreted, and even obeyed. Premonitions are often presumed to be the protective work of ancestors. Anastasia and her sister were once at a movie when Anastasia got a feeling of dread. She grabbed her sister's hand and pulled her, protesting, to the streetcar. At home, they just had time to join their stricken mother in the ambulance. Anastasia credited the premonition to the abiding concern of her mother's mother, Mami Muli (Grandmother Dead Woman) for her family.

The appropriate feeling is the essence of ritual. Virtue and luck are expected to "match." Anastasia put it like this, "You do the right thing because it's good luck." Feelings associated with the message of luck usually follow Machvaia custom and the recommended *vorta* (right) and moral action. In keeping with the principles of purity maintenance, for example, washing his face in the morning helped Stévo feel lucky.

But only saints are perfect and, whenever one of Lola's family or the other Machvanki I knew forgot to fast on Friday or on any other weekday promised to the Saint, she excused herself without remorse. "I guess I didn't have the feeling." Or, "Saint knows I meant to." In terms of effective ritual, feeling and intent must go hand in hand.

## Misfortune and Jealousy

Those who are good are not always lucky, and anyone can have a run of bad luck. Machvaia seldom blame themselves or the mistakes they have made for their misfortunes. They prefer to project, blaming inherited luck, blaming Americans who have no heart, or blaming the ill will of "those other people," meaning other Gypsies. In regard to attracting jealousy, Lola told me, "It's best to be *prosto* (ordinary, simple), not *puchardé* (puffed up)." When her parents and family first arrived in America, everyone was *prosto*: "We were all poor and miserable; we didn't even know the language." Now the trick was to be high class and "big," without becoming insufferably proud and therefore hated.

Not all Machvaia are successful at avoiding jealousy and envy. The more reputable and powerful are often more accomplished at the recommended behaviors than those less fortunate. When I slyly asked what I might I do if I felt jealous, Lola recommended expressing the feeling frankly and "bringing it out." Direct expressions of jealousy indicate the wish to emulate the other. Praise offers the gift of respect, and puts the receiver up into an ascendant position, thereby benefiting both parties, and creating the basis for a new understanding.

Nearly everything involved in earning money eludes the certainty of good outcome. Like many European Gypsies, Machvaia operate in the unofficial margins of the business world. Their methods are designed to offer as little competition as possible with powerful Outsider institutions or the territories of other Roma readers. To keep good luck, the identity of Outsider clients, and the arrangements with the police and the city council must be kept as secret as possible. At public events, the Machvanka is frequently asked, "How's business? Are you making any money?" These days, in fact, since the cost of living has escalated, it is easy to say "Not good." But earlier in the last century, when asked how she was doing financially, the reader was well advised to be discreet. Otherwise, other fortune tellers, including her impossible-to-refuse relatives, were apt to move into her territory, copy her advertisements, and steal her customers—this happened to several women I knew. Or they might achieve a similar result and ruin her luck by projecting angry, jealous thoughts. But cursing, Lola warned me, was no job for amateurs. Owing to the process of automatic retribution, good going to good, bad to bad, curses, when undeserved, can boomerang and "fall back upon my house."

## *Dav Armaiya* (I give a curse)

Machvaia consider words and intentions to have a profound and communicable effect. When angry, Machvaia are inclined to curse, calling upon their ancestors for assistance. They curse members of their families, of other families, the dead, but never the godparents or the holy saints. A curse can be spoken or unspoken. Primarily an act of volition, the strength of curse or oath is expected to correspond to the degree with which it was felt. I understand many people of European heritage were, and perhaps still are, afraid of a Gypsy's curse.

Intense and unexpressed emotions relating to romantic love, longing, or acute grief are believed to emit a negative power and detrimentally affect the well being of the individual and the family. Rage and jealousy lead to curses, bad luck, ill health, and suspicions of witchcraft. As Gropper (1975:168) writes, "Gypsies believe that any strong negative emotion, such as hate or envy, generates a disharmonic force field in the universe that attracts more disharmony (Americans would say 'evil')."

Placing a great emphasis on the unseen, Machvaia connect intuition and feeling, strong thoughts (*zuralés ginduria*) and willful intention, as well as the omens seen in dreams and visions with their luck. Perhaps this is because, having lost the Brahmin experts who knew the ancient words and rituals, they learned, when trying to cope with trauma, to focus on the unseen. Reconstructing their history is impossible, of course, as Romani was not, until recently, a written language, and none of the Machvaia I know seem aware of written Romani. In addition, by temperament, the people invariably prefer to move on from the past. But some of the Gypsies' centuries of escape and abuse are documented in European laws and records. During their experience as helpless Romanian slaves it might be supposed that VlaX-Roma lacked much opportunity to express vengeful thoughts, other than through a silent curse.

ON OCCASION, as she became old and sick, Lola referred to an intuitive sixth sense Roma are reputed to have, and which they do believe they have, and complained, "In my heart, in my body, I can feel someone is doing me damage." A curse (*armaiya*) involves intent, whereas a witch lacks this awareness. I couldn't tell which, curse or witchery, Lola had in mind when she referred to someone doing her damage, and maybe she didn't know either. But that's when she ordered, cursed, or prayed a countering defense with "Leave the bad luck to go away and the good luck to come back."

Rituals associated with "perfect" Saints are, of course, particularly sensitive to an angry curse. Years ago during *slava*, Old Kaboka got a telephone call from her younger brother, Nick, asking her for money. When she refused to sponsor any more of his good-time trips to Mexico, Nick cursed her St. George *slava*, yelling, "Pish on your table, your lamb, your candle." Kaboka had no choice: she threw the defiled lamb, food, candle into a plastic sack, tossed it in the garbage, and told her guests to go home. "The *slava* is over."

But a brother is a brother and, later, when Nick, possibly drunk, was driving and his car rolled over several times, Kaboka said, "he didn't get hurt. Knocked his shoes off. But he didn't have a scratch." Kaboka was anxious to explain to me that the accident was not owing to any ill will on her part. "Honey," she said, "When he did that, cursed my *slava*, I was praying that The God and the Dead Ones would protect him, him first and then me. Which they did."

## Ineffable Luck

A life that is lived in accord with *romania*, Sutherland writes, comprising "traditions, customs, ideal behavior, morals, beliefs, rituals, and attitudes" (102), as well as ritual cleanliness and generosity is expected to bring *baX* (1975:282). To this I would add the aforementioned auspicious items, the Machvaia preference for ranking, and the matching of like to like, good to good.

But the Machvaia have an expression, "Too good is no good." Machvaia must look for luck in the danger and uncertainty of America where, as they say—from the standpoint of Machvaia morality and Machvaia custom—"anything goes." Knowing what is lucky and not-lucky so often presents a quandary. As playboy Ephram put it, "Things like clothes, charms that seem to be lucky for a person. Why? Who knows? A rabbit's foot wasn't lucky for the rabbit, and he had four of them."

Sometimes even stepping outside *romania*, breaking the Rom law, brings success. "Following the feeling" can lead the people in unauthorized, but rewarding, directions. It did for Bahto, Lola's former husband. When his family arrived in the States, their world was wagons and horses, and the most they could travel was five miles a day. But young Bahto, against his father's better judgment, insisted on buying an automobile, and they began to camp in towns and put up their tents in vacant city lots. Instead of farmhouses, women gave readings in storefronts. Cities were full of potential fortune-telling customers, the legend of the "like gold" Machvaia readers was born, and the people were on their way. (See examples, Miller 1997:22–23)

In 1940, Alexander Petrović, a medical doctor, wrote of the Serbian Gypsies that "every man has his luck, some better, some worse . . . So the greatest wisdom in life for the Serbian Gypsy is to discover who and what (person, animal, or thing) brings him luck, and to keep that person or thing for himself" (41). As luck is only found in outcome, the character of luck is necessarily after-the-fact. Luck is whatever works, which is usually the culturally valued or what has previously proved advantageous. But when it isn't, the enterprising must rely on the message of feeling. The uncertainty of what will be lucky, the gap between performance and outcome, and the question of how much, or how little luck there will be, turns every enterprise into an adventure.

WHEN, A CENTURY AGO, the people traveled as wanderers and nomads, no more than a few staples, cooking oil and coffee, could be stored and carried. It was a matter of one wagon, two horses, a heavy load of children, and as few possessions as possible. With little but their wits as capital, the people trusted to the moment's bounty. They lived in hope of what might lay around the bend. They wished—remember, wishing has power—for fresh water and a land generous with produce. They believed in the good power of their luck.

Historically, luck beliefs explain much about the people's willingness to risk new ventures and to deliver themselves speedily from unpromising ones. Leaving the unpleasantness of the past behind, they rationalize it as luck, and forget it. The power of desire and unfolding of feeling leads them to begin afresh. The power of the Dead Ones affords unseen protection. The rituals and beliefs surrounding luck suggest, in part, how and why the Gypsies, so often strangers in hostile foreign lands, have persisted for a thousand years and occasionally prospered.

# The Romany Church

THAT FIRST SUMMER OF FIELDWORK in Seattle, I occasionally took my daughter when I visited Katy's First Avenue storefront. Leslie, at sixteen, was the same age as Katy's daughter Sophie. I suspect Leslie's willingness to visit Gypsies helped Katy construe me as less of a threat.

At first, whenever I stopped by the First Street storefront, Katy's Kalderasha husband was out, according to gossip, dating American women. "No good, a playboy," was how Lola put it. Respect rests on shame-aversion and the willingness to be discrete. But Ephram disappeared for weeks, returned as he liked, and his disregard for a cover-up left Katy to deal with the scandal. When any of the Roma called, proud Katy was required to answer something like, "No, he's not in and I don't know when he will be back."

Then, in the fall, Ephram's girlfriend was suddenly out of the picture, and Ephram was back with his family. Curious about my presence, he followed me out to the car to ask what I was doing. "Religion?" Ephram stuttered as he opened my Volkswagon door. "You want to ask us questions about our *religion*? No kidding? We have a religion?"

Later, after she had divorced him, Katy admitted that when Ephram rented the brown-shingled house and said they were "going American," she went along, figuring it might prove a distraction from his obsessive career as a playboy.

AS I WAS THE APPARENT EXPERT on religious matters, Ephram called to say he needed written evidence, a "Bible Romanes." Inviting me over for three kinds of pie, a table of cakes, wine, beer, and boiled-to-black Gypsy coffee, he ordered his family to submit to interrogation. Roma who dropped by were offered the usual hospitality and required to "Sit and answer the Djuhli's questions."

But the family was unused to explaining the unexplainable. Humiliated by the frank direction of my questions, at least half of which were verboten topics—the Dead, the Devil, bad luck, *choXani* (ghosts)—they defended themselves by remaining in motion, flying through the room, changing the subject. Unintelligible answers and showers of giggles exploded from the curtained doorway. Vocalizations of "Gimme That Old Time Religion," the family found, invariably cracked me up and halted my questions. When Ephram went outside to show a car to a prospective buyer, a ten-minute silence followed. I folded my notebook and left.

THE NEXT DAY, Ephram called to apologize and promised his family would try again. "Saints are guardian angels," little Julie lisped, and the silly flyaway family flapped their arms and crowed like roosters. Then, while Katy left to give a reading, Steve, the son with the missing wife, showed me some of the latest Gypsy dance steps. Meanwhile, Lana waltzed out the door on her way to the market, Jelly John behind her, while the oldest girl, Sophie, curled a forefinger at a passer-by without success. I was rising again in exasperation when Papusha, somebody's cousin, whispered, "We pray to the Saints for health and luck."

The distractible family returned to the fray, and I asked them which was more important, health or luck? "Happiness," Steve said, signaling Sophie to refill my coffee. Ephram appeared in the doorway and, hearing the topic under discussion, thoughtfully repeated "happiness" as he settled into the only armchair, crossing his ankles to feature his new two-tone shoes. "Happiness is getting what you want the very moment that you want it, neither sooner nor later, don't you think?" He glanced winsomely at me for backing.

"You should know," Katy glared, and offered me a piece of cake from Julie's birthday party, which Ephram had neglected to attend. Pleased with himself and the progress of his bible,

Ephram went to get the pencil stub with which I was instruct-
ed to write the story of their "true believe."

They began with what they thought I expected, all the
scenes that could be remembered from biblical Hollywood
films. Opinion differed as to whether or not Charlton Heston
had enough aplomb to be Moses, who they described as "a very
big man." "And good besides," Katy added, taking a cigarette
out of her apron pocket and trying to help. When I asked how
they knew what was good, they said good was the right thing to
do, that they lived by the lessons of the generations, and, when
in doubt, they asked the *phurotem* (elders).

No priest; each Rom was the priest and guardian for his
family. No church; the home shrine was their primary place
of worship. No serious crimes like murder because Roma are
nice, Jelly John promised, proud to be so nice that he bent his
fat waist to kiss his sister's hand, and she archly fanned her
short skirts in curtsey. No sin, although no one liked a crying
kind of face. Then Ephram pointed at the television screen,
the unrelenting media eye on the sins of America, and promised that what he saw there was forbidden to occur in his
house.

Katy sniffed.

After that, Ephram took the lead, standing up to test the
sound of his message. "Take this down!" he directed. "This
isn't superstition any longer. Call it cosmology!"
Cosmology? Had he been reading anthropology?

I SOON REALIZED THIS was quid pro quo; trade and nego-
tiation would be the name of the game. In the unity of a hard-
won understanding, my job was to furnish them credence in
the Outsider world, to create, if not invent, the expected categories of goodness, evil, sin, something akin to a religion. I
would underwrite the official version of the New Romany
Church and, in the meantime, collect the research material I
needed. Sworn to secrecy and buoyed by our mutual need,
heady with an upbeat combination of complicity and acceptance, I felt certain to have passed the fieldwork test. Now,
decades later, I find it was the truth of that moment. No
longer.

Ephram took my amateurish pages to the Seattle City Council. He traded them for a license that gave his brown house church the official go-ahead. Renting his uncle's new truck and ringing doorbells, announcing that money or furniture would be fine—"It's for a very good cause, God, and tax deductible"—Ephram collected donations. Katy was re-christened, appropriately enough, Sister Charity. Sister had less aptitude for her role than expected. Ephram criticized her dress, her headscarf, her coppery-colored hair, her tendency to lapse into Romanes phrases and English gutturals when counseling clients. He said she looked more Gypsy than minister, and she said he should advertise as the Holy Father: "You got children all over the world crying for their father." On a continuing high of good expectation, Ephram stockpiled folding chairs. "Mass production is the American way to do business."

THEN, ANOTHER OUTSIDER caught Ephram's bad luck eye, and he was over the hill and gone again. The yard grew to prairie grass; the church sign disappeared. Lola tossed her hands in the air. "He can't change. That's his luck." Sometimes *baX* is destiny.

# Chapter 5

# FOOD

## "Did You Eat Today?"

"Eat!" Lola would command as we enjoyed our afternoon supper. "Eat! You'll get sick if you don't eat!" she said, taking the best bite off her plate and putting it, without comment, on mine. *Xabé* (food) sharing signifies the give and take of kin relationships and bonding.

Providing food creates a climate of caring. Whoever feeds you, particularly cooked food, becomes like a mother. Machvaia mothers seldom refuse their children food. One time, Katy's daughter-in-law got up in the dead of night to walk ten blocks to MacDonalds, she said, to buy the Big Mac her three-year-old son demanded.

Most of this past century, the ghost of hunger put the edge to accumulation. The concern with getting enough to eat is reflected by their standard greeting. Instead of an American hello, Machvaia would ask me, "Did you eat today?"

As a BaXtali (Good Luck Machvanka), Lola was determinedly optimistic. But even she managed to recall times so tough that "the cupboard was bare and the children was crying for food." The Machvaia focus on food is underwritten by their origin myth about the Church of Cheese: the people got so hungry they ate their church!

In the past, food sharing served a larger purpose. Once it meant a fair and equable distribution and involved the health and well being of more than the immediate family. The people traveling in groups *po drom* (on the road) stopped mid-afternoon and each tent prepared a stew over their fire. The people moved convivially from pot to pot, talking, laughing, sampling. If nothing was available, belts were tightened and any verbal reference to food was avoided. Then, Lola explained, "We lived on air."

Before the days of Public Assistance and Aid to Families with Dependent Children, obtaining food was apparently a challenge. Slender people were conceived of as impoverished in a general sense and the cause for some concern among their relatives. Beauty of physical form was understood as plumpness, the certain sign of good living. Corpulence was associated with strength, success, good health, and good luck—a visible attribute of merit. The honorific titles of Baro and Bari connoted, and do so still, the masculine and feminine for big, great, and powerful, both literally and figuratively.

Baro George of Los Angeles, whose reign ended in the Sixties, was portly. He is, in living memory, the most illustrious example of an effective Machvaia leader. Having made mysterious arrangements with the police, he "owned" a large piece of Los Angeles and doled out territories. Despite the fact that fortune telling was illegal in California, as Baro, he could assure these families a "territory" and legal protection.

MACHVAIA SAY, "BREAD IS SUCCESS." Bread refers to life, need, and sufficiency. Special breads are cooked for Christmas, on the New Year, at Easter, and whenever the mouth wants them. At *slavi*, a long loaf is placed upright beside the giant *slava* candle. At a lineal *slava* (saint-day), the father and son may pray for the health and luck of the family with a round loaf of bread. At a birth celebration I once attended, the mother-in-law baked a gold coin in *pogacha* (flour, salt, baking powder) bread; whoever got the coin in their piece was expected to have good luck. In those days, throwing bread into the garbage was forbidden. Leftover bread was given to birds; birds have a close connection to the beloved ancestors and the Other World. Even yet, at the end of the year of mourning, in the manner of a goodbye snack, the Dead One's candle may be stuck in *pogacha* bread upon a silk handkerchief and sent on a little raft down "a river that runs."

When Katy finally left husband Ephram and moved to her Pike Place Market storefront, I often stopped by to enjoy the table drama, the plate-to-plate redistribution, the gallant exaggerations about how the spoils were won. Katy's seven-year-old daughter Julie skipped around the block looking for coins on the sidewalk; little Jelly John manfully lugged his shoeshine stand to the corner; Sophie gave a plate of food to the homeless man who brought us a pound of coffee; clever Lana and her mother told fortunes in exchange for shopping bags of day-old vegetables. Everyone helped, ate, enjoyed. In the days when single Katy was raising her family and making a living, each afternoon meal was a triumph.

## Food as Brotherhood

What is eaten is taken into the body; it becomes the body. Eating together confirms that commensals are equal in respect, moral rectitude, and purity practice. Eating together demonstrates solidarity; an act of physical incorporation, it suggests political incorporation. Eating together enacts ideals of brotherhood and equality. It says we are all together in this moment at this table. We are all the same.

This system of beliefs is apparent at *krisa* (Roma court and law). If everyone present eats with the defendant, he is restored to acceptable community standing. If not, he is stigmatized and ideally avoided by all the Roma. For those not in attendance at the trial, the critical information is whether or not, before the men left the courtroom, they drank coffee or whiskey with the defendant.

Commensality is a mix of the moral, the political, and the prophylactic. On any social occasion, denial of commensality, either by failure to offer food or drink, or by serving the guest a beverage in a cracked or discolored cup, constitutes insult. Decades ago, when I headed an exploratory research project on the topic of Washington State Gypsies, a leading Tacoma Kalderasha family and I were served coffee in this demeaning fashion. In response, we coolly smiled and ignored the compromised service, leaving as quickly as we could. Realizing this Spokane family was unwilling to participate in our project, we settled for revenge. Failing to take a sip or bite when a drink or food is offered suggests the host is impure, possibly diseased, and no longer worthy of respect.

Besides the moral "goodness" required for commensality, food is associated with intimacy and rapport. It isn't enough to fill the belly; the taste, the mouth, and the senses are to be exquisitely sated and the *odji* (stomach/heart), the center of being, seduced to a ripe satisfaction. Regarding ingestion process, all conditions—the preparation, the nature of the company—must be favorable. Coffee is a bit of a fetish among the Machvaia. If the cup and saucer, the taste, the cream, the server's attitude is inadequate in any way, the guest may refuse it.

Harmony is ritual's keynote. Whenever anyone at the table can't eat, gets sick, receives bad news and lays down his fork, no one eats. Everything is subject to contact, and contact concerns both the visible and the felt. Ruled by this susceptibility, the people are unable to eat with those they cannot tolerate or stomach, or any place they don't feel entirely comfortable. To share a meal in the communal Machvaia fashion is truly to eat in unison and together.

One time when I stopped by Katy's unannounced, she had an older Rom her children called Kako (Uncle) Spirako as a guest. He found he couldn't eat his dinner in my presence. Everyone at our table had started, but he sat holding his fork in the air, unable to proceed, most likely because I was an Outsider, and he had never before eaten in a Gypsy home with an Outsider. To do so is forbidden, unlawful. As we sat, not eating, the conversation continued. I wanted to go to my car, but Katy said no. After he left and the table was cleared, Katy tried to deny the significance of what had happened. Patting my hand, she weakly explained, "Times are changing. But he doesn't know you."

## Food as Desire

Machvaia believe that each adult or child ought to get whatever he wants in this life and that other Machvaia, being of the same connected bloodlines and history, the same *vitsa* luck and sympathetic heart, are obliged to help.

The gift of hospitality was once underwritten by disease sanction. Guests that left the table hungry for an item of food were vulnerable to *poftarniko*, the fasting disease. Until the past several decades, Machvaia obsessed about their guests' satisfaction for this reason. "Try this!" the hosts would urge. "Have some more!" they pressed. For if the eye had spied, the nose had smelled, the stomach longed for something on the table—and sometimes the item of food was recalled and desired later—*poftarniko* might ensue.

A Machvano I met in Seattle told me, "If a person doesn't get a bite of what he wants, he will get sick. That's right. Gypsies do." As an example of how this might happen, he said he and some Kalderasha men had gone hunting in the San Juan Islands. "Jimmy George was fixing this rabbit. He'd salted it and rubbed it with garlic—he's a great cook—and just about the time it was roasted, he had to go to the car for something. His brothers, to be funny, threw the rabbit into the brush. Well, it wasn't really that funny because Jimmy couldn't eat anything after that. He was *poftarniko* (fasting disease). He wanted that particular rabbit."

Certain Machvaia lineages, like the Machvaia Stevens and the Lees, are known to be easily *poftarniko*; if they see something on the table they want, they must eat it. Women who are pregnant, or the very young, are especially susceptible to the fasting disease. Pregnancy is known as a time of eccentric desires. When Duda, Lola's daughter-in-law, was pregnant with her daughter Gina, she had a craving for a splash of gasoline on ice and, if she hadn't taken a little, she might have, she confided, "thrown the baby out early." For reasons of *poftarniko* danger, anyone in a beginning life stage, a child, pregnant woman, the just-married couple, should avoid ending-life-stage events, and particularly the *pomana*, the death commemoration. Machvaia explain that they might see some item on the table, want it, and get sick because they are not allowed, by tradition, to eat it. Indeed, regarding a pregnant woman we both knew, Lola said, "It will be bad for her if she eats it and bad for her if she doesn't."

Those who become *poftarniko* constitute a significant danger to themselves and a threat to others. "They see it, need it, have it on the mind, and they suffer." Those selfish and unfeeling Gypsies who fail to satisfy the gustatory needs of others can find themselves and their extended family haunted by hostile and powerful *poftarniko* Dead Ones.

I was told terrible tales of the fasting disease, "all true." In one story, a hungry daughter-in-law, busy serving her family and her elders, hadn't time to eat. She was found dead the next morning. *Poftarniko* was to blame. When an autopsy was performed, the amazing power of appetite and the human will became clear. Food the daughter-in-law particularly wanted, but had not eaten, was discovered in her stomach.

Children seem especially susceptible—Lola told a poignant story about a two-year-old *po drom* (on the road) who hungered for the half moon. His mother sang to him, scolded him, then she beat him to stop his crying. She tried everything she knew, even offering him a banana, not the easiest fruit to find when they were traveling. But the child knew the difference; he died, Lola assured me, of *poftarniko*.

How to avoid *poftarniko*? Lucky Lola claimed she had never been *poftarniko*. "If I see something at the store and I have the money, I buy it. If my heart wants it, I get it."

## Food as Hospitality

Hospitality is giving, and giving is meritorious; it is the nature of food, Machvaia say, to be shared.

The people will spend weeks preparing for the festive three-day *slava* (saint-day). Food is offered to the Saint with the prayer for health and luck; minutes or hours later, that same food is offered to all the Machvaia present. (According to Hindu custom, the food has become sacred leftovers and eating them confers a blessing.) Sundays, the Machvanka lights a candle and places a bit of food and an offering of coffee next to the household shrine. At *pomani* (commemorations), generous tables of food are offered to the ancestors. Whenever the thought of a Dead One comes to mind, honor can be paid with the prayer, "*T'ai tanglal mulo* (To have before Him),*" accompanied by a bit of fresh coffee poured into the saucer, or the clean sink, or on a green grassy mound outside. On Memorial Day, Machvaia like to picnic on the family graves, offering whatever the Dead One especially enjoyed, including cigarettes.

I learned that hospitality yields advantage to both the giver and the getter. In the 1990s, whenever I was staying with Katy and her new husband, she invariably cooked us a handsome breakfast of eggs, toast, bacon, and potatoes. Once, in return, I asked if I might take the family to dinner? Katy assured me that reciprocity wasn't necessary, that she offered me breakfast because I was her friend and her company, that her efforts were "putting me in her power." The upwards direction is everything to Machvaia and, as Mauss

(1990:74) points out, in archaic societies, "To give is to show one's superiority, to be more, to be higher in rank."

IN THE 1970s and 1980s, nearly all the Machvaia appeared to have money and they repeatedly offered their peers good times. Machvaia believe in generous tables; they believe their women can provide them.

In the 1930s, "Madame Butterfly," an entrepreneurial Machvaia *bori* (daughter-in-law) of only sixteen who had married into a Yovanovich family, received the unheard of sum of one hundred thousand dollars for her fortune telling services. Her accomplishments enhanced the reputation of the Machvaia *vitsa* among American Roma and set a challenging precedent for all Machvanki breadwinners. By the Sixties, Butterfly's story (she was arrested, went to jail, came out, and managed the same coup again and again) had become endemic. The Machvanki became described as the "big money" women. Whatever the income source—selling a house, a car or boat, collecting brideprice, collecting on insurance, or receiving Aid to Dependent Children—gossip gave the family fortune teller credit. Some readers even enjoyed cultivating a mystical, rather witchy, character. Once, when I was staying with a family of modest means in Los Angeles, the Machvano complained that he hadn't the money for tomorrow's golf. To our mutual amazement, his wife walked around the block, came back with a hundred dollars, and refused to say how she got it.

WHEN I FIRST BEGAN MY STUDY of the Machvaia, several evenings a week I drove the few minutes from the University District to downtown Seattle and Katy's storefront. When I knocked, no one answered. So I walked through the unlocked door into the back of the store where, in competition with the television, the music was playing. After that, I never bothered to knock.

Asking Katy about her open door, she explained that at any time of the day or night guests might drop by for a cup of coffee and her home must be open to "all the Roma," thereby confirming the moral character of the inhabitants—"That shows we are living in the good way." As in the time of traveling and tents, Katy's home and her family were continually on display and at the service of other Roma.

Whenever I arrived at Lola's door, she ran to the kitchen for coffee, cream, sugar, and a snack. She taught me in a most concrete fashion that Machvaia hospitality has to do with the virtue of sharing, that the arrival of guests requires food and celebration.

When I commended her on making me feel so welcome, she explained tersely, "that's the Machvaia way." Hospitality was the happy lesson of *po drom*. Back then, according to Lola, whenever other Roma families were met on the road and found they spoke an intelligible Romani, they might camp for days, sometimes for weeks. The party lasted until the food, the drinks, and the money were gone, and the property owner had lost all patience. No one wanted to break the spell, to say goodbye, to end the bliss of being together. Circumstance, not intent, "broke us up," Lola told me. The vagaries of luck and the whims of the crazy Outsiders were to blame. Otherwise, no one would ever choose to part—Lola sighed, overcome with nostalgia—not from "the people they love and always want to be with." That the meetings on the road were perceived through an alcoholic haze made no difference. Nothing is as true as the truth of experience. Happiness arrived with the wine, with the warmth of meeting people starved for gossip and eager to escape the rigors of traveling. The infrequency of these meetings worked like a charm, the valorous impression lasting, repeated in song and story, blossoming into myth and legend. Those people never seen again became especially mythical. The unforgettable moment was easily achieved, for that was the time when the people knew they were special, the kind The God had favored, whose talent was to have the most enjoyable and unforgettable parties.

## Food as Festivity

Not until I had moved to the Bay Area did I fully understand the spiritual import of pleasure. Sometimes individually, sometimes as a group, the Machvaia men made the rounds of California homes to be fed, celebrated, entertained. Diplomats without sashes, they left the house early to go about their visits. They left to other welcomes so they might recount, on their return, how beautifully they were served and how much they were appreciated. They discussed Machvaia affairs, a prestigious topic, and collected the merit of admiration and liking. Was the host family in need? Were they living ethically and in accord with Machvaia precepts? Visits like these connected household to household. As Katy's live-in guest, I would hear the news of the day studied, sifted for meaning, reinterpreted, and phoned to other households.

Families with more than one daughter-in-law-in-training generally rose in reputation. The young women would clean, cook, keep the children out of sight, and offer their best singing and dancing entertainment. In the days of open-door hospitality, "seeing each other in the good way" was paramount.

Enjoyment ranks high on the scale of life's worthwhile possibilities, and the life of the Machvano was theoretically one of enjoyment. Described as a playboy, a king, the Machvano played his role to the hilt. Some men even did so without the backing of much money. Such is the force of myth.

On my visits to Los Angeles, I sometimes stayed with a famous Machvaia partying pair, Leo and Srécha. The couple were said to exemplify the best Machvaia values, arriving early at the public events to offer service, always noticing what was needed and helping out. My nights on their living room couch were fitful, however. The flat was in line with a major Hollywood freeway on-ramp. In sync with the vehicles passing nearby, the walls shook, thundered, and roared.

The Machvaia described Leo with favor as a kind man, unpretentious and good-hearted. (I would add he was charismatic.) Whenever he wasn't fishing or golfing, he was visiting other households. Served in the formal hospitality fashion, he would ask how things were going, confirm the report through personal observation, and, by sharing and pleasing, create a reserve of community good will. His hosts were honored to see him, and even more honored to feed him. Leo had little money for other entertainments. Srécha had been arrested so many times that telling fortunes had become high risk. But, despite their depressed economic circumstances, Leo was never described as being poor and bad luck. Popular from coast to coast, he was a veritable King Midas in terms of friendship. The men of Los Angeles pooled their money to take him wherever they went.

Over their protests, and because they really needed the money, I insisted on paying the couple a nominal amount for room and board. The money went directly into party food and hospitality. I was there one evening when nothing remained for our supper, and Srécha closed the window blinds. While the eager guests we didn't have the heart to turn away banged on the door, she and I hid out together in the back room with a box of stale crackers and the television.

## Hospitality and Djuhli (American Woman)

Lola took me everywhere, to all the ritual events. Although eating together, Machvaia and Outsiders, was forbidden, I was, nevertheless, wined, dined, entertained, and treated with the same courtesy as Lola. Young girls honored Lola with presentation dances; as her companion, I shared the glory. Was it by virtue of some special unknown powers that Lola managed me this show of acceptance? Was it her age and importance as a high-class BaXtali woman that gave her such amazing clout? I assumed it was both.

Not until I had moved to California did I learn how Lola's younger son, the laughing Miller, had explained my presence. He said he told the Kalderasha, the other "tribes," as he called them, that I was Lola's nurse. Pleased to have put one over on those who had often made his life a misery, he thought it a great joke: "Who would refuse an ailing old woman the attentions of her nurse?" His news dismayed me. I had mistakenly believed I was gaining in popularity and cultural expertise.

Whenever I visited Lola, she welcomed me royally. But the distance between Machvaia and Outsider became a painful matter to us both when I tried to reciprocate. Having moved into a new Seattle apartment, I invited Lola and Katy to a house-warming party. While pouring coffee into my recently purchased Wedgwood cups, I explained they were new, and I had just washed them in my brand new dishpan. Lola's cup hovered at her lips, and then she set it down, despairing; "I'm just not used to it." Humiliated, she asked me to drive her home immediately.

The apparently less exalted Katy returned with me to eat, drink, and then stayed for several hours. Recently, when I asked Fatima why her mother-in-law Lola had failed to eat what I prepared, she explained it was likely Lola couldn't believe I had observed all the customs regarding food management, that despite my desire to emulate what I had learned about purity and defilement, I hadn't been trained from childhood, like a Machvanka.

Yet Lola and I often dined together in restaurants. Lola preferred well-lighted and "fresh" looking eating places where she could observe the preparation. Her mother, Stanya, however, and "all the other old people," she assured me, never ate in restaurants; to them, American restaurants were "*nai latchi* (not good)." The caste-like separation between Machvaia and Outsider is backed by *vužo* (purity) custom. Repeatedly, over the years, I have heard the terrible tale of the non-Gypsy dishwasher who had dropped the dishrag on the floor, picked it up, and proceeded to wash with the same, now defiled, dishrag. Nevertheless, for reasons I cannot explain, restaurant eating and party catering are the Machvaia fashion of today and undoubtedly of the future.

IN 1971, Katy moved to California a year before I did and became, much of the time, my frequent chaperone at Machvaia parties, celebrations, and commemorations. Seldom did I try to explain the word anthropologist, a dismayingly difficult concept that gave the people the idea I was a spy, and reminded me that I was, in a sense, a voyeur. But, somehow, only on two occasions did a Machvano complain about the impropriety of my presence to my face.

Once when we were staying in Sacramento, I heard Katy explain me as *poftarniko* for the ceremonial food—that was a good one! But was she believed? Several times, she told the women that I had baptized her children, which was patently untrue but very effective; godparents must be treated "like God." (Later I did baptize two of her step-grandchildren.) Often, in the face of perplexity, I would try to explain that I wanted to write a "good story" about Machvaia which, I promised, would offset all the usual lies and misconceptions. This seemed to make no impression whatsoever on my audience; they had no interest in reading books. In any case, I could see my opinion, as an Outsider, didn't matter. The people recognize passion and, like their tolerance for different religions and exotic beliefs of every kind, honored it with some compassion. They said, "I pity you"—apparently for my impossible task.

As the years passed and I became a familiar face in the Bay Area, the people would introduce me in the following manner: "This is Djuhli (American Woman)," adding the clincher, "She understands," which provided me a gilt-edged guarantee of acceptance. Eating was part of every get-together and, knowing the taboo against eating with Outsiders, I was always somewhat apprehensive. The people gave me so much, in so many ways, and all I had to give them in return was my affection. I loved a few, and liked a great many; liking has power and the people make a habit of reading intention. Nevertheless, I think the main reason I was tolerated was owing to the people's generous nature, their ingrained hospitality, their basic need to give and share. Despite all contrary ruling regarding Outsider avoidance, I now believe I wasn't summarily given the boot because of the good will, inclusive fellowship, and spiritual implications of the very public moment.

# Katy in Oakland, the Heyday

IN THE EARLY SEVENTIES, although she "didn't want to do it; I'll be lonesome without her," Lola arranged for Katy's marriage to King, the younger brother of another daughter's husband. King drove from California to Seattle with his children, Pinky and Fonzie. He picked up Katy and her two youngest, Julie and Jelly John. Lola got the brideprice, $1,500, which aggravated her youngest son. By tradition, Miller should have made the arrangements and received the money. But, as Katy pointed out, Miller hadn't even attempted to find her another husband. Indeed, he found it hard to lose any of the women in his family. To marry, both his gorgeous daughters were forced to elope.

The following summer, I arrived in Oakland and found Katy transformed into a dedicated gardener. She immediately took me around her yard, pointing out all the fruit trees and flowers. That evening, we sat on her front porch, breathing the scented air, drinking iced coffee, and listening to our favorite songs on her boom box. Pleased to be back together—I planned to look for an apartment nearby, in San Francisco—we agreed that life seemed very good.

BOTH KING AND KATY had been married before, and consequently had no *abéav* (wedding). To mark the occasion, Katy's older sister's family took them to dinner at a restaurant and gave them her blessing. Several years back, King's former wife Sadie had run away with a much younger man, taking two of their four children and leaving King, who worked a forty-hour week as cook at a diner, with daughter Pinky as housekeeper and her brother's caretaker. Sweet-tempered Pinky was pleased with her new family, and eagerly turned her responsibilities over to Katy. She seemed the typical American teenager of the time, testing makeup, wearing jeans, going to rock concerts, collecting and playing records.

The East Bay area was full of King's former in-laws, and Katy, despite the Machvaia ethic of "being good with each other," worried about how, having lived since she was seventeen in Seattle, she might be received. At public events, she hardly recognized her aunts and cousins. When, in July, she gave a *slava*, Katy asked me in private if I thought anyone would come? I was there for the preparation which was extensive and took weeks, and during which Katy kept talking to herself about the number of plates, how many rented chairs, the amount of salad to make.

But the turnout was handsome, over-filling the house and flowing out the doors. Many in the Bay Area came, including Sadie's relatives, her mother, sisters, her cousins, one of whom explained, "We felt bad about King, when Sadie left him." The people came with the will to make a party: they danced, sang, and talked until the wee hours. It was my introduction to party-time success, the euphoric bliss of brotherhood and bonding. As Katy and King had no formal wedding, it was the community's way of showing they wished the new couple well.

KING GOT KATY A BOOTH AT A LOCAL FAIR. Sunday afternoons, she told fortunes. Otherwise, those happy months in Katy's household were spent on more important matters. We bought new shoes, lipsticks, nail polish, and earnestly studied the effect. We canvassed the entire Bay area for fabric yardage, stockpiling it, stacking it in one living room corner. Each week, Katy and I drove to the dressmaker to be fitted and measured. We tried to conform to the current fashion without being slavish. We were obsessively concerned with our entrance and how we looked. We intended the first impression at the doorway to convey the visible evidence of very good luck.

Over years, the style of Machvanki dresses has changed from the traditional two-piece with ruffled blouse and fifteen yards in the skirt, to piano pleats, accordion pleats, to a patterned and draped A-line wraparound of nylon crepe in florals, paisleys, polka-dots, and animal prints. This was followed by a fetish for fur collars and cuffs, and sparkly sequin jackets. By the Eighties, formal ball gowns were the rage. I would chase Lola's youngest granddaughter, Little Gina, who arrived in spectacular Cher-like dresses by the designer Bob Mackie, around the hall with my camera.

For me, the Outsider, and Katy, so recently returned to her tribe of origin, it was a career in promotion. I was meeting Machvaia and gathering fieldnotes; Katy was meeting Machvaia and becoming reacquainted. Within a few months, we were current on all the gossip and regarded as invaluable company. Our phones rang day and night with invitations and queries: "Will you be there?"

IMAGINATIVE THEMES WERE INVENTED: a Golden Gate Bridge wedding cake that festooned several tables; an engagement party with the Cinderella bride-to-be arriving by horse and carriage; a "music of five countries" wedding; a giant Los Angeles *slava* with a dozen *slavaria* (*slava* celebrants); gifts for the Dead One that required a rental van as transport to the house of the man who "took the suit." An increasing amount of food was provided by buffet and sit-down dinner, three days of meals for those attending *slavi* and weddings, even more tables and tributes honoring the beloved ancestors. Rituals exploded in size and elegance, and nearly every family seemed obliged to confirm their good luck with style and flourish; hosts might even provide their guests' airfare. We were either getting ready for a party or reviewing the last one attended. Recalling that more bountiful time when rents were low, telling fortunes a lucrative enterprise, and food stamps readily available, one Machvanka explained, "We had it and we showed it."

I call this, the Seventies and Eighties, the heyday of Machvaia ritual. I consider it a time of communitas, a joining of hearts and minds much as Turner describes in *The Ritual Process* (1969:97), a time of "giving recognition to an essential and generic human bond, without which there could be *no* society." It was certainly a time to have fun and, simultaneously, sharing it, to create the benefit of harmony and good luck. Machvaia believe health, virtue, money, luck, and status all come in a package—the good and lucky in sync with more of the same. Opulent parties and rituals enhanced many reputations; these were built, advanced, and some, of course, lost luster. Then, the ethic of seeing each other "in the good way" was continually reinforced by an easy sociability. The women made the money; the men spent it on good times.

# Chapter 6

# SAINTS AND SLAVI, POSNO AND FRIDAYS

## Saints and Miracles

In the Gypsy universe of exceptional powers and beings, Saints are *devlesko* or "up" on every scale. All purity and goodness, Machvaia saints never penalize or punish. Saints are like The God, helpers to The God, and pretty much the same as The God. Saints are a reason for great celebration. Conceptualized in human form, they must be treated with deference and ritual consideration. Saints have never been married, never felt the good and bad of human existence, never been mean, jealous, or mad. Man, on the other hand, is both an angel and a devil. Machvaia attribute the more excessive examples of evil they see on television news—the Columbine killings, for example—to the Devil. Machvaia say they know about evil. Gypsies have endured centuries of savage mistreatment at the hands of their fellow men, an abuse that continues, on occasion, into the present.

O Beng (the Devil) is associated with *Bi-BaX* (literally, without luck), with Prikadja (the Demon of Bad Luck), with Bi-Wusho (the Unclean One), with imposing and large, dark bodies of water (in contrast to *nevo pai*, new water that runs swift, clear, and clean), and with Hell. Hell, however, as a contrast to Heaven, seems a rather questionable notion to the people—"Some say it is hot, is that right, Djuhli?" Whenever life proves overly challenging, the Machvaia enjoy pointing out to me that "Hell is here on earth." I was also told that "the Devil is part ghost." Like the names of the dead, the name of the Devil is avoided. Decades ago, Roma spit inside their blouses or knocked on wood when they heard it. Words have power and when asked about these unlucky matters, the people were aghast. "For Heaven's sake, Djuhli, don't say it!"

The God was, in the past, a rather amorphous concept who started everything in the known and unknown universe; He was Maker and Origin, and then, it was supposed, He let whatever might follow take its course. He was Sky, Sun, Moon, the Clouds, the Weather. As the ultimate of all on earth, He was considered too remote, too "up" to attend to the personal and human.

But that idea was under pressure of change by the time I met Lola in the 1960s. She told me about a dream she had in middle-age. In the dream, an old man with long white hair and a beard, possibly, she said, The God, rocked in a circle. He pointed his cane at her walls and made each wall fall down. Although illegal by Machvaia rule, she took this as evidence that she should hire an American lawyer and get an American divorce from her abusive husband. Afterwards, having seen someone who might have been The God, or a relative of The God, in her dream, she referred to Him on a daily basis and said she felt "adopted." Confronted by crisis, Katy was inclined to blame Prikadja (Demon of Bad Luck) whereas Lola usually addressed The God, "Oi, Devla!"

MACHVAIA ARE A CENTURY AWAY from Machva, Serbia, where they apparently celebrated *slava* in much the same fashion as the Greek-Orthodox Serbs. Andrei Simić (1978:91) writes, "The *slava* is a very old custom in the Balkans, and it may have even sprung from pre-Christian forms of ancestry worship or cults of household gods . . . its first historical mention was in 1018 A.D." Machvaia *slava* is much like the Serbian *slava* in ritual outline. But the cosmology is somewhat different. For one thing, Machvaia saints are totally divine and have no human history. For another, there is no Serbian priest, or any other kind of priest, to bless the bread and the proceedings. Instead, Machvaia enjoy more direct divine support.

NOW, AMID ALTERNATIVE RELIGIOUS MODELS, the challenge to Machvaia belief has encouraged revitalization miracles: several Saints spied in trees; the California saint that cried; the notable visits of Sainte Anne to Svetsaika (Saint-woman) Kaboka in which the Sainte reportedly advised removing liquor from the *slava* table and avoiding the subject of money at ritual events (*slava*, Christmas, New Year's Eve were, and still are, considered ideal days to tell fortunes or initiate a money-making venture); the nearly invisible appearance—only one Rom claimed to see him—of the God who ordered the women to resume wearing the symbol of their married state, their head-scarves, something that, by then, seemed to be of interest only to the newly married. When, years ago, I questioned Katy's son about the report of a miracle, he said, "Every few years, the people start to disbelieve and a Saint appears in life to remind us."

In the Seventies, Duda could hardly wait to tell me about Svetso Danny of New York who saw The God in his shaving mirror.

God talks to him. Svetso (Saintman) sits in a chair in the front of the hall and the empty chair beside him is for The God. A halo floats high around Svetso's head and his forehead looks bright. I hear he looks like The God's brother. He's not like Kaboka. He won't take money. He tells people what The God says. He can heal people; he healed one crippled, one cross-eyed, and some people who were sick. My sister-in-law was dying of leukemia and he stayed with her three days. He only ate wine and fruit; he slept on new sheets. When he left, she got eighty percent red cells and the white cells went down. You gotta believe, you got to have faith in anything that you do or it won't work. Through Svetso, God commanded the people to bring back traditional customs. The women to fast and not to comb their hair on Fridays, the men not to shave. And no more jewelry, makeup, bright colors, wigs for commemorations; no more elves and Buddha statues in the shrine, no more adopting the American lifestyle, and no more pool playing or gambling.

A month later, Sabrina, Duda's daughter who was seventeen and already smart and worldly, had this news about Svetso.

Now we know what really happened. Svetso's wife was expecting some big money that day and the client didn't show up. So Svetso, in a temper, broke all the shrine statues and left the pieces in the bathroom-that's bad. Later, his wife retrieved them, wrapped them up in one of her nice head scarves, and bundled them into the attic. The next day he was standing in the bathroom shaving and The God appeared in the mirror. God said, Why did you do that to me? Svetso was so surprised he ran up to the attic. The God followed him and said, "I never died like my son (Jesus). So nobody got my picture. Only you get to see me and nobody else." That's what my cousin told me and she lives in New York, same as Svetso.

And Svetso? Sabrina says, "The word is out he is a fraud. They say he's in the crazy house." But later, Sabrina's cousin saw Svetso at the racetrack, betting on the horses. In truth, they say, he isn't Svetso any longer; he's back to just Danny.

SEEING SAINTS, ANGELS, AND GODLY BEINGS is considered a favorable portent regarding the future. As a young man Bahto found a leprechaun sitting on the pump handle of a well, and called the others. But the Little Man disappeared. Thereafter he was regarded as a lad of great promise. When Bahto grew up and became rich, the sighting was confirmed as divine premonition.

As in Irish folklore, Machvaia associate elves with money. When she was a new *bori* (daughter-in-law), married to Bahto, Lola remembered a miraculous visit from the Money Elf. Outside the tent, Lola could hear a noisy party; inside, Lola, recovering from a bout with the virulent 1918 influenza, was surprised by a visit from the Money Elf, ManushchoRo BengoRo (Manchild Little-Devil).

"The size of a quart milk bottle, right next to my pillow. I called my *sokra* (mother-in-law) and He disappeared." Seka, her mother-in-law, told her that if she had snatched the Money Elf's hat, and kept it, she would always have money. "But I didn't know," Lola said. "Later," Lola added with regret, "I met a woman whose purse and pockets never ran out of money and she said she did that, hid the Money Elf's hat."

One late fall day in October, 1978, Katy, resplendent in gray silk chiffon and long ropes of pearls, accompanied by her new husband King and me (in an old sweater; I hadn't realized the import of the occasion), followed a line of cars to a little church near Stockton to

70

find the Sainte statue that was reputed to cry. She didn't cry during our visit, but that, Katy said, might anyway have been unlucky. When I asked Katy what she was praying for, she said for the life of her daughter's mother-in-law, who was seriously ill. Then she arranged my hands together in prayer position and added, "For all the terrible things happening in the world that you see on the news."

On the way out, Katy broke off a branch of the vine hanging over the church doorway to take home to her shrine. Katy likes to collect fruit, blossoms, tree limbs, whatever grows that strikes her as auspicious. Contact and proximity are everything in the Machvaia line of thought, and Katy described the power in these green branches as, "Something alive that grew big and made a blossom near the Sainte that cries."

Milano, a runaway gay Gypsy (See Chapter 15) who lived in San Francisco for most of his life is the most successful runaway I know, and this despite not having a wife's monetary support. He, like so many Machvaia who exist, in large part, on an intuitive level, has remained vulnerable to the extraordinary and the marvelous.

It was written up in the *Desert Post* in Palm Springs. People saw God's face in a tree stump.

I went with my sister (Janet, who had cancer) and my cousins. It cost six hundred round trip. Janet had a customer who lives in a condo where the tree is. The customer picked us up at the airport and drove us inside, past the security guard.

Janet saw angels right away. But it took me awhile, maybe fifteen minutes. Then I saw a woman with a veil and a child in the cold frost; she was moving through the tree-another tree, not the one with Christ's face. I hit myself and closed my eyes. I can still see it. I was so in awe, so overwhelmed, lost. Then the security guard came and threw us out. There were ten of us with cameras.

We played the videos at the house. We could see angels, a little boy only an inch high, a little house, two saints waiting for the boy to come in. Huge faces coming out of the trees, crosses, candles, angels. It was like TV.

The next day, during lunch, the rest [cousins] decided to leave. But Janet and I decided to stay. We think it's something like an extraterrestrial.

I thought to myself that a miracle might be anywhere. So we didn't bother the security guards and went across the street. We saw them out there too, three angels floating and two walking. Angels. Other things flying around. A huge hand appeared. The sky was different colors. Suddenly, an image out of the sky, a six-foot-high angel or saint dressed in a flowing robe flew off from the street into the trees and started to glow. Hosts of angels. One went right through me!

## Slavi

Lucky Lola, who lived in continual expectation of largesse, explained how, when she was a young mother preparing for *slava*, the Saint being celebrated would help

> When we had the family together, we celebrated Svet Nikola. I never had to buy anything except the candle and the music. My customers would bring the rest, the food, the beer, the chairs. The *slava* brought everything we needed. Women brought bolts of material, and I made dresses, all the same, for all my girls. Everybody said they looked so pretty.

Lola's niece, Rose, told me about how, early in the last century, *slava* was celebrated by her family. For the Svet Jovano (St. John) *slava*, her mother's brother Pero would drive from Sacramento to San Francisco to help.

> When they say *slava* today, it isn't the same. Just the word meant something so great. It took days and days to prepare. We didn't have filo pastry to buy for *gushvada*; we had to roll the dough. No American food of any kind on the table. No American baked goods or canned stuff.
>
> Pero used to come and fix the pigs; they'd go to the farms, then to the butcher to clean it all up, then to the bakery. Do you know how many hands it took? We'd start at

night. The man of the house would say, "Get up and start cooking." Hours and hours in the kitchen. For the *sarma*, you'd find the biggest cabbages. Our heads had to be covered with hankies; we had to be neat, a smile on our faces. No one dared use a bad word. Hours and hours in the kitchen for two or three days. The *sarma* had to be perfect. We'd have to make the bread. The beets boiled and fixed in vinegar, garlic, oil. Salads; greens are *banka* (money). No one could go to the table until they blessed the things and lit the candles. And all the people would sit down. At *vitchera* (night before the main *slava* day), all the men got drunk. Pero used to love wine.

The women had to have their clothes ready, everything brand new, with long skirts. It was a very holy day. *Vitchera* you didn't dress up because you're cooking. But no one had a bad word or bad thought. *Slava*, the music was always Gypsy and Serbian music. The boys would play guitar and the women would dance Gypsy-no American dancing. Nobody sat at the table except the old people. There were a lot of old people then.

Us kids didn't dare go close to the table. I see kids now at the table before the old people. That was war, fighting, before. If anyone used a bad word or some *boriohri* (daughter-in-law) passed in front of the father-in-law or didn't bring that drink right, or bring that coffee right, big trouble used to start. It was all respect, men and women. People were so particular in those days. That's how things have changed.

*Slavi* are three-day events. At the *vitchera* (night before), the family cleans, cooks, prepares, and may have guests in to drink, talk, and help. The man of the house will wash his hands and light a little, pre-*slava* candle.

On the main *slava* day, the family bathes and dresses in "fresh" clothes-all new, skin side out, including shoes and underwear, if they can afford them. Fasting, no food, no coffee, no smoking "so we will never be hungry," continues until about noon. Then, with the sign of the cross, the *slava* candle is lighted from the *vitchera* candle and the Saint is asked for health, luck, and money, "*sastipé, baX, tai lovensa.*" The family offers the Saint a glass of whiskey or wine or black coffee; whiskey is *baX*, a good luck item. The Machvaia say, "Whiskey makes us strong." Plates full of food are connected to the divine by the burning incense that circles the table once (the incense circles three times at *pomana*).

Katy described incense as tree tears; it smells like pine. Incense can be used anytime to purify, to banish sickness and evil, and to scare away ghosts. Lighted incense is part fire, and fire is a blessing that clears away fears. The fire of the candle "opens the way," and invites the saint; the smoke from incense sanctifies the area. As Anastasia once put it, poetically, "The candle is the instrument, and the incense is the music."

According to the Halperns' description (1972:113), this rite of candle and incense is similar to the Serbian *slava* ritual.

THE NEWLY PURCHASED *SLAVA* candle (*mameili*), usually an imposing three feet tall, is set in wheat stalks and corn seeds for reasons no one could tell me, but that likely relate to fertility and plenty. The candle must be beeswax. Bees, beeswax, honey are all very pure, and therefore "up." The beeswax candle is also associated with money and "busy like a bee" industry. The *slava* candle is never blown out, but rather put out with a drip piece of beeswax at midnight and lighted again the next morning, which Machvaia call the third day.

After the customary washing and purifying, the *slava* candle can be re-lighted on holidays, Friday fast days, and Sundays, "To bring the blessings of the Saint." Lola's daughter-in-law Fatima assured me she did this, "if I don't forget." In return for the gift of cleanliness and good thoughts-the service of hard work, *baX* food and drink, new clothes, new water, new soaps, and a just-purchased *slava* candle, the purity of fasting, the gift of fellowship, irresistible music, the happiness of movement and dancing-the boons of *sastimas tai baX*, good health and good luck, are prayed for and expected.

*Slavi* and other Machvaia rituals seem similar to Hindu *puja* in their central characteristics: bathe, light incense and a candle, offer the godly being earthly sustenance; then drink, pray, and hope for the best.

Two *baXtalo* (lucky) food items are never omitted from the feast table: *Sarma*, a spicy, hot dish, a cabbage roll stuffed with meat, rice, and tomatoes; and a rich and sweet cheese strudel, *gushvada* in Romani. Lola showed me how the latter is made. She spread a fresh cotton tablecloth on the dining table and kept rolling, patting, and pulling the dough out, trying to keep it even and whole until it thinly covered the table, a tricky process that, in the days of camping, was done on head pillows covered by fresh tablecloths. Then, she rolled the dough up over dots of cottage cheese (or apples, raisin, nuts), as well as sugar and butter until it made a long snake, which she looped into a pan and baked in the oven. The *baX* foods are believed to have a healing power, and they are prepared whenever the people feel the need. In the past, to avoid *poftarniko*, satisfying any passing desire for *sarma* and *gushvada* was regarded as critical to good health.

BIBI, LOLA'S SISTER-IN-LAW, told me that during the days of camping her father put a small glass of whiskey in the center of the round *pogacha* (special bread) and, together with her oldest brother, turned the loaf around three times. Then the father drank a bit of the whiskey. The two then turned the bread three times in the opposite direction, and her brother drank from the glass. This custom likely relates, as in Serbia, to those *slavi* celebrated for male Saints and inherited through the patriline, father to son, with a focus on the household head. (A Machvano with only daughters can pass his *slava* on to a son-in-law.) Each patriline *slava* day features meat or fish: St. John and St. James, barbequed pigs; St. George, a ritually slaughtered lamb; and St. Nicholas, a large fish. To honor the household head, the heads are decorated with ribbons and coins and left intact, to be saved for the third *slava* day when the man of the house eats the brains, if he can-most now refuse.

APPROACHING THE SAINTS, who are perfect and pure, requires the ultimate effort at matching. On *slavi* (saint-days), the people's actions are to be harmonious, respectful, and generous, to demonstrate good thoughts (*lachi ginduria*), empathy for others (*žhav*), and the soft heart (*kovlo ilésko*).

When I was living with Katy, we began preparations weeks before the *slava*, never arguing, always agreeing and trying to "satisfy" one another. Saints being "all good," in keeping with the Machvaia emphasis on the unseen and emotional, and the importance of every contact, we strove to create the matching *latchi* (good) mind-set. According to Katy, the inside was more important than the outside: "You have to be really nice and decent to get close to the Saints."

Weeks before the *slava*, the lists and the cooking began. Food was arranged for and prepared; the house was industriously cleaned and painted. When everything was perfect, we were ready to welcome our visitors. And we got plenty of visitors. At my first *slava* in California, the music, singing, dancing, and the camaraderie confirmed success. The Saint, Katy said, could not refuse to accept the invitation. Machvaia saints, it seems, "do love to party."

"Saints want you to celebrate them. They want you to have a feast table. They want to come and have fun."

## Taking a Saint

Saints are either lineally inherited or "taken" during a health crisis. As to the latter, after lighting a candle, black coffee or whiskey is offered and the supplicant promises to celebrate the Saint whenever His or Her *slava* day arrives—Bibi always followed the Greek Orthodox calendar. The sick who recover will celebrate this Saint annually for as long as they live. It is a conditional contract: if the patient dies, the contract is broken.

Men often take one of the male saints for reasons of illness. But because She is a woman and "She will understand," women usually prefer Sainte Anne, particularly if a child is involved. Machvanki claim that Sainte Anne is the grandmother of the Jesus-god and, like all Machvaia grandmothers, old, powerful, wise, and respected. (Nevertheless, and despite this compelling evidence, I am told that no Machvaia saint ever had sex, or a sexy thought, or a family.)

At Sainte Anne's *slava*, the meat dish is lamb. She is associated with a church in eastern Canada, Sainte Anne de Beaupre, where, it is said, miracles have occurred. Nearly every month, Rose, who lived on the East Coast much of her life, sends the church money and receives vials of holy water for her clients. Sainte Anne is celebrated on July 26th, and by more Machvaia than any other saint. Saints John, George, James, and Nicholas may or may not be represented by picture or statue, but Sainte Anne is nearly always represented by a colorful Byzantine print of a young woman with an infant. Katy had three gold framed pictures of Sainte Anne, all the same—one so faded that it might well have traveled with her grandparents from Serbia.

AS *SLAVA* is mostly for good health, enthusiasm for *slava* has waned as the people's confidence in modern medicine has grown. Miller was in his sixties when he began going to the hospital regularly for twice-weekly dialysis treatments. In 2000, Miller said, "I stopped celebrating *slava*. *Slava* wasn't doing anything for me." A few years later, his daughter, Little Gina, brought me up-to-date:

> The only ones doing *slava* now are the older people, mostly, and it's usually a little thing in the house. No more *slavaria* (multiple celebrants) and big halls. No banquet room—now they cost thousands. Years ago, you only paid a hundred. Money was easy then. Easy to get everything you wanted. We all had money, we had parties, we had *slavi*. Now, instead of having good times, you have to work just to live, to survive.
>
> Now, the people will still do it if something wrong (sickness) is happening in the family. Then they must.

Once, Saint George was expected to send little children pre-*slava* dreams of green meadows and baby lambs. The dreams were a reminder to the family that the Saint was ready for His celebration. But fields and lambs are beyond the purview of children raised in cities, and the sacrifice of lambs has fallen out of favor. The last time Machvano Stévo killed a lamb was 1967. The family kept the unhappy animal jammed in their apartment's closet for several days. His children all fell in love with the lamb. Stévo admitted he had become attached to it too. Such crying when *slava* arrived! Such a mess to clean up! No one could eat! "It didn't feel right," Stévo confessed. "I don't know how my grandfather did that."

## Posno and Slava

*Slavi, patchiva* (parties honoring a particular person), and weddings are celebrations: the ritual tone is happy; music and dancing are encouraged. But of these three rituals, only *slavi* involve the purity of a Saint and a morning *posno* (fast) before the candle is lighted.

*Posno* is the rite of purification that brings the applicants into the more spiritual and "up" status. The more *vužo* (pure) state is mandatory when approaching the higher beings (see Chapter 13). *Posno* is, Katy explained, an offering. "We fast to give thanks."

"We fast to give us happiness in life and health."

"We fast to help us make money."

*Posno* avoids anything with blood. No *maklo* (greasy) food is allowed, no meat or meat-derived products like butter, cheese, or milk. What the people seem to miss most is the cream for their coffee. And cigarettes; smoking is taboo during *posno*.

Celebrating male saints involves an entrée of barbequed pork, lamb, or fish. Specifically, there is Svet Jovano (John), January 20th, who baptized the Jesus-god, a *slava* celebrated by the Pavlovich, Yovanovich, and Stevens lineages; Svet Djurjev Dan (Saint George), May 6th, who killed the evil thing (dragon/Devil), a primavera *slava* inherited by the Lees and Merinos; Svet James, October 26th, the half-brother of the Jesus-god, a *slava* inherited by the Aratso, Marikeshti, and Johns lineages (Old Persa and others also call it Bari Parashtui, Big Friday, for reasons unknown); Svet Nikola (Nicholas), December 19th, who protects ocean travelers and fishermen, a *slava* inherited by the Todorovich and both Adamovitch lineages.

At the meatless fasting *slava* of Svet Nikola, the table menu is simple: fish stew in oil, tomato gravy, nut *gushada* made without butter, cabbage slaw, green salad, navy beans in oil with bell peppers, meatless *sarma*, fruit. The people I sit with often complain: "Why do we eat this stuff?" [Power and purity of being is the answer.] The large fish centerpiece of the *slava* table is served the third day.

FIELDWORK, OF COURSE, was full of surprises, most of which I didn't write down and promptly forgot. However, one I remember well dates from 1980 when, encouraged by Lappé's *Diet For a Small Planet* and the trauma of a life crisis, I became a vegetarian. Some of my meat-eating Outsider friends were obviously annoyed at the inconvenience; a few demanded to know why; most wondered if I had seriously considered my nutritional needs.

But the Machvaia didn't appear concerned when I took only vegetables and fruit from the feast table. Perhaps they thought I was fasting to earn a boon? Perhaps they found my fasting activity *devlesko* and in line with my obsessive interest in ritual and belief, and all those difficult questions about matters they had never before had to consider? No one asked me why I stopped eating meat. Instead, the Machvanki quickly explained to the servers, approvingly, that I ate only vegetables. Their nods and smiles my way indicated their increased respect.

## Fasts and Fridays

Like the Serbian Gypsies (Petrović 1938:72–3), Machvaia call Easter Bari Patradji. They say she is a Spirit, and that eating meat on the Friday before Greek Orthodox Easter is bad for Her; "That's why we don't do it," they say. Some older Machvaia begin Bari Patradji with a Big Posno (fast), forty days of fasting by avoiding something they like. For example, Dinah gave up coffee, her favorite beverage, and kept calling me for suggestions of what she might drink in its place.

Eating meat and meat by-products is also "bad for the Lady/ Spirit" called Bari Parashtui (Big Friday). Usually celebrated on Friday, the people say that if She wants you to do it, and you don't do it, She appears in a dream to remind you. Then, "We take care and give thanks." To "take" Bari Parashtui, the householder promises to avoid all "greasy" (animal related) items for a specified period in return for a boon. The fast of Bari Parashtui is not a celebration, as it doesn't include dancing or music, and usually only lasts until sundown.

Much like a stereotypical old-time Gypsy, the Lady Parashtui has long, black hair; on Fridays, the women told me, you shouldn't comb your hair, or cut your hair, or shave. Suggesting a particularly close identification with this goddess, it is said that if you do, you will be pulling Bari Parashtui's hair. Some who "get" the feeling also celebrate Bari Parashtui on other days. Katy's oldest daughter did, every Monday and Wednesday, as well as Friday. She wouldn't tell us why; it was a secret, she said, between her and Bari Parashtui. But the number of Parashtui's celebrants has dropped, and at present only a few of the faithful keep Her fast. She was mostly associated with health; Her fast was usually observed during health emergencies, which, as mentioned, have become more of an Outsider medical system issue. As the ever-progressive Lola said, "We used to do that, but now we forget."

## Rituals in the American Church

Baptisms and funerals are like a hello and a goodbye to Outsider world. They are the only Machvaia events involving Outsider priests and churches. Perhaps there was a time in Serbia when it was mandatory to observe these rituals, and the people have continued. Machvaia predecessors may have lived a long time in Serbia; a few of the elderly still go to the Greek Orthodox church for baptisms and funerals. At the now more common Catholic church funerals, the people never seem to know The Lord's Prayer and cannot, when asked, join in its recitation. Nevertheless, the people assure me, they are closer to The God than Outsiders because they have more belief—Machvaia kinds of belief, which, despite the saints' statues and icons in their household shrines and their required church attendance for baptisms and funerals, are only nominally Christian.

For Machvaia, baptizing is said to give a baby a name in this world. Baptizing is expected to quiet an infant's crying and provide the benefit of health protection. Godparents become responsible for the health and well-being of the baby they baptize, a responsibility that will extend throughout the lifetime of the principals. When Dukey, Lola's grandson, fell into a coma, the couple who baptized him was required to to go to their godson's bedside and pray for his recovery—even though doing so required that the Machvano leave his own dying father's bedside.

Baptizing brings the parents of the baby and godparents into the special relationship of *chivrimos* (co-godparenthood). Special respect for the godparents, who are ranked "up" by their godchild's family, must be observed. They are doing the family a *sevahpo* (favor) and are to be denied nothing. Each addresses the other as their *chivrea*. Between the two *chivrimos* families, marriage is not allowed.

In terms of seating and respect offering, Machvaia rank godparents first, then their grandparents; they say, "Godparents are like god."

The ritual begins with the baptizing pair, on arrival, throwing candy to all the small children. Then they outfit the baby in an entirely new suit of clothes, including underwear and socks, and carry the baby to a church. In the past, the parents didn't accompany the baby to the church, but now they usually do. There, the baptizing couple can give the baby any name they choose, although most stick with whatever name the parents have been using. When they return home, the parents throw a party honoring their new *chivrea*.

## Household Shrine

The *svetsuria* (saint things) in the shrine suggest the promise of the sacred, the powerful, and the lucky. Saint things should be inherited, be a gift from revered elders, arrive by means of a serendipity, or selective, intuitive choice: "I knew she wanted me to buy Her." At minimum, a shrine must include a saint statue or picture, a candle, and incense. It is invariably located in an area described as "nice" and where nothing defiling is likely to occur. I have seen shrines on the dining room buffet, in the hallway entrance or a hallway closet, above the kitchen door, or in the isolation of a reading room where Machvaia expect the presence of saint icons and candles to expedite the reader's success at fortunes. [The Los Angeles Kalderasha who Marlene Sway (1988:57) mentions didn't seem to regard their icons with a similar reverence. Perhaps they didn't depend on divine help when giving readings; perhaps they had no Catholic clients; perhaps they were pulling her leg.]

In 1982, I visited two sisters in Stockton who had recently lost their mother to cancer. Among the numerous sofas for sleepovers, I got the one in the dining room, the thoroughfare to the kitchen, busy with people passing through. Their shrine, in the far corner of the room, was protected by curtains which could be closed

81

whenever a "shameful" event, such as sexual intercourse or un-
dressing, took place nearby—saint statues do have painted eyes!

Although the sisters lowered the curtains at night, it wasn't really necessary. Like the other guests on the overstuffed furniture
in the other rooms, I never changed to night clothes, which would
have been improper. Instead, I removed only my skirt and shoes,
and slept in my slip on pillows and sheets that I carried in my car—
all the Machvaia I knew did this. I was told that a modest woman,
in those days, wouldn't undress completely, even when sleeping
with her husband. Yet, on another occasion, a Machvanka I had just
met beckoned me into her bedroom and, swearing me to secrecy,
showed me with delight a black lace nylon nightgown she had recently purchased.

In keeping with trends in America, fortune-telling has changed
since the Eighties. Currently, many Machvaia fortune-tellers in California are as likely to "meditate" or "think healing thoughts" on the
client's behalf, as they are to "pray." Pretty Bobby recently gave up
statues, even her favorite, Sainte Anne, when she works. "Now everyone is a psychic, no more palm readers." Amber, a distant cousin,
refers to her work as psychic therapy and although, in the past, the
cost was whatever the traffic would bear, she now charges a fixed
rate for her time—like a licensed psychotherapist.

During our days in Stockton, several fortunes were told next to
the shrine, as proximity was believed to bring good luck to the
money making enterprise. I noticed that only if the client expressed
an interest in a particular statue did one of the sisters work that saint
into the fortune she was telling. In my experience, modern shrines
tend to display a large number of saint statues when the primary
clients are Latino. The Stockton house was located in an inland
agricultural valley, and the bulk of my hostesses' clients may well have
been Latino. Their shrine was a bit short on items that were popular in the San Francisco area where I lived at that time (fat porcelain
babies, the Chinese elders, and golden Buddhas), and was instead
decorated with the following:

*Top tier*

Hand-crocheted pink roses. A Universal Life Certificate
authorizing the owner to perform the functions of a minister.

### Second tier

Pictures of a jeweled half moon and holy cards, mostly Our Lady of Guadalupe with halo. A statue of Christ with hands open and outstretched. A green Irish elf of plaster. A branch from the eucalyptus tree an hour's drive away that grows near the church door where we found the Saint that cries. Hard candy in a dish. Several small birthday cake–type candles.

### Third tier

Statues of the holy family, Mary, Joseph, and Jesus as a lad. A statue of Svet Jovano (St. John, the Baptist, the family's patrilineal *slava* saint). Two female statues, almost certainly of Sainte Anne. A little girl angel figurine that the sisters said "is so pretty." Another framed Universal Life Certificate made out to one of the sisters, Barbara Adams. Four Catholic-looking holy cards, all women. A box of French incense.

### Bottom tier

A large *slava* candle burned down to half size. A large elf statue. A picture of Jesus pointing at his open chest with the heart revealed. (Lola once described this iconic picture as the god with open-heart surgery.) Four female saint statues. A picture of a female saint surrounded by angels. A deck of cards in a basket.

To the left of the corner shelf was a large framed picture of a queen with a crown giving food to the poor. To the right was a familiar picture of Jesus praying on the Mount of Olives and a gold sculptured picture of the Last Supper. I asked the sisters if they knew the associated Bible stories. They didn't. They were unconcerned when I told them about another name on the back of an icon they called St. John. The *devlesko* intent is there, and that is what matters. Halos and crowns, it seems, emit the *vorta* (right) vibrations. The sister who sometimes calls herself Barbara said, "Who cares about their names? They all bring good luck. If they don't, you get rid of them."

I wandered into the empty living room. There, pictured in a faded hand-colored photo, was the sisters' dead mother, much younger than when I knew her, a stranger, sleek, red-lipped, small-waisted, triumphantly uncaring, unmarked by the crying need for *slava* candles, saints, and miracles. In front of her picture was a half-filled glass of water, a vase of flowers, a single dried fig, and one chocolate bonbon.

# Chapter 7

## HOLIDAYS, PARTIES, AND GIFTS

### Holiday Celebrations

Holidays, for Machvaia, signify renewal, fresh beginnings, and a chance at better luck. Easter, Christmas, and New Year's are celebrated as three-day rituals similar to those of their Serbian Gypsy forbears. Machvaia use the English term "holidays" and—except for the Fourth of July, which puzzles them—celebrate the same major ones as their American hosts, but in a slightly different fashion. Mornings they pay homage to the ancestors; afternoons, they have fun.

DAY ONE, THE FOOD IS PREPARED. On New Year's Eve, and, in the past, at Christmas, *nevo* (new) luck arrives through the door with the First Footer. At midnight, the First Footer—Bibi called this person the Bolazniko—steps across the threshold to wish the family *baX*. As what happens at the beginning of the year is believed to characterize that entire year, the First Footer must be someone considered lucky and therefore capable of transferring merit. When I was living with Katy, I was asked to play the First Footer.

Day two, no smoking, eating, or drinking is permitted until a breakfast has been offered to the *mulé* (ancestors). The table should include "everything, all the sweetness and the goodness"—pastries, fruit, salads, some greenery, flowers, coffee, and meat (usually pork chops, ham or bacon). Plates for each of the honored ancestors are arranged on the table, blessed with *tumuya* (incense), and the prayer *des anda vas* (you give from the hand) given verbally or silently. If the family is in their mourning year, they light the newly Dead One's candle and, ordinarily, someone eats as proxy for the Dead One. Inspired by the image of the dead Christ on the cross, some Machvaia have even adopted Jesus, whom they call the Mulo-God (Dead God), as intermediary with the Other Side and light the Dead-God's candle in tribute to the ancestors.

After breakfast, the candle is moved into an estimable position in or near the shrine. Then, the *slava* candle can be lighted; *slava* is for the benefit of the living. Friends and relatives arrive; the merriment and music can begin.

ON THE THIRD DAY OF CHRISTMAS, New Years, and Easter, the leftovers, already dedicated to the ancestors, are ideally taken to one of the Machvaia cemeteries in Sacramento, San Jose, or Los Angeles to be arranged on the family gravestones. These are gala affairs. Picnicking near the graves of the ancestors is the opportunity to talk with beloved Dead Ones a bit, to remind them of the luck connection. Flowers, food, and candies are shared. Machvaia say, "the Dead are always with us."

EASTER, CALLED BARI PATRADJI, is the most significant, the most *devlesko* (godlike) of the major holidays, and requires the most time and care in preparation.

I recently asked Gina, Lola's granddaughter, if the younger Machvaia continue to celebrate Easter. She said this:

> Everybody still celebrates Easter. They do it at home. Mostly, now, it's family and a few friends. You exchange red eggs. You celebrate. Everybody does Easter in one way or another. Give a little feast in the morning. They have to do something—it's the Easter holiday.

The name, Bari Patradji, suggests that Easter, the Patradji Spirit, is female but She is never represented in a human form. Eggs are symbolic of the continuation of life, and, on this holiday occasion, the eggs associated with Easter link Bari Patradji to the Dead Ones. Shiny red and green Easter eggs—red eggs are primary—combine the power of rebirth with the increase of happiness. (Red represents happiness and protection, and green represents happiness and money.). Among the food items on the Easter table are the invariable *sarma* (cabbage rolls), *gushvada* (strudel), and a sweet butter/sugar/egg Easter *pogacha* (bread) topped with red Easter eggs that have been dyed the night before. Katy would make several of these bread and egg dishes. She would give me one, and then we would visit other households to wish them luck and exchange red eggs. The next day, the third day, we drove to the graves with our egg/breads.

BIBI WAS ALREADY OLD when I lived in the Bay Area and she remembered so many Serbian words that I initially suspected she had been born in Serbia. Bibi called New Year's "Sveti (Sainte) Podja," whereas most Machvaia say "Nevo Biersh." She called Christmas "Svet Bodzhiko," like the Serbian "Baro Božiko" (Petrović 1938:73). When her family first came to America, Bibi said, celebrations were relatively simple, and *slava* was ordinarily celebrated for one day, not three. She also recalled that shortly after their arrival the family adopted Memorial Day with memorial picnics on the graves. Thanksgiving has been added, she noted, simply as a family party, with no breakfasts for the dead.

Years ago, Bibi said that the *slava* of St. George and the celebration of May Day began at dawn with a trip to the river for a community bath of "the main people—not the children or the daughter-in-law." On St. George *slava* morning, the branch- and flower-crowned lamb was sacrificed and roasted. According to Bibi, "you kill the lamb like St. George killed the dragon." She went on: "Father said, 'I kill this lamb in honor of St. George.'" Then they gathered lilacs because "those were the flowers for the day." Where the leaves were plentifully thick, the cut branches whisked drops of fresh water on the people to send them bounties of good luck.

## Parties and Gifts

As mentioned, *patchiva* are parties designed to honor a special person. Luli gave a *patchiv* for the son she hadn't seen since infancy, not since she left his father on the East Coast and moved to California forty years ago. *Patchiva* demonstrates caring and puts the *patchiv* person "up" on the scale of respect.

Years ago, beloved Singing Sam Stevens and his family drove across the States from New York to San Francisco, stopping to play, sing, and entertain Roma along the way. Lola's son Miller ran into Sam at a restaurant at Fisherman's Wharf and immediately invited Sam to a *patchiv*. Sam and family stayed at Miller's house. The San Francisco Roma got together to rent a hall and hire a band. Sam's beautiful music, I was told, made an evening of unforgettable memories.

SEVERAL DECADES AGO, the people began to celebrate their children's birthdays with a party of cake and sometimes ice cream, to which the extended family and Machaia neighbors were invited. Unless the gift was a gold coin or money, any presents received were immediately passed around and shared. Normally, however, there were no presents; the real gift was to be invited and to attend. To go to a birthday party showed you honored the child and the family.

Generally speaking, parties are now mostly given for children and the elders aging parents and grandparents who are nearing the Other Side. A man I knew, Chally, had three grown sons who one year threw a family birthday party for him—cake, coffee, the gift of several watches—and then took him to Las Vegas for an overnight. Chally doesn't gamble, but was extremely proud that his sons cared enough to spend some quality time with him.

UNTIL RECENTLY, Machvaia children were encouraged to grow up as quickly as possible and appeared disinterested in childish toys. Children felt essential to their family's comfort and survival, and their lives had a rich sense of purpose. Whenever I visited Katy's Seattle storefront, her children worked with a will to get the afternoon meal to the table.

At that time, children respected their elders and emulated Machvaia adults. Lola's grandaughter Gina was only three when she broke her candy bar into pieces and passed the bits around the room. "See?" Duda said proudly. "She understands."

Currently, as in many non-Roma homes, the toys most likely to be popular are handheld electronic games, fancy cell phones, and computers. Machvaia teenagers spend their days chatting online. Exercise is not a priority. Public school, if attended, seldom goes beyond grade school and, until old enough to drive a car and run errands to the store, there isn't much to keep a child occupied.

# A Birthday Party, 1976

ARRIVING AT ZONI'S, I found her son Danny, his brother, and a cousin sitting on the porch of their Spanish-style bungalow, home from school, but locked out. Although I was already an hour late, the party hadn't begun. Good, I thought to myself—good that I didn't come on time and have to wait.

Danny climbed into my car and I wished him a happy birthday. He smiled winningly and asked me what I brought him. Learning I brought nothing, he candidly explained that he was hoping everyone would give him money so he could take karate lessons, that a dollar would be a lot. I gave him two and, happy as a clam, he invited me to sit with him on the porch. As we climbed the stairs, his little brother and cousin hollered that they have jimmied open a window. The lights went on in the house. The phone was ringing.

Danny excitedly chatted non-stop. His mother Zoni was out with his uncle, Miller, and Miller's wife "on business" and would be back soon. Among Machvaia, business always has priority.

Danny had high expectations that all his friends and local relatives would come. He showed me the cake in the refrigerator, a giant sheet iced with a plane, a sailboat, and the Golden Gate Bridge, reading "Happy Birthday to Danny from Mom." I began to make coffee in the Mr. Coffee machine.

Katy, Danny's aunt, arrived first, followed by her stepson and husband King. Then Miller, Duda, their children, climbed the stairs, Zoni dragging behind. Zoni was tired, "too tired to cook," she says as she flopped grocery sacks on the counter.

We prepared hot dogs and pop, and fixed the table. Everyone gave Danny money. Katy asked if he'd rather wait until she finds a shirt and a pair of pants, but he said no.

The men were served first, and the children were handed hot dogs. The women joined the men at the table and the men passed us mustard, hot sauce, and chili peppers, saying, "try it" and "it's good." So Zoni doesn't feel bad about failing to cook a more elaborate birthday dinner, we assured her our simple meal was delicious and just what we wanted.

Danny's friends arrived, four friends he made at a private grade school he attended in Golden Gate Park. After setting off some firecrackers in the back yard, the children left for *Zims Coffee Shop* to eat away some of the karate money.

ENCOURAGED TO SHOW HIS HOME MOVIES, Miller joked, "Sit down and be comfortable because this takes about three hours and you're going to be very sorry." We watched shots of the plane flying into Alaska, Miller and friend shooting moose, flying out, and then flying in again with Duda and Long Nose and his wife, this time to set up a fortune telling *ofisa* (office) at a fair in Anchorage.

Then, the children came back from Zims, and they pointed to the screen. "Look, there's Sabrina. She's little. Lally. How cute!" Lola, Zoni, Katy, and Miller's mother, appeared on screen and we all sighed in unison. Katy wondered if it was safe, before the last *pomana*, to see her looking so alive. It was what Lola, my dear old friend, would have called in her usual understated fashion, "a little sad moment."

The projector was put away and we lit the candles on the cake, singing "Happy Birthday" so many times that Danny became red with embarrassment. We ate, we talked, we laughed, and then the phone rang.

IT WAS CUSTOMER CALLING FROM SEATTLE. She had just taken twenty-six sleeping pills and was calling to say goodbye. Duda covered the phone and screamed for Miller to take the other line and call the police. Then she asked the customer why she took the pills, and the poor woman said nobody cares. Her son doesn't call, her husband has left her, and she is alone. Duda shrugged her shoulders in exasperation; another example of how foolish Outsiders are.

Miller grabbed the phone and said:

"We love you, Christine. We were looking forward to your visit this week. Why didn't you get on the plane and come here when you felt that way?"

Duda took the phone; meanwhile, Miller, having already called the police, dialed the Seattle Fire Department on the other line. Duda soothed her client:

"Now Christine, have you got any coffee? You've got to stop crying. Everybody loves you and me most of all. As long as you got friends, you got no problems. Get the coffee and bring it back to the phone."

Suddenly, Duda screamed, "No! No! Don't go to sleep! Christine! Christine!"

Finally a voice answered. It was the police. They were taking her to the hospital. Duda and Miller hung up and they both turned and looked at me accusingly. Miller burst out that no one should live alone, that "it's not normal to live alone." Then Miller and Duda invited me to spend the night.

BY THEN, EVERYONE WAS EXHAUSTED and Zoni announced she had made more coffee. Danny wanted me to eat more cake: "You just had such a little." Time tends to fly in the company of Machvaia and it was suddenly two in the morning.

I kissed Danny happy birthday and, on my way to the car, he waved energetically from the porch. Since his three older siblings returned to New York and to their father's family, he, at eight, was the man in a single-parent household. Racing down the steps, testing the car door to make sure it locked, he gave me some of the Gypsy advice that, as Lola would have put it, is better than money. The people don't believe in challenging luck with unnecessary risk. Danny cautioned me to call them when I arrived at my destination and to "be safe, drive carefully going home."

# Chapter 8

# ELVIS AND TRAVOLTA

## *Chelimos* (Dance)

Machvaia admire elegance of movement; they critically appraise others and themselves, asking, "How does this look?" Everyone practices dancing; they begin as children, observing themselves in mirrored walls, attending to the beat, the turn of the wrist, the line of the shoulder. The people dance for any reason whatsoever. "To dance," I was told, "you don't need lessons, you just follow the music." The music calls, the dancers answer.

In Seattle, by Lola's arrangement, I would chauffeur the Machvanki to downtown nightclubs twice a month. There, the women played at weaving in and out of the other dancers, greeting strangers as they passed, making jokes, experimenting with different personae. Katy was, for a ridiculous moment, The Statue of Liberty, twisting her scarf into a crown and her short umbrella into a torch. "Look! Look at me!," she sang. When we got up to leave, those around us begged us to come back soon. We had made their evening memorable, they said, adding, "And be sure to bring your mother!" They were quite taken with Lola, declaring, "She's so much fun!"

Lola's bedroom closet floor was covered with dozens of dance shoes in all colors, mostly high heels or high wedges. She liked to dance in the style she described as Serbian, one arm straight up like a swaying signal, her feet taking quick, authoritative steps. She danced, she said, "because I can"; dancing, in her opinion, was as essential as eating. To dance was Lola's tribute to being alive.

After moving to San Francisco, I would fly back to Seattle on holidays to see my children, my parents, my siblings, and to visit Lola. During my 1974 Christmas visit, Lola pointed to the new pair of shoes in the open box on her television set. "These are for dancing," she confessed, taking them out to show me, and then glancing down at her swollen ankles she added ruefully, "when my legs are better." I remember those shoes so well, pretty black suede pumps, open-toed with flat bows—I stared at them as I waited for Lola to heat our coffee and return, realizing she was no longer likely to dance because her heart was failing. An era, a dance of life, was ending.

DANCE, ACCORDING TO SPENCER (1985:28), is a highly social and leveling activity. Citing Turner (1969:126) cf. Langer (1953: 204–5): he writes that dance "contrasts with normal everyday life, taking the dancers out of their structured routine and into a realm of timeless charm. In their ecstasy they literally stand outside."

At Machvaia celebrations, everyone who can, everyone who is able bodied, should dance. At the last engagement party I attended, a young man said "*Patchiv tuchi*" to his grandmother, indicating the respectful nature of his gift, and offered the guests a smoothly elegant North African dance. Some time later, four young Machvanki laughingly bowed and faced a table of older women in a karaoke song and dance. Presentation dancing begins with a nod or wave of respect in the direction of the person honored. During the dance, the audience may stand around to clap the beat, join in a bit; they feel their bond of beat and blood with the dancers.

BUT THE DESIRE, OF COURSE, must be there. Early in my studies, I made the mistake of inviting Lola and Katy to a Christmas cocktail party at my brother's. After telling fortunes, they fruitlessly tried to dance with everyone, all the partygoers who were holding drinks and standing around, somewhat stunned. We left early. Going home, Katy announced her discovery, "That's the American way. No dancing."

IN SEATTLE, where I began my research, I immediately responded to the dancing. Apparently it runs in our family; my daughter taught ballet, my granddaughter danced with the Off Center and the American Repertory Ballet companies.

In California, women I didn't know beckoned me to the floor and we had a wordless freeform conversation, mimicking, innovating, making eye contact, laughing. With a sweep of the arms, a torque of the hip, there was bonding and aesthetic pleasure. According to a neuroimaging study (Brown and Parsons, 2008:83), dancing activates the Broca's area in the frontal lobe classically associated with speech. They write that the interaction of "the representational capacity of language and the rhythmicity of music . . . allows people not only to tell stories using their bodies but to do so while synchronizing their movements with others' in a way that fosters social cohesion."

Ehrenreich (2006:10–11) calls dancing in the streets, which is the title of her book, a collective ecstasy and what Victor Turner in his famous study *The Ritual Process* (1969) saw as "an expression of communitas, meaning, roughly, the spontaneous love and solidarity that can arise within a community of equals." Pointing out that civilization offers few forms of communal emotional connection, she presents a persuasive argument for a return to the collective joy of festivities which may include drinking, gaming, some efforts at costuming, as well as dancing. (254–260). According to Ehrenreich:

> To submit, bodily, to the music through dance is to be incorporated into the community in a way far deeper than shared myth and common custom can achieve. (24)"

## *Musika* (Music)

The prolific Robert Bellah (2006:158) quotes Walter Freeman, The Origins of Music:

> Music involves not just the auditory system but the somatosensory and motor systems as well, reflecting its strong associations with dance, the rhythmic tapping, stepping, clapping, and chanting that accompany and indeed produce music. (2006:412)

Bellah also mentions that the ethnomusicologist Bruno Nettl (2000:472) has concluded the "earliest human music was somehow associated with ritual."

GARTH CARTWRIGHT (2005:233) traveled with Gypsy musicians in the Balkans and claims, "Since time immemorial music has been the Gypsy gift to the world," adding:

> Music is a sacrament. This has been true for thousands of years of human history, save the last hundred or so. Today it may primarily exist as entertainment, simply another commodity, yet the mechanisms of music, how and why it affects us the way it does, are still mystical. Good music carries an incredible, invisible strength, one that communicates with the human heart and can act to inspire in so many ways, none more so than as an anti-oppression agent, slicing through prejudice and ignorance . . . Grief, melancholy, frustration, dissatisfaction, alienation, loss of family, economic insecurity, a sense of powerlessness against unjust power, of being a commodity rather than a person, of losing your roots, such is the subject matter of Gypsy song . . . (2005).

Current living conditions for Gypsies in the Balkans may be different from those in the States, but, for years, the Machvaia songs sung at the table were unbearably sad, the men pulling out the final notes, leaning against one another for support. At times, a solo stark with feeling hushed the conversations, stopped the drinking and the dancing, and filled an enduring pause with the tonal shadows of the past.

EARLIER IN THE CENTURY, when the people were traveling, Lola said that the men's guitars helped the people set up the tents, water the horses, and light the fires. In the Sixties, in Seattle, the men adjusted their guitars to a minor key and played, making up amusing lyrics to suit the situation and the moment. The people's genius for emotional and intuitive feeling is readily expressed in the music/dance venue; the people celebrate being together with song; they follow the direction of their feelings with dance. These tendencies seem characteristic of many Gypsies. Williams (1992) points out that Leblon, who studied Gitanos, defines flamenco's most distinctive characteristics as "free rhythm, absence of exact correspondence of text and music, preponderance of performance over material, that is, of emotion over form, the latter shaping the former" (87). The motif of personal inclination and feeling is apparent during *kolo*, the Machvaia wedding dance, each dancer stepping to a somewhat different beat.

A Slovakian Gypsy woman, Ilona Lacková, had a father who was a musician. She wrote, in her memoir of 1999, that "when someone wants to say something in a song, no one can get offended or angry or mock it." Also, to express something impossible to say publicly, "he'll sing it in a song. A song is sacred and untouchable." In her Roma group, "the most sought-after husband was a musician and the most sought-after bride was a girl from a musician's family (71)."

## Stayin' Alive

During the heyday of Machvaia parties, the stylized disco dancing from the film *Saturday Night Fever* became immensely popular. Mimicry is adulation and, at nearly every event, the floor would clear, the band would play "Stayin' Alive," and each member of the male chorus line became John Travolta. For more than a decade, lads from three to thirty danced as a unit, emulating the great Travolta. Parents even managed to smuggle their three-year-olds into *Saturday Night Fever*.

Eventually, a Los Angeles family invited the Outsider John Travolta to the ritual commemoration of their teenaged son, a lad who had worshiped Travolta. When the arriving crowd found the kind-hearted Travolta at the memorial table, they went wild. Miller's oldest daughter, Sabrina, then a teenager, claims she saved the star from the ensuing stampede by quickly escorting him out through the kitchen.

From the Seventies into the Eighties, no party was complete without the excitement of several "Saturday Night Fever" renditions. While dozens of Travolta "wannabes" flung their arms with attitude and tapped the beat in synchronized measure, the older women with whom I was sitting frowned and, ringed hands clasped to chests, caught their breaths in foreboding. Sensing the fast winds of change, they pensively recalled the time that no one danced better than a Gypsy and the only reason to copy a foreign dance was to show how it might be improved or adapted. I understood what they meant. Ranking is what Machvaia consistently do, and emulating Travolta in such fashion proved the Machvano dancer and Travolta were becoming a match—no longer two disparate kinds—at least when it comes to dancing.

A few years earlier, a Machvano had assured me that "God loves Gypsies best." The reason he gave for this formidable statement was the people's sublime ability to sing and dance their way into a musical and *devlesko* (godlike) field of wonder. Music, singing, and dancing have a deep significance to Roma that goes beyond the purview of ordinary experience. Nevertheless, the overwhelming enthusiasm for Travolta's dancing provided, I suspect, the final death knell to the old beliefs that Machvaia were without peer in the song-and-dance category, and that "no one has a better time than a Gypsy."

## Those Hips

Once Singing Sam and Hollywood John were the Roma Pavarottis. As I have mentioned in Chapter 7, when Sam and his New York singing family came to San Francisco, Miller showed them particular honor with a *patchiv*, the feast of respect that is offered those of superior value. During the Machvaia heyday, Tom Jones and Englebert Humperdinck were also popular; Lola's daughters and I would fly to Las Vegas to be in the audience and pay a fortune for front row seats.

Even old Lola was not immune to Tom Jones's charms. Gina said her sister Sabrina was only six when Grandmother Lola, dressed up "fancy" in sequins, took her to a Tom Jones concert. Carried away by the music, Lola pushed aside the guards, jumped onstage, grabbed the singer, and kissed him directly on the mouth. Some way, little Sabrina got lost in the turmoil and tried not to cry until the police found her.

Returning home on the bus, in keeping with the joy to be found in the direct expression of feeling, Lola sang Tom Jones songs full voice. This, Sabrina admitted, embarrassed her even further.

BY THEN, ELVIS PRESLEY, the singer whose fluidly suggestive hip movements resembled those of the young Machvaia men at weddings, had been a favorite for some years. (Some claim that Elvis was part Romnichel, or British Gypsy.) On my first trip to California, I found that many Machvaia Elvis look-alikes had adopted his name and hairstyle, his manner of dress, and at nearly every party insisted on singing, as best they could, the same tunes as Elvis. Unfortunately, it was years before I considered Elvis any challenge to the status quo. At the time, the novelty of so many Machvaia in one room, the noise, the musical comedy atmosphere overwhelmed me, and I gave the Elvis copies too little of my interest and attention.

But singer Elvis has been an even longer lasting influence than the dancing Travolta. Of course Elvis gained the advantage—he died, becoming, to the Machvaia way of thought, all indomitable spirit. Since then and for decades, the media has promoted Elvis's continuing power; he or his ghost is regularly spotted around the world. Elvis mimics are still playing nightclubs. At Graceland, the single most visited home in America, save the White House, non-Gypsy pilgrims pray before the Elvis gravesite.

AT LUNCH WITH KATY AND HER COUSIN sometime in the Nineties, I was dumbfounded to learn that some of the Machvaia people have even adopted Elvis Presley into their divine pantheon of saints!

As Katy said:

> They hold him so great. Everybody knows he was so good, the best music, the king of rock and roll, the king in our lifetime. Might be something to it. I saw on TV, how a man took a picture of the brightest stars and connected the dots. He found Elvis Presley in the sky. He [Elvis] was in his waggle-hip pose.

Cookie responded:

> I celebrate Elvis Presley's birthday. A lot of Gypsies do. I go to the park and put a table. Light a candle [this act connects the supplicant with the Other Side]. He brings me luck. I've

**101**

had good luck ever since I did this. It started when I found a little pink petal on Elvis' picture frame. It was there for days, always fresh. It fell off and began to wilt. I picked it up, held it in my palms, and it got fresh again. That meant I should celebrate him.

Then Katy stunned me further with the following information about Mara, a distant cousin with whom we often chatted during the Seventies, when we went for a late breakfast at a popular coffee shop in Berkeley.

Remember Mara, married to Jumbo? She was in love with Elvis, cherished him; she had pictures of Elvis all over her house. She lit candles, she put food for him. People say that's why she killed herself, to be near him.

Technically speaking, of course, Elvis was no Gypsy saint. For one thing, a saint is sparkling clean, pure, absolutely good, and never married. Elvis was none of these. But his movements were graceful, he was remarkably good looking and he sparkled onstage with rhinestone-studded vests, diamond rings, gold chains, and spotlights. Moreover, the people agree that his singing was perfect: "I always feel good when I listen to Elvis."

In particular, Rose told me, "You never know what is in this world. All the people hold him so great. Not just Gypsies. American people see his ghost all over. Everybody knows he was great. The best music, the king of rock and roll, the king in our lifetime."

[Pause]

"You like somebody, you like somebody."

*Chapter 9*

# GHOSTS, GRIEF, AND ANCESTORS

## Ghosts

When Lola's people first arrived in America and didn't know a word of English, "We heard sounds, strange sounds. Mostly at night." Night is the time the Devil walks and Martéah, the Angel of Death, is near. Even fearless Lola confessed that "nights, when I was little, we were really bothered by ghosts. Sometimes the wagon would shake and turn over. My aunt saw a big floating cloud face with bright yellow eyes looking in her tent flap."

One of the first things the people wanted me to understand was that, "Gypsies see ghosts." America in the early 1900s was apparently profligate with ghosts. Frightened horses would whinny and tear at their ropes, and the men would have to calm them. If it was daytime, the Gypsies could try to outrun the ghosts. But ghosts prefer the dark, when the woods and road were black, and moving the wagon was treacherous. Once, a Machvano had to wrestle with a ghost who tried to strangle him. He showed the others the marks on his throat, and later he was said to have lost his mind. But now, having buried several generations of their own dead in American soil, the Machvaia appear to be better defended from "foreign" ghosts.

The people began telling me ghost stories, mostly relics from the days of traveling. An elderly Machvano from the Yovanovich lineage related this about the ghosts of his childhood:

> We camped near a house we didn't know was haunted. We
> stayed there two nights and the first night we weren't

**103**

bothered. But the next day, all us kids went into the house and played, and I think we woke them up. That night we had trouble, ghosts. Our big dog fought with them. He fought until all the corn stalks around us were crackling. My father shot in the air three or four times, hoping to scare them. Then we heard violins and dancing in the house. But we couldn't see anything through the windows. So father made a big fire, as big as he could. He carried us out of the wagon and up to the fire. My brother was big and he got to hold the torch. Father played the old Serbian tunes on his guitar and we danced. We danced for courage.

Another of the innumerable Machvaia ghost stories I was told effectively underwrote the taboo concerning intimacy with Outsiders:

Two boys were driving home from a movie. They were heading back to the campground when they saw an attractive young girl in her nightgown walking down the highway. Stopping to pick her up, they asked what was wrong? She didn't answer. One of the boys tried to make love to her, but her flesh was cold as ice. Something wasn't right with the girl, both the boys felt it. Then she got out and disappeared. At the next town, they were told that a girl had been killed at that place some years ago. I know one of the boys; he grew up and he's my uncle. And that is true, a true story.

This ghost story concerns the problem of what Lola called "loving too much" which, as she explained, easily becomes *farmitchima* (bewitchment), a serious condition that can lead to death, or worse:

When I was living in the South, I met a Gypsy woman who was 100% haunted—Brazil is where this happened. She told me this story, about how after her husband died, he couldn't leave her alone. If you cross a big water, you're supposed to lose a ghost. So the woman packed her little things and took a boat to America [North America]. But she didn't get away. The ghost stayed beside her. It kept bothering her dreams. It kept her from getting married again. When she would think of another man, an accident happened. The ghost couldn't give her up. She thought the ghost had hitched a ride on the top of the boat to America, somewhere high, maybe on the flagpole.

More recently, a ghost visited Shinkie, Lola's distant cousin, in a dream:

I never really saw it, but I came very close—I was shaking and the memory vanished like the ghost. I didn't want to let anyone know something was wrong because what you believe [or hear, or say] can hurt you. So I said nothing, just got up, made coffee, and turned my mind to other things. That day my daughter fell and broke her arm.

If it wasn't a *tchoXai*, a female ghost, Shinkie presumed it might have been an ancestor, someone in her bloodline, trying to warn her about something, from "the Other Side."

IN SEATTLE, LOLA OFTEN CALLED to tell me her dreams— ghosts often appear in Machvaia dreams. One such dream sounded suspiciously like the film, *An American Tragedy*. In the movie, Montgomery Clift kills his pregnant girlfriend, Shelley Winters, so he can marry the glamorous Elizabeth Taylor. It's quite a melodramatic story and held Lola's interest during several retellings. In one of Lola's versions, the killer dies in the end because of divine retribution, an automatic power that comes "from The God" but requires no personal involvement on His part. Another evening, Lola told me the killer dies when the Shelley character's angry ghost comes back and kills him. In traditional Machvaia belief, the power of a ghost is not something to mess with.

A series of bad dreams will require remedy. Daylight, company, incense, are said to "take away fears," and Katy assured me that the need to protect her small children makes any mother "as strong as Superwoman." But bad thoughts bring bad things, and, to avoid ghosts, it is best to avoid graveyards and death-related topics, like war, major disasters, including many of the accidents and incidents regularly portrayed on the evening news.

IN THE OLD DAYS, BAPTISM was associated with vitality and health; even today, it is a health protection. Some time ago, a Machvanka called me to ask if I would baptize her ailing mother. Her mother, she said, kept dreaming of ghosts; she couldn't sleep, and was getting sicker. I didn't know what to say. Dinah was a woman older than me by several decades and, at the time, I didn't have a job, the money for plane fare or the amount needed to buy Dinah the required baptism outfit, a complete costume change, skin side-out. So I called another Dinah for advice. She had a different solution to Dinah's problem.

> When I dream of the *mulé* and it's past the year [of grieving],I get up and throw nine lighted matches behind me, over my shoulder, saying "Let the night close behind them."

Ghosts are called *tchoXani.* Many scary ghosts are *but tchoXani.* Ghosts are people who died with real hate and/or evil in the mind, Lola told me. Ghosts are those who die before they "have the chance to live," before they become parents, grandparents, before growing wise, respected, old, spiritually advanced, and before they have experienced all of their luck's good and bad possibilities. Unfulfilled lives and unfulfilled desires throw the universe off balance. People who are cursed, who commit a horrendous crime and never repent, who die with revenge on their mind, who "wished and wished, but it didn't come true," and those too passionately attached to the living may be condemned to remain on earth and suffer. In return, as ghosts, they cause suffering.

The nature of ghosts, or a ghostly presence, may be ambiguous, and depend much upon the point of view. Of late, there have been times when those open to risk have employed the unknowable to good purpose. Peggy Lee's little girl Peaches was heard talking to a ghost in another room. Peggy Lee called her sister and the two watched the lights and shadows play on the ghost room wall "like a movie." Some of the images looked like clouds, some like ghosts, one like a saint. The sister's husband walked in and read the saint's shadow as The Devil, after which, dismayed, he prayed to see a saint. A strange smell, not unpleasant, floated out of the ghost room. Peggy Lee decided this might be her good luck: "Peaches doesn't seem scared."

That very afternoon, a customer voluntarily brought Peggy Lee the thousand dollars she was owed from years of previous readings, money she had stopped expecting. Peggy Lee decided the ghost was on her side: a little girl like Peaches. "She likes us and visits us in dreams. This is a good house for money."

The next year, however, Peggy Lee passed the house along to her brother Frankie and, the first night Frankie's family spent there, his baby boy fell out of bed and cut his eye. It was Christmas, cold, and hard to find a doctor. The next night, the lights flickered and they heard a funny noise. When the tree caught fire, the family escaped to a motel, and never went back. The ghost, they said, must only like Peaches.

In any case, immediately after death, the behavior of a beloved Dead One has particularly ghostly aspects. Not having embarked as yet on the final journey, He or She is around somewhere, perhaps lingering nearby, and may indulge in short-lived tricks like transforming into a crow, a bee, a dog, even a fly, and startling their grieving relatives. Shortly after Lola died, I was cautioned not to injure the bee that kept buzzing by my ear. Zoni, Lola's youngest, waved a little cigarette smoke harmlessly toward the bee and told me, "Bees make honey and wax. Bees are lucky."

The next Memorial Day in Sacramento, Lola's daughters and I, sheltered by a tree, were picnicking on Lola's and Bahto's side-by-side graves. We doused the area with soda pop and wine. We carefully arranged a bean burrito in the middle of Bahto's American business name, John Roberts, in metal letters. Nearby, the niece she raised cut Muli (Dead Romni) Rachel a piece of homemade chocolate cake. Mulo (Dead Rom) Piggy was, I noted, a two-beer-and-pretzels man. I pointed out a crow flying away with the candy bar I had offered as gift to Lola. Birds are a winged connection between earth and sky, the living and the dead, and when the crow had settled on a nearby tree branch, Lola's middle daughter assured me that the theft was, "a good thing. We think She [the Dead One] will get it."

AS RELUCTANT AS THE PEOPLE ARE to release their beloved dead completely, so do they feel that the Dead One may not want to go. Talking about the Dead Ones can be construed as encouraging their return to the earthly dimension. Sometimes, when I broached the topic of death and Dead Ones, the family ran from the room. Once, in a manner that felt quite like a warning, Katy slowly, pointedly told me, "The dead are dead, and let them be dead."

According to Patrick Williams in his insightful book, *Gypsy World: The Silence of the Living and the Voices of the Dead* (a translation from the original French), speaking the name of the *mulé* fails to pay them homage. Among the French Manuš, the blanket of silence around the dead is the living's gift of honor (2003).

THOSE WHO HAVE A LONG AND LARGELY lucky life, like Lola, who die easily and without fanfare—Lola died in her sleep of a heart ailment, or, Katy suspected, of an overdose of sleeping pills —are unlikely, the people say, to become ghosts. Nevertheless, no one intends anyone in their *vitsa* to go on that final journey with a residue of bad feeling. It is critical to attend the dying and ask for forgiveness, or at least see the Dead One and ask and offer *Yiertiv tu* (forgiveness). For who can tell in what manner or degree one may have offended another in this life? And who can tell for certain if the Dead One was truly satisfied and content before embarking on the final journey? Without warm thoughts and the exchange of forgiveness, the dead may drag the cumulative weight of unresolved bad feelings "like rocks," and lack enough buoyancy to pass through the gates to the Other Side. How easy, then, to become a ghost! Indeed, the distinction between alien, angry ghosts and the beloved ancestors who are their kinsmen's advocates can incline to the obscure.

After death, whenever the name of a Dead One is mentioned, "*T'alierto* (I forgive you)" respectfully follows.

As Bahto lay dying, he refused to give his daughter-in-law Duda the peace that comes with forgiveness. Lola admitted, "We felt bad for her." During the year of mourning, Miller and Duda kept seeing signs and having dreams; as they slept, Bahto Mulo (Dead Rom) threw the pans out of the kitchen cupboard; the cleaning lady's little daughter announced she had been playing with Bahto in the bedroom: a man who looked like Bahto repeatedly caught the bus down the block. When Bahto Mulo appeared in a dream asking, "Where is it?" they realized he wanted his shaving mirror—which they had forgotten to include among the *pomana* offerings. At the last *pomana*, Miller offered a mirror with the proxy suit of clothes and the visitations became less frequent. But Duda kept having nightmares. When their house burned down, Miller and Duda moved, and the nightmares stopped. Their little daughter Gina supposed Bahto Mulo might not know where to find them.

## All Gypsies Go to Heaven

Ancestors are of the most exalted status; invariably described as good, they receive more respect of the honoring and memorial kind than any of the living. In an effort to bridge my incomprehension, Lola's daughter-in-law explained, "The Dead Ones are like holy people to us."

Death, to the Machvaia way of thinking, is a perfectly natural phenomenon in the given order of things for *but thiem* (human beings of all kinds). "Die young and have a good-looking ghost," was once a popular expression. Dying is a kind of promotion: no matter how misbegotten and maligned the Dead Ones were in life, when they die they become perfected in memory and incorporated into the ideal.

A quick and easy death is considered the crowning glory of a long eventful life. Atarino, Lola's father-in-law, died in the right way. Lola said:

> He ate a good dinner the night before, soup, meat, dessert, and he died in his sleep. As soon as we knew, we lit the candle. That's our belief, so he'll have light in the next world where it is dark. The Gypsies that were camping just over the hill came to keep us company. So we won't get scared. From all over the country, the people came for seven days.
>
> Before he died, twenty-six cars drove with him to see a heart specialist. But the man couldn't do anything for him. Atarino knew he would die. Atarino sent the word ahead for the people to come. Most had already started. We built a huge fire at night; it was warm during the day.

Death has serious theatrical possibilities, and I could well imagine Mulo (Dead Man) Atarino in the most dramatically important moment of his new career, sitting up in the direction of the tent flap to greet his visitors, the living Machvaia and the Machvaia dead as well—for the ancestors are believed to come and pick the Dead One up, so "He won't be scared."

THE PEOPLE HAVE A TERROR OF BEING ALONE, and dying alone was once considered, "the worst that can happen." Zoni, Lola's youngest daughter and the one who called me Peio (Sister), died in her forties. Dear Katy tried to console me, saying, "When your time comes to go, Zoni will be waiting. In our belief, they keep you company so you won't be scared. They take you with them."

Those who are grieving require company too. Once, everyone tried to finish what had been started, the entire tribe except for those unavailable by phone, too sick to travel, or too far away. Back then, as I was assured by a Machvano of the proud Adams family, "We had good hearts. We were respect." Rituals were on a smaller scale; the *pomana* (commemoration) table offering was simple, whatever was available at the country store. "Maybe apples, oranges, walnuts, bananas, jelly beans, and hard candies, all laid on a big tablecloth on the ground, over some clean straw, and that was it," Bibi said. At that time, the Machvaia people were fewer in number, no more than several hundred, and there were more *pomani*, six a year, instead of the current three. When the people traveled by horse and wagon, attendance at these events was tortuously slow and difficult. But somewhat at a loss in the strange Outsider world of America, the people were aware they needed the backing and support of one another.

ALL GYPSIES GO TO HEAVEN, I am told. Heaven is heaven "because you get to see the people you love, your parents, grandparents, friends." Heaven is heaven because it is "the place of peace, without pain or suffering." Heaven is "up," as is the Other Side, The Sky, and The God, and these were, for the *phurotem* (elders), pretty much "all the same."

DEATH, THE END OF THE JOURNEY OF LIFE, is the beginning of the cosmic journey. For six weeks after the burial, the dead relive all the major events of this life, traveling to see all the people they loved, and visiting all the places they wanted to visit but didn't get the chance. At the conclusion of *krisa* judgment, on their way to the Other Side, the *mulé* pass through a gate (or two) where those they loved and knew will greet them. A Dead One who lived a long and fruitful life, being already spiritually advanced, is believed to travel fast and arrive on the Other Side expeditiously. By the end of one year, all Dead Ones, no matter their history, should have become ancestors, the guardians of tradition and protectors of their descendants.

According to Paul Thomas (n.d.:40), in India, "the soul, on its departure from the body was made to appear before Yama, the god of death, where it was judged . . ." In a similar fashion, the Machvaia Dead Ones, before passing through the gate, are judged by a heavenly *krisa* of their dead peers regarding "what happened," the good and bad merit of their lives, and this automatically devolves on their descendants as *baX* or *bi-baX* (without luck) inheritance. As in Brahmanical belief, dead relatives require their kinsmen's help on the journey, an encouraging push on their way to heaven. Machvaia who are grieving in the recommended fashion are said to help their dead relative get a better review by the *krisa* in the sky.

To facilitate a favorable judgment, Machvaia make frequent offerings to prove that they care and haven't forgotten. Gifts for the dead are much like what was enjoyed in this life, for the Other Side is much like this, the rich are still rich, those who were popular in life are popular in heaven, and their *vitsi*, lineages and bloodlines, are the same. Food, drink, money, flowers, as lavish as can be afforded, are offered by the mourning family at *capella* (chapel wake), the funeral, the burial. More food, most particularly fruit (the fruit tree is symbol of perpetuity as it doesn't die when the fruit is picked), and fine clothes (traveling on death's journey is said to wear them out) are given at the six-weeks and one-year death commemorations (*pomani*). The new clothes required for the *capella*, or lying in, are presumably still fresh at the three-days-after-death *pomana*.

ON THE HOLIDAYS OF CHRISTMAS, New Year's, and Easter, a fine breakfast is served the recently Dead One (see Chapter 7). But even after the liminal post-death year, whenever the Dead One comes to mind, an offering of the last bite on the plate, or a spill of coffee, *Des anda vas* (You give from the hand), is in order. If you take a bite or cut into food and a crumb falls, that indicates a Dead One wanted it. Leaving the last bite on the plate for the 'hungry ghost" was, at one time, recommended. Even yet, a bad dream or a bad feeling indicates an offering to the *mulé* is required. A gift to someone, anyone, in the name of the dead, is one way to deal with grief, one way to pay the Dead One honor.

Jan Yoors (1967:237) remembers his friend Pulika buying the best horsewhips available from a peddler and distributing them "among the startled horse dealer *Gaje* [Outsiders] in silent offering to his dead brother whose appreciation of a good snapping whip was well known among the Lowara."

Fat Annie's mother died thirty years ago. But Annie still honors her mother's birthday each year with an annual party.

When, at a *pomana*, I asked about giving food to the great-grandparents who died before she was born, teen-ager Pinky, Katy's step-daughter, said, "We don't know Them. We never met Them. But, if the *mulé* see Them, we know they'll give Them some."

## Bloodlines and the Dead

Ancestors are the living's courage. They are a form of insurance in a world the Machvaia didn't make, seldom understand, and so often cannot control. Available whenever desperation calls them to account, ancestors are their kinsmen's defense against the Unknown, the final barrier against the forces of darkness. When you call on your luck, the Dead Ones hear. If you curse someone "with real hate," as Lola put it, you involve the dead. The people say, "The dead are always with us." The dead are what living are becoming and eventually must be —all spirit and awareness. And what the living aren't, eternal and invincible.

Machvaia ideas about the dead have some similarity to Indian beliefs. Regarding Hindu ritual, Veena Das writes that "though the ancestors have the power to cause great harm, they also have the potential to bestow wealth and progeny on their descendants [and] they have to be propitiated so that they may grant these boons to their descendants" (1977:16).

*BaX* AND THE WORK OF DEAD RELATIVES often appear to be one and the same. Machvanka Duda, who was her dead father's favorite, had dreams of him on occasion. One summer he "showed up" several nights to indicate which horses would win the following day at the race track. During her memorable Bay Meadows visits, Duda made thousands of dollars on long shots. In keeping with custom, good-hearted Duda split her winnings with her companions. The local Machvanki welcomed an invitation to accompany her to the races, to share her luck, to receive a transfer of Mulo (Dead Rom) Gitsa's merit.

Ancestors warn their families of impending dangers. Years ago, Katy was riding in the passenger seat of her car, her youngest in her lap, when another car slammed into them, and her baby boy was killed. Just before they hit, Katy saw her dead mother-in-law's face through the windshield. "That was a premonition," she said. "She tried to warn me. Often before something bad happens, I see or feel something is wrong."

AFTER MY FIRST STUDENT YEARS IN SEATTLE, I began traveling summers to meet more Machvaia. I was on expedition in southern California when Lola's grandson Duke, a young man in his twenties, overdosed and fell into a coma. Invited to help, I moved in with Boba, Duke's mother. Perplexed by his curious condition, I heard a Rom describe Duke as "dead, but not dead, and wired up like a stereo."

Word went out across the nation. The hospital halls and lobbies filled. Boba's telephone rang day and night. Because Duke's life peaked out so early and what happens to one of their children, particularly a lad from a good family, might happen to them all, the alarmed women queried me, the visiting Outsider, about American "diseases," or addictions. "What is this dope? How does it make them feel?" "What would you do if your son was doping?"

Later that week, we were sitting in the kitchen area, all Boba's sisters, her sisters-in-law, some visitors, and me, when Boba remembered a dream. Two nights before the overdose, dead paternal grandmother Nata had appeared in Dukey's dream and told him to get her stocking, and, laughing, he complied. A simple dream with the most ominous implications. Those long dead should be at peace, in need of nothing. Stockings are a woman's intimate apparel and inappropriate for a grandson, a male, to handle. The difference of sex, authority, and age compounded insult. The women agreed Duke's laughing betrayed a critical lack of awareness regarding the dream's tragic import. The sock/shame was Nata's warning to stop the shame of dope. Unfortunately, Duke hadn't heeded Nata's warning.

The dream was told and retold, over the phone, and to the visitors. In the language of dream reversal, Duke's laughter indicated he would be crying soon. Boba disagreed. She attributed Duke's drug problem to the noisy expressways and increasing traffic in an area once quiet, fragrant, and green with orange groves. Boba blamed cars: "It's the machines. The machines got bigger and stronger."

But the people found considerable solace in the dream. They said Dead Grandmother Nata was handling the situation. Duke, neither dead nor alive, was being held in abeyance for a final decision by the jury in the sky.

The women relaxed. Heads and voices lowered. It was a moment of triumph in an episode bleak with depression. The crisis was happily relinquished to those who are All-Knowing. The power of drugs, "dope," the incomprehensible foreign custom, had been effectively denied.

Time dragged as the days passed. The ancestors took too long and the dream ran out of meaning. Portents ensued. Lola, who was still in Seattle care-taking Miller's children, wistfully called to tell us about the small *chiriclo* (bird) that pecked at her window, the needle-nosed bird that comes like the breath out of the body to warn of a relative's death. Lola's daughter Keka said her eyes had itched for a week —itchy eyes meant trouble. Keka spent hundreds of dollars on phone calls to find out how everyone in her family was doing. Another time, we were in the kitchen, having breakfast and listening politely to a distant cousin describe the black cat she saw on the back fence driving in. Up all night at the hospital, visiting Duke, Aunt Kaboka, formerly reknowned as Saintwoman, was in no mood for idle surmise and irritably responded, "What's this cats business? You watch too much *Creature Feature!*"

FOR THOSE NEAR THE DYING AND THE DEAD, dreams and apparitions are the rule. A year after Lola gave one of her younger daughters to the George Adams family in marriage, Diane became seriously ill. Lola and Zoni took the train from Sacramento and, at midnight, a cold wind whistled down the aisle. The train lights blinked, off, on, off. "Wait," Lola hollered. "Wait for me!" That was when, Lola said, she knew Diane was dead.

> The evening before the burial, Lola was staying at her brother's house. It was warm and summer. By myself on the front room sofa. I couldn't sleep . . . cause I was waiting for her to say goodbye. Then, there she was, flying down like an angel, coming to me and all drifty in white chiffon, her black hair open to wings around her head. An angel! I ran out to the porch and called "Diane." And she moved away. I heard my voice singing this song I never knew before, My Truly, Truly Friend. The louder I sang, the higher she flew. She got so high, she disappeared. Higher and higher. I never forget that. I saw her clear as I see you now. My brother came out and asked what was wrong? I told him nothing. I kept that for myself all these years. She came because she had to.

After the vision she had of her dead daughter floating in white, Lola often assured me she had never been afraid of ghosts. "I say to myself, maybe it's only Diane." Lola also wanted me to know that "Ghosts are mostly fear. So I am never feared."

Ancestors also function as the community conscience. No matter what they were like in life, when dead, they become the guardians of custom, responsible not only for protecting descendants, but also keeping them on the straight and narrow. This is much like the point Turner (1977:28) makes, that the ancestors serve "a mediating function concerned with keeping the social structure of the system going in its characteristic form, with all its moral and jural rules, by acting as a punitive sanction."

Children who die, however, do not become ancestors. Innocent, pure, and inexperienced, they are unsuitable as ancestors.

Instead, their parents are usually offered the meager comfort that "God wanted your boy. He was too good to live." Like their time on earth, a child's post-death rituals are abbreviated.

## Sickness and Dying

In the Sixties, when the word spread that someone was sick, Roma gathered at the hospital. I was still in graduate school when Zorka was hospitalized for several weeks. The University Hospital called me to discuss the growing chaos, the Gypsies' constant questions, the overflowing lobbies and bathrooms, the crowds in the hospital corridors, the cars with California license plates in the parking lot, the families who slept in their cars. A young Gypsy girl had walked into an operating room during an operation! A typewriter was missing (it was later found in another office).

Meeting with the staff, I explained that what they found chaotic was actually organized into *vitsi* and families, respect shown and received. But I didn't, as yet, comprehend the poignancy of the people's courage as, owing to their sensitivity to contact, the place of the dying and the dead has serious disease- and ghost-potential for the living. Nor did I explain that it was up to the living, holding together, to keep Zorka's vulnerable relatives from being swept away "like crumbs" by the inordinate dimension of their grief; indeed, one daughter-in-law was already covered with scratches. In such situations, the Angel of Death is perceived to be very near and, as the author Gypsy Vishnevsky writes, "nobody knows what she or he might do to themselves physically . . ." (2006:147).

The many Roma at the hospital did try to pick up after themselves and made efforts to keep their children, except for the necessary trips to the bathroom, outside the building. I tried to explain to the staff that the Roma came because they cared "with all our hearts," as Lola put it. But I don't think the Outsiders were impressed.

Had it been a decade later in my research, I might also have explained that medical establishments were an Outsider mystery: medical terms, procedures, the way the body works unfathomable; the doctors' lack of warmth so frightening that some Machvaia never went to a doctor. When Mileva of Oakland was sick, for example, she gave her daughter-in-law a list of symptoms, and the daughter-in-law had the blood tests at the doctor's office—Mileva never got an accurate diagnosis.

ONCE, MACHVAIA HAD MACHVAIA DOCTORS. But the Machvaia medicine women who knew about herbs were all dead and gone by the 1940s. By the 1970s, after a series of miracle cures involving penicillin, drugs and the medical establishment were reassessed, then followed by a pill-popping period when a lot of medication was assumed to be better than a little. Once, when Šrecha had a fight with her husband Leo, she stayed with me for a week in my San Francisco studio. Unable to find her usual preference—whatever that was—she took all my birth control pills, three months worth, in one dose. Soon after, perhaps owing to my lack of pain medication or sleeping pills, she moved on to Oakland and her daughter's.

After several Machvaia died of overdoses, including, the following year, my dear friend Šrecha of a stroke, the people became more wary of medication. Now, going to the hospital is not necessarily considered a death sentence. Now, having universally agreed that doctors *can* heal—although, as Miller claims, some just want your money!—some Machvaia tend to jump from one doctor to another, expecting instant results. Now, to avoid ruining relations with a doctor they like, or causing problems for the hospital staff, or sending concerned relatives into bankruptcy with the cost of motels and the required "out of sight" hospitality, the Machvaia often keep their illnesses away from public awareness.

## Žaléa (Grief)

One winter afternoon, after the exhaustion of a twenty-four-hour hospital visit, tears welled and pooled mascara down my cheeks. I was hiding behind a tissue when the Machvanki noticed. Apparently I had the right look, blotched and swollen. The women circled tight around me in approval and support: "Look! The Djuhli! She has a heart. Like us."

Fatima, Lola's daughter-in-law, remembered a time long ago when, at the burial of Big George's mother, the people walked all the way, miles and for hours, to the graveyard. The women, she said, were in tears, wailing, long hair down, shoes falling off their blistered feet, and no makeup. "We looked like a disaster area, a national disaster," she giggled.

NOWADAYS, MOST MACHVAIA DIE IN HOSPITALS. Before, when the people died in tents and wagons, no Roma would make use of those death-associated structures, believing the Dead One leaves behind a dying essence that poses a contact danger for the living. Outsider contacts, Outsider ghosts, as well as Outsider curses, are believed to have less potency because, "We don't know them and they don't know us." Nevertheless, when moving into a residence previously occupied by Outsiders, the Machvanka still douses the rooms with incense to clean out any resident ghosts, and then washes everything she can with Lysol.

According to the literature, death beliefs and rituals appear remarkably similar from one Roma group to the other and, in this respect, are particularly enduring. Examples are the Gypsies in France (Maximoff 1960:12–27), Wales (Myers 1943:93–5), and Sweden (Tillhagen 1952:19–54). As a child, Jan Yoors traveled part of each year throughout Europe with a Lowara Roma family. He writes that when the elderly Tshukurka died, his tents, pillows, and rugs were burned, his plates and glasses destroyed. "Nothing should remain in use that was used by him and that he had been attached to" (1967:236). In America, Machvaia prefer to evacuate the *ofisa* in which someone died, and permanently dispose of the furniture and clothes. In earlier times, Bibi told me, items belonging to the dead were sent on a raft down a clean flowing river. Now, most Machvaia live in cities and they are more likely to take the Dead One's clothes to a dry cleaning establishment and never pick them up. Clothes and other items intimately associated with the Dead One may also be wedged in the branches of trees in a city park. The household furniture is usually moved into a storage locker, and forgotten.

After a Machvaia death, if the family doesn't abandon their living quarters, the mirrors may be covered and all the standing water thrown away in case the Dead One might continue putting these items to use. The next of kin must wait three days to comb their hair or change their clothes and, until the first *pomana* (commemoration), no one should wash or shave—the productive bubbles and suds are associated with the living and life. When Lola was a child, the next of kin waited longer, until after the burial.

The amount of time devoted to grieving is ideally in keeping with the bloodline relationship to the diseased. In earlier times, these proscriptions lasted as long as one year; now, for many, six weeks is more than enough. The mourners pay attention to how they feel. Regarding mourning periods, Williams (2003:9) describes those of the French Manuš as "variable: mourning lasts as long as the mourners decide, and they each make their own decisions." Currently, in the States, music, advertisements, and movies are broadcast in stores and elevators, and other unexpected places. Avoiding music is, for the urban Machvaia, difficult, if not impossible.

THE GRIEVING TURN OFF THE MUSIC in the car, on the radio, in the house. The grieving can't dance, wear red (unless very ill and needing protection), wear makeup, go to movies; they can't watch television, count their money, measure anything or be measured, cut, dye, knead, wrap, bake, roll dough, or make repairs. Certain activities associated with normal life are taboo: combing, painting, singing, whistling, playing the guitar. Pickles, black pepper, and hot peppers are removed from the kitchen area. The grieving can't eat chickens—one Machvanka told me chickens are ghosts!—turkey, or eggs; eggs, are associated with Easter, rebirth, and beginnings. They can't cook *sarma* or *gushvada*, food associated with *slavi* (saint-days) and celebrations. During the year devoted to grieving, no one of the Dead One's lineage should be married; a transition concerned with the beginning of life is bad luck in an era of death. The family's period of grief, *žaléa*, is formally broken by the last *pomana*, the one-year, but any period of grieving can be ended by singing or dancing. Some like to pour a glass of wine on the ground and say, "This is the end of *žalea*." But it is the music, particularly singing, playing, or dancing along with music, that changes the modality from grief, announcing that happiness, the happiness of life, the good and bad of life is back.

Ideally, grief should end at the end of the year; to grieve too much or too long is said to pull the Dead One back to the land of the living.

# Halloween, 1997

SO, WHAT ABOUT TODAY'S YOUNG MACHVAIA? Do they still fear and honor the Dead Ones? If the party I attended in San Jose in 1997 is any indication, not in the same fashion or as much as before.

Believing as they do in the virtue of celebration, the arriving Machvaia pioneers readily adopted major American holidays, with Halloween and the Fourth of July as the general exceptions. But on October 31, 1997, a Halloween masquerade party was hosted by several Canadian Roma whose grandmother had been a Machvanka. Brothers and wonderful dancers, they had recently married Machvanki from the San Francisco Bay area. The party introduced the Canadians to their new community and was well attended.

Young Machvaia, along with a few middle-aged adults from important lineages, came dressed as magicians, pirates, cartoon characters, story book characters (including fairies and Alice-in-Wonderland), vampires, Vikings, Indians, movie stars, and rock stars. One young woman glided through the room in gold and jewels, a beautiful and aloof study of the queenly Nefertiti. The portly Joker (from Batman fame), his red mouth laughing, bounced from one friend to another, glad-handing. I almost didn't recognize George, Miller's son and Lola's grandson, in his three-bobbing-headed ghost costume. Two Roma from Los Angeles, cleverly painted and costumed as the rock group "Kiss," won first prize in the costume contest. I took dozens of pictures.

But the most popular costumes were those of priests, nuns, and ghosts! Emulation is never taken lightly, and dressing like a priest or ghost was once an unimaginable folly. To Machvaia, emulation is *contact* and any type of contact may be contagious. Several decades back, the people told me priests were to be avoided for the reason that "they pray on the dead," meaning they were in frequent contact with potentially dangerous Outsider ghosts. Only on the communal occasion of baptisms and funerals were priests and Outsider churches something the people would willingly dare.

DOES THIS INDICATE THE LOSS of fear of ghosts among the younger generations?

A loss of fear of the power of bad luck or contagion?

A loss of fear of the authority of the Ancestors, which is, in a way, the authority of the elders and Machvaia law?

The end of the Ancestors' immutable powers of punishment and protection?

ONE FEARLESS AND LOVELY WOMAN with an antic sense of humor particularly stunned me. She had recently lost her valuable fortune telling territory in the town of Fremont to another Machvanka. The former Fremont fortune teller came to the party as a Dead One, dressed in sparkling tiara and earrings, white sequined gown, chalk-white makeup on her face and arms, and carrying a limp bouquet of cut flowers. The banner across her chest read "The Late Miss Fremont."

# Chapter 10

# COMMEMORATION OF DEATH

## Pomana (Commemoration)

No matter how attenuated the powers of the ancestors may have become during the latter part of the past century, they were, and are still, honored and beloved as parents, grandparents, family. With little time for preparation, the first *pomana*, at three days after a death, is brief, even hasty: a simple meal in a restaurant or a barbeque in the parking lot at the funeral parlor. The six-week and the one-year *pomana* require a proxy and, except for the difference of tone, are quite the same ritual. The six-week may be rife with tears while the last, consistent with the Dead One's arrival at the place of peace and no suffering, tends to be celebratory. After Lola's last *pomana* at the Hyatt on Union Square, her daughter, daughters-in-law, and I sat in a line outside the kitchen, feeling smug. The proceedings were judged a great success with more than a hundred attending. The guests had dressed in their best, brought their smiles and good thoughts, and looked, we agreed, like angels. Afterwards, Boyd led us into the adjoining banquet room where we sang "I Left My Heart in San Francisco."

SPICES AT A *POMANA* are forbidden; seasoning might overstimulate the Dead One and, when I first ate at a *pomana* in California, the food struck me as incredibly bland and tasteless. But, as with most things, times are changing and now the food at *pomani* is often catered.

Once it was the men's job, the women helping, to prepare the main dishes for *pomani* and *slavi*. *Pomana* food was cooked in five pots and among the five main dishes were pork and rice, lamb and string beans, and beef stew, each piece cut into small chunks as if to accommodate the Dead One's deficit chewing strength—at least that's what I liked to imagine. Poultry—birds that walk better than they fly—was considered inappropriate, a taboo that includes all the morning breakfasts honoring the Dead One. At *pomani*, the women wash and polish boxes of fruit, lots of fruit, everything available, stacking it into a continuous pyramid at the table's center, along with a variety of drinks and desserts.

Fruit, like eggs the fruitful symbol of rebirth, has affinity with death and the promise of life everlasting. Before fruit became available from all over the world and at all seasons, Machvaia celebrated a First Fruits picnic, usually in a park in July, to herald the annual arrival of the season and to honor their ancestors. Only after offering fruit to the ancestors, *des anda vas* (you give from the hand) at this picnic, could the summer fruits be eaten.

AT *POMANA*, a proxy eats for the Dead One and should be similar in age and status; someone the Dead One liked is even better. When Dora Nellako (Nelly's daughter), the famous unmarried Machvanka of the wealthy New York Adams family, died, she appeared in a dream to strenuously object to the proxy choice, an unmarried woman whom she hadn't known well; "Why did you pick her. I didn't ask for her. I don't like her much." There were no more dream complaints when Betty, a married friend, was chosen instead. Machvaia have no specific term for the proxy. Instead, they say, "So-and-so is taking the suit," emphasizing that the clothes and the memorial are intended for the Dead One.

For male proxies, the suit is a business suit and hat, everything new; for females, the suit is usually a jacket and a dress, or jacket, skirt, and blouse. The material should be fine; the color and cut flattering, and black is usually avoided. The result should be "beautiful, rich-looking." Like the godparents' gift to the baby at the baptism, the gift of proxy outfit must be "complete," and include fine new underwear and shoes. To be chosen as proxy is an honor; to agree to perform the role is a favor of considerable merit—*chéres sevahpo* (you make a favor). Those who attend the *capella* (chapel

**124**

for the Dead One) and the *pomana* are said to be showing their respect.

Before all the guests arrive, the table is set with pictures of the Dead One, fruit, desserts, drinks, plates, and tableware. Reserved for the Dead One/proxy, the china and silver at the head of the table is especially fine, the setting wide and surrounded with a sample of everything— the proxy's job is to sample all the edibles, though this often proves an impossible task.

Gifts for the Dead One are arranged in tiers nearby. The generosity of the gifts reflects on reputation and rank. Charley Adams of Los Angeles was rich and well known. In my forty years of fieldwork, he was probably the closest to an Ashundo Rom (Heard-about Man) of anyone I met. When he died, Barbara Miller's son took the one-year suit and, afterwards, retreated to Marin County with the spoils, which were so much and so many that I heard he was required to rent a walk-in storage locker.

*POMANI* BEGIN AFTER SUNDOWN when all kind of spirits are about. After the food arrives, hot from the kitchen, a Machvano with a pan of burning incense circles the table three times in the counter-clockwise direction. Incense, usually purchased at a church store, is said to "cleanse and open the way" for the dead to come and eat at the table. Trees are powerful, pure, signify the upwards direction; Katy describes incense as "fresh tree tears."

The incense smoke and fire, an awesome power, also sanctifies the "suit" before the proxy puts it on, usually behind a screen. Following this ritual treatment, I have been told by several women that, in place of the proxy, they momentarily saw the Dead One.

Two men start at the head of the table, circling the table three times in opposite directions with fistfuls of slender lighted candles, chanting the name of the Dead One, hollering something like, "Let this be for Rachel in heaven, this suit, this table," or "This table is for Rachel, the child of To'ma and Lara." In order to protect the living, the candles, which are at least forty in number (with the Dead One's candle, the number would be an uneven 41) are stuck into loaves of bread, as many as the bread will hold, and spaced around the place settings—they were inserted in watermelons at one *pomana*.

Candles are said to "light the way." During the days of camping, there were no chandeliers or streetlights. The fire in the middle of the camp and candles challenged the dark. Now, in the brilliance of a lighted hall, I am told, the practice of so many candles is sometimes neglected.

THIRTEEN IS CONSIDERED A LUCKY NUMBER for Machvaia—in part, perhaps, because it is unlucky for Outsiders. But the number might also relate to the thirteen found in some Hindu death rituals. Khare (1975:31) mentions the gifts on the thirteenth day to the thirteen Brahmins who are invited to a pakka feast honoring the dead. The gifts include "a glass, a plate . . . a spoon and bowl, umbrellas and wooden staffs." The Brahmins usually pass these items along to the priests. Indeed, the Brahmins and priests behave as proxies as "these gifts . . . are in fact given to the dead for his comfort in the other world."

Machvaia associate their good luck with the number three as well; three people usually go to buy the suit in which the Dead One will be buried; three men make the funeral arrangements; two men carry the burning candles around the *pomana* table three times. Uneven numbers are said to provide protection and the day chosen for the six-week and the one-year *pomana* must be an uneven number somewhat in advance of the actual due date. It is becoming popular, in fact, for the one-year to be held earlier and earlier; the last one I attended was more like nine-months. Nevertheless, it was called, and regarded, as "the one year."

At one time, weddings were taboo on Tuesday, Sunday was the ideal day for a *slava* (saint day), and Saturday was considered best for *pomani*. But since the people began renting halls and had to compete with the Outsiders for the weekends, these preferences are frequently overridden.

BEFORE THE PROXY IS SEATED, the Dead One's candle is relighted, the same candle as that used at the moment of death "to light the way to the Other Side." It was burned at the head of the coffin in which the Dead One lay during the week of *capella* (chapel). The day of the funeral, after the Dead One's leg bindings are cut "so She can travel easy," the death candle is snuffed with a piece of its own wax.

The trip to the church for a brief service is followed by the burial at which the candle is lighted again to evoke the Dead One's presence.

The 'light-for-the-Dead One' candle will be lit at each *pomana* until, after the last, it is left to burn itself out, often on the grave. Once it was placed on a little raft with some food, some of the Dead One's clothes, and sent to sea or down a river. Fire and pure water are powerful, cleansing, and *devlesko* (godly); they connect the living with the Other Side.

BY TRADITION, the Romani eulogy begins with 'Kama, Shona, *tai* Devla, A *šun!*" which in translation means, "Sun, Moon, and God, Listen!" These are the words I most often heard during my years of fieldwork. According to this summary translation by Ronald Lee, a Canadian Kalderasha Rom and writer, they are likely an ancient Roma tradition:

> Sun, Moon and God, hear me! This table which I place before [Dead One] may it appear before [Dead One] in heaven. May the people who eat from it become humble in his honour. May they themselves remain healthy and may his god carry him into heaven. Thank you, God, for what you have done for us on this earth. (1968:25)

For a people who now live in cities, the sun and moon have lost considerable meaning and it is currently hard to find anyone who includes all the preceding. More recently, I have heard Sainte Anne addressed. Devla (God), once primarily associated with the Sky, Sun, Moon, the weather, is usually part of the current eulogy and seems more frequently mentioned on a day-to-day basis with the passage of time. Listing as many lineage ancestors as can be remembered has become popular; owing to the tendency to forget ancestors beyond several generations, the list is never very long. At one of the last *pomani* I attended, Machvano Billy repeated the following three times:

> Kama, Shona, Romalé, Chavalin (Children); This is for Egi to wear here in health and happiness and for Bobé to wear on the Other Side.

The spoken eulogy is a moment of solemn attention, more solemn than, possibly, any other ritual moment. The usually voluble guests even stop talking, stand and listen.

DURING *POMANA*, the seated proxy begins eating a moment before the other guests. In the past, the male guests were first to join the proxy—I remember times when there was nothing left for the younger women to eat. By the good living mid-Seventies, men ate at the sanctified table and women were often served at surrounding tables. In the Eighties, the older men were usually allowed a head start, but women quickly joined them. Now, everyone walks over to the table at about the same time, and often there are adjoining tables; no one is left hungry. After the delay required by the preceding rituals, the food is cold and not particularly appetizing. But it must be eaten, and what can't be eaten, must be taken home—boxes are provided—and eaten there.

It is *nai mishto* (not good), however, for those of the same family and bloodline to remove anything from the hall—the deceased may follow. The sanctified leftovers nobody wants are wrapped in plastic bags and disposed of with care.

During the meal, the guests are inspired to shout, "What we eat here, may Lola eat in heaven!" "What Bobé [proxy] wears in good health, may Lola wear in heaven!" This might be echoed by "*Prosto!*" which was usually translated by those I asked as something like "Up, up, and away!" But I got a variety of answers and perhaps, at this point of time, we can assume that *prosto* means whatever the Machvaia might wish for the Dead One.

IN 1999, I left California and, except for visits, most of my contacts with the Machvaia community are now by phone. I call to keep in touch and learn the news. In 2000, when I called to ask Fatima in Los Angeles what *pomani* are currently like, she answered.

> *Pomani* are still elaborate. Can't do it for less than seven or eight thousand. I don't know why they're so expensive. *Pomani?* Now, when they give the clothes, it's got to be something. I think I heard that when Charley's daughter died, Rita got a mink coat, diamonds, real jewelry, a trousseau. But

not as many *pomani* because people live longer. It's the new technology of today. That's why they aren't dying. Before, they used to die like flies. Now they don't.

This view reflects Fatima's personal experience. She comes from a lineage known for bad hearts and dying young. A willful and intelligent women, she managed to survive several bypasses and to give up smoking, carefully followed the directions of her Cedars-Sinai medical doctor, and outlived all her siblings. Fatima died in 2007, in her eightieth year, and I truly miss her.

On occasion, when I wouldn't drive her where she wished to go, Lola used to say that I reminded her of Fatima.

# Chapter 11

# HAPPINESS AND WEDDINGS

## "Giving" and "Getting"

*Abéava* (weddings) are the most exciting of all Machvaia party occasions and they enlist the largest turnout. The people come as advocate and witness; they dress in their best and brightest clothes. They drink, eat, give *dahro* (brideswealth gift). Weddings are the opportunity for the young and unmarried to meet, to look over prospective spouses, to slyly pass out telephone numbers. Elders discuss which girl looks good, which girl might "stick" (stay in a marriage). Everyone who can, dances. At weddings, while the people stand around to clap a welcoming beat and smile, the young men show off with the wedding dance of athletic squats and kicks, rhythmic finger snaps, sexual shimmies, thrusting hips.

The overriding purpose of Machvaia life is to raise children *vorta* (right), which means in accord with custom, and to see that, in time, those children marry Machvaia. Nowadays, the young are more often involved in choosing their mates, but getting children married *vorta* is still the overriding concern.

THE WEDDING RITUAL TRANSFERS the bride from the family who "gives" to the family who "gets." By tradition, marriage is patrilocal, bringing the bride into the purview of the family who "gets." Marriage, therefore, has a potential for luck increase—or loss—that most affects the groom's family. Machvaia say something like, "Marko is giving, Zharko is getting." Or, "Zharko lel bori"—Zharko [in this case the groom's father or grandfather] takes a daughter-in-law, suggesting that the daughter-in-law will now belong to

**131**

her new family—*bori* (woman married into our family) describes her impersonal status. Because kinship is traced cognatically, through both the mother and the father, the acquisition of a bride will bring several new lineal bloodlines and accompanying luck prospects into the "getting" family.

Increased income is also expected; until recently, girls usually didn't marry until they had fortune-telling experience. Given a "location," a place to tell fortunes, the new bride was expected, preferably within the year, to return the brideprice cost incurred by her family of marriage. The adult role of the Machvaia female is breadwinner and provider, as well as caretaker of the home in a manner consistent with Machvaia purity standards. In Lola's day, a good daughter-in-law was said to be "good in tent, and good in town," which would include both household duties and business. The greatest gift of all, of course, to the "getting" family, is the promise of a new generation.

Everything seems to depend on the married woman. One of the duties of the new *bori* is to "settle" her husband. Whenever a family has trouble controlling an aging bachelor son and paying for the escalating costs of his leisure entertainments, the people agree the cure is marriage. "Get him married. Poor man."

AT ONE TIME, first cousin marriage was a *baro ladjav* (big shame) and the guilty couple was required to avoid public events. Marriage to someone with whom the families were in *chivrimos* (co-godparent relationship) was also forbidden. But, these days, the penalties devolving from these shames seem often overlooked.

IN SEATTLE, I remember when Stévo, a low-income Machvano with six sons to marry off, complained, "Marriage is the biggest risk a Gypsy takes." This surprised me; his lifestyle seemed, to me, endemic with fundamental risk. But then I discovered that if, out of pique, a bride goes back to her parents, repents and returns to her family of marriage, it can cost both families thousands in fines, plus the cost of sponsoring *krisa*—particularly if the girl keeps repeating the process. In the meantime, family secrets are spread, ugly rumors grow, and the families involved lose respect and status.

Stévo often complained he didn't have enough daughters to help him with the brideprices needed to marry his many sons. As it turned out, two of his three daughters ran away with men from other tribes, returned, and ran away again; and he failed to accumulate the money that might have paid for estimable Machvaia daughters-in-law. These are not trivial matters. To his mind, he failed at the most important task of his life, which was to insure the good luck of future generations.

DESPITE HER HISTORY OF MARITAL PROBLEMS, Katy still tells me that a wedding day is the most romantic day she can imagine. Romance feeds on perversity and one reason that the wedding occasion may be so exciting is the possibility of disaster, the elusiveness of the final outcome, and the way these can benefit, or damage, everyone involved, including ancient bloodlines and entire extended families. There is a lot riding on Machvaia marriage.

Harmony is prerequisite for public events and a messy divorce that leads to fights over children, unpaid fines, and enduring vendettas can isolate the principals socially. Until a divorce has been finalized, until all conflict between families is resolved, those involved are well advised to stay at home. Enmity of any kind inhibits the attendance of both extended families.

But after an interval that allows tempers to cool—a year, maybe longer—the more powerful and reputable family usually prevails and begins to accept social invitations, while the less reputable family becomes increasingly isolated. Failure to attend Machvaia ritual occasions can, in succeeding generations, lead to a family's marriage into more accommodating, less conflict-ridden situations, with other Roma. New *vitsi* have undoubtedly been born, over time, in such a fashion.

WEDDINGS ARE STILL A RISK. Today, wedding arrangements are still agonized over and discussed from every angle; rumors multiply about the character of the principals and omens abound. Now, as before, at the least sign that fate or luck isn't wholly in accord with the proposed arrangements and that all portents aren't auspicious, the people call the wedding off. In 1985, Bibi had second

thoughts about the wedding arrangements she was making for her
live-in grandson.

> I don't know about this *abéav* (wedding). I been losing
> things pretty much lately, my jade bracelet, the papers for
> the [rental] house. Now I hear my sister had a car accident.
> Those are all bad signs. It [the prospects for a successful
> marriage] doesn't look good. *Hatchiares* (you understand)?"

## Kaboka's Wedding, 1920

Lola thought she must have been eighteen or nineteen when Kaboka, the daughter of Zharko, Bahto's first cousin, got married in
Sacramento to Todoro's son, George Lee. Then, she recalls, the
people were traveling; their roomy tents, all colors, faced toward a
giant bonfire in the center of the camp. Large American flags
flapped high on tall flagpoles. Lines of flags, the flags of all nations,
were strung between the tents. The wedding lasted five days. The
music was an American band with the Gypsy boys filling in; the dancing was *kolo*—the wedding line dance. Pigs and lambs were roasted
on spits turned, most of the time, by the children. There were barrels of beer to drink and plenty of whiskey and wine. The men wore
American-style suits; the women dressed in ruffled capacious skirts,
aprons, over-blouses, much like they had worn in Serbia. Kaboka's
American-style ankle-length bridal gown was covered with lace. In
the yellowing snapshot I have of the young bride Kaboka, she appears to be wearing thick-soled boots underneath her belling skirt.
  Lola continued her story:

> Then, Kaboka got her hair combed up and tied with gold
> coins. Then they put the scarf [her mother-in-law tied the
> scarf of the married woman around her head] and she went
> around to the tents with a pail of water. The men dippered
> the water on their hands and face. They threw in a little
> money, you know, into the water; that was for good luck to
> the marriage. But now that we rent a hall, I don't see them
> doing that [passing around the pail of water] any more.

# Bibi's Wedding, 1924.

Several years after Kaboka's wedding, Lola's sister-in-law Bibi got married in Portland, Oregon. By then, most Machvaia families were traveling in big touring cars. When I interviewed Bibi in 1977, she described her wedding half a century earlier. She began with the color red; red is said to bring "happiness and protection."

> My first-day dress was American Beauty red; mother gave it.
> My bride's dress was white organza; three women sewed it.
> The veil was made of silk flowers, many colored flowers, and
> a little hankie hanged to the shoulder in the back. No, it [the
> veil] didn't cover my face—that would be bad luck. There
> were sixty tents, Machvaia and Kalderasha, and some people
> came a long way. My father loved me very much. So he asked
> for an extra thousand [added to the brideprice]. That's so he
> had traveling expenses in case he heard I was having a bad
> living and he had to look for me.

When the Machvaia were nomads, marriages were often hastily arranged between families who met on the road. After a day of partying, one family might ask the other for the hand of their daughter in marriage; brideprice would be given, and the two families became *Xanamikuria* (in-laws). The second night (called the third day) was the night the couple slept together; without this step there is no marriage.

> Bibi: Here's what they do. They take your clothes and put a
> white slip underneath and you go to bed. That petticoat has
> to show blood on it the next day to show you are a virgin.
> Then they make a flag out of the slip the third day and wave
> it on the pole to prove you are a virgin. Not any more,
> though. Nobody wants to know that!

The next day, three young girls braided Bibi's hair with gold coins and bound her head with a *diklo* (scarf). The bride and groom had to eat a little salt and bread off the other's right knee, most likely as the promise of future sustenance. In those days, the bride often cried throughout the three-day ceremony, in part because the difficult life of the daughter-in-law was reason enough to cry, but mainly because families traveled across continents and sometimes national borders, and the girl might never see her natal family again. (I couldn't, however, imagine the woman I knew as Bibi who seemed dismayed at nothing crying at her wedding.)

A small engagement ceremony (*tomniala*) at the tent or house of the bride's family usually preceded the wedding. This visit tactfully sounded out the possibility of further arrangements. If given the go-ahead, the discussion of brideprice and wedding arrangements was accompanied by a formal ritual offering of *ratchiya* (bottle of whiskey or brandy) tied with a red ribbon and gold coin. Now, if possible, a big *tomniala* party is in order, the details are worked out on the phone, and both families agree on the particulars, which, according to the financial circumstances of those involved, can be a simple dinner or a three-day celebration with hundreds in attendance.

## Fatima's Wedding, 1942

When I traveled to California and mentioned Lola's family, I often heard stories about Fatima, the "Glamor Girl Bori," as she was described by some who had been to her wedding. Fatima married Lola's oldest son Boyd and the marriage has lasted, a blessed and auspicious sign.

In 1983, I asked Lola's niece, Rose, about Fatima's wedding:

When Lola and Bahto had the storefront in Sacramento, they got their first daughter-in-law. The people even wrote a song about the wedding. How rich Bahto was: how he got the daughter-in-law Fatima: how he gave a very high price for the girl. She was quite lovely, Fatima. She had a delicate look without makeup—we weren't allowed makeup in those days. And how Lola wanted a special dress like no one ever had before, sapphire blue with silver beads. It cost at the time maybe five hundred dollars, which would be like three or four thousand today. They dressed her in many outfits, making a really big wedding. Then the people wrote this song about how rich Bahto and Lola were, and how they dressed the beautiful Fatima.

In 1998, I repeated the previous story to Fatima over the phone, and she said:

Not so. Another example of the Gypsy imagination. You know how stories are always growing into better stories. I'm not that kind. I never lie or blow things up, even when I should. My mother made my dress. It was gold spangles—at that time, no one wore spangles. I don't remember any song.

Then I called Katy:

I don't remember any song either. But people have told me about it. So someone probably made that up later. I do remember Fatima was a glamor girl. Red hair and light skin and very elegant. Maybe it was her more than the dress. But the people always give credit to the father-in-law.

Today, a formal wedding lasts three days, the first two given by the groom's family, the last by the bride's. Days one and two, *kolo*, the wedding line dance, winds into and out and across the room, the community enthusiastically traveling around the floor with the bride. The arm-on-arm, arm-on-shoulder line dance, each participant doing their own steps, grabs people from their seats, drops them off, and stops only to start again with a different format, mostly men, or mostly women, or mostly relatives, etc. *Kolo* tells a story throughout the wedding, and everyone who can is expected to participate, to show they support and celebrate the marriage with the spirit and style.

A staff tied with a red *diklo* (scarf), bells, and gold coins is carried by the line's leader. Formerly, the staff noisily called for attention, vigorously struck against the floor and off the beat of the music; I associated the staff's thrusting motion with male dominance and the priapic male principle. Now the staff, called the *bariako*, is short, no longer than a broomstick, and waved overhead. Anyone, except the bride and groom, can pick it up and start another *kolo*.

Nowadays, the bride and her family may arrive to loud cheers, processional music; then *kolo* grabs the bride into the line. Sometime during late afternoon, female relatives or in-laws-to-be take the bride away to help her into her white bridal gown. This done, her "wedding godmother," a woman chosen as an ideal marital example, a woman married only once, will run with her across the floor to the groom's side of the hall. A mock argument ensues over imaginary brideprice amounts—the real brideprice has been paid—and the gatekeeper godfather, husband to the godmother, escorts the bride through the invisible wedding gate. Then the godmother pins the veil and crown on the bride, and the groom's family leads the bride around the room in another celebratory *kolo*.

On day one and day two, after the dinner has been served, a *dahro*, a contribution, a "help," is collected from the men's table and the total announced. The equality of the men, their united concern and good wishes for a happy marriage, their investment in the continuation of their *vitsa* is symbolized in the giving of *dahro*.

By the 1960s, when I began my study, the *dahro* tribute from all the male household heads was heaped into a hollowed-out loaf of salted bread, "to make sure the couple always has bread and salt." Now that sustenance is no longer such an issue, the bride herself collects the *dahro*, properly not bridewealth, according to Spiro (1992:114), as it goes to help the groom's family, in an elegant container. With each gift, the Machvano is given a *diklo* (scarf) from a collection of colored scarves or white scarves, the latter a recent innovation suggesting purity. The exchange of *dahro* for *diklo* is like the company's pledge of support and approval, echoed by the bride's pledge of obedience to Machvaia law and fidelity to her new family.

Brideprice is a method of sealing and legalizing Machvaia marriage and in no way a commercial transaction. At one time, to avoid confusion with mundane matters like income, the brideprice amount was couched in terms of lira, instead of dollars.

MOST OF THIS PAST CENTURY, in part because boys are considered more sexually driven than girls, marriages were arranged when males were as young as fourteen. The practice of getting children married young on the premise that they would grow up together and, in the process, learn to love one another, wasn't always successful. Katy told a story about her young male cousin, Googie, who in the 1930s married an older woman who proved too ambitious for her own good.

Katy (1999): When I was little, I lived with Grandma Seka. In some ways she was kind, in some ways she was mean. And she wanted her own way. My grandfather was a very quiet and generous man [to the extended family and beyond]. She was the one who used to tell everybody what to do and what not to do.

In the house with us was Dolly, married to Pacific Rob, and [cousin] Googie. Me and Googie grew up together, went to school together, we are the same age. Googie had married an older girl—he was only about fourteen. He was really afraid of her. When the parents tried to put them together, he said, No. I don't want to sleep with her. I used to tell Nastassia [his new wife] not to bother him: "Don't do that to him. Let him take his time and get used to you'" But he just didn't like her. He was a little boy and we were all just kids and we joked around. He was too young. And that went on for a while.

What happened was this: the Old Lady [Seka] used to send Nastassia to the *ofisa* and she began to suspect that Nastassia was taking money from the hiding place where we kept money, pretending she made it that day. The first time, she said she made a couple of hundred. And, when she gave it to the Old Lady, Seka said, 'Oh, that's very good, my dear.' Nastassia kept doing that until the Old Lady got smart and marked the bills she was saving. Nastassia took the marked bills and said she made the money in the *ofisa*. I guess she wanted to please Seka.

When the Old Lady found out what Nastassia was doing, she called Nastassia's father and told him his daughter had a customer who had asked for his money back. She said she needed $5,000 to give him. [Machvaia have a rule, when requested, to give the money received for readings back. To do otherwise can result in lawsuits, bad press, and cost a

**139**

reader her territory.] While the father was coming over, Seka dressed Nastassia up real nice, fixed her up, and, after she got the money, gave the father back his daughter. She said, "We don't want her anymore." She gave her back and she got the entire brideprice back. [The usual amount returned at that time was a thousand.] Seka was a pretty smart old lady.

And Googie was so happy, he was dancing. Then, after awhile he got older. And then he got married. But that was the end of Nastassia.

# A Wedding in 1995

At an Adams/Yovanovich wedding, the party given the first two days was sponsored by the groom's family. The hall was large, the ceiling high. Five-foot-tall bouquets showered a rainbow of flowers and colors across continuous tables that banked the walls. Several barbequed pigs were displayed between tiered cakes. The largest cake was centered between water fountains with glowing hearts and Kewpie dolls that topped flower-wrapped Corinthian columns. Fronting the stair-stepped cake were Barbie and Ken, in wedding regalia. (Because Machvaia children usually don't play with dolls, these icons don't carry childish connotations.) Strung across the tables and the decorations, pinpoint lights flickered like a thousand electric candles.

A nine-piece band played a medley of music: Gypsy, Klezmer, Rock and Roll. Whenever the band played "Hava Nagila," someone grabbed the wedding staff, festooned with bells and a red scarf, and began another *kolo*. Pulling everyone available into the line, picking them up, dropping them off, snaking around the floor with much laughing and shouting, the dance wound through the hall, casually avoiding the toddlers running ahead of the line.

This bride didn't arrive at the party in red, in keeping with custom. Instead, she wore black sequins, and later, white chiffon, finally changing in mid-afternoon into her wedding gown. Hair down and full, the sign of the Shei Bari (presumably virginal and unmarried Big Girl), she was a continuing fashion statement as, the next day, she made her entrance in a white designer dress. The third day, her dress was a marabou-trimmed brilliant red—the traditional going-away color.

Forty years ago, no one paid much attention to the groom; he was like a baby-faced nonentity at a ceremony featuring the transfer of a young woman from one family to another. But, at this wedding, the groom, already eighteen, was not the least shy and retiring. He wore the customary red diplomat sash beneath his tuxedo jacket and circulated socially around the room. By day three, the sash was gone. The gossip was that he and the bride had been talking to each other on the phone for over a year and—who knows?—maybe meeting in secret.

THE FIRST DAY, I was sorry to miss the moment when the wedding godmother runs the bride across the floor to her new family and crowns her. To find out who the godmother was, I had to ask at least a dozen people. The crowds were thick, the celebrants kept milling about, and, until the bride emerged from the throng, veiled and smiling, to be led around the hall, again in *kolo*, I couldn't get close enough for a picture.

The gate, the run across the floor to the groom's family, the veil and crown, are small steps to what Van Gennup would call the marge, a stage of ritual transition. As mentioned, the nomad bride often lost all touch with her family, becoming completely dependent upon her family of marriage. *Po drom* (on the road), the wedding godparents provided the bride's family some assurance that another family, besides the new in-laws, was invested in their daughter's well being.

Each day, a breakfast, a lunch buffet, and a mammoth dinner were provided, as well as the music of various live bands.

The wedding gown, a Louis Quatorze dress, had puffy exploding sleeves above fitted elbow-to-wrist lace. Hoops made the skirt nearly as wide as it was long. The bride wore a bouffant veil, a spectacular diamond crown, and a necklace of heavy twenty-dollar gold pieces that swung past her waist. Carefully maneuvering her lampshade skirt, the bride moved with some difficulty and couldn't do more than a slow walk during *kolo*. But the bride cannot refuse the *kolo* line, and this one did her best.

THE SECOND DAY, the bride wore several wedding dresses, including the Louis Quatorze; the groom still wore his red sash; the band played on; the people ate and drank; they partied.

By evening, while cutting the towering cake, the bride's gold coin bracelets, her necklace, and her veil continually got in the way and had to be meticulously and slowly readjusted. With cameras flashing, the groom fed the bride and the bride fed the groom. Then, in a scene that reflects the greater equity of the pair and the growing importance of the two-person bond, the groom poured champagne into silver goblets, and the pair linked arms and drank. As the power of the extended family has declined, these innovations emphasize the couple's new relationship.

After dinner was served, a dowry was again collected from the men's table. I was impressed by the style with which Redondo (of Redondo Beach) and his son were said to "help." They gave a small chest of fifty-dollar bills, a long string of pearls, more jewelry, and an uncirculated gold coin. The man who was collecting, a Machvano with a good-humored gift of gab, called out crazy amounts, making jokes, holding the items high, listing them. Then, someone in the "taking" family poured Redondo a drink, and gave the Redondo family a reciprocal gift, in keeping with custom. Opened, this proved to be a gold evening bag containing a silk scarf.

The collector continued around the table, passing out scarves, the bride following and banking the money in a gold plastic box. Then, as this was the second day and the last day of *dahro* collection, the total was announced, and the people agreed the amount was auspicious, almost enough to cover the cost of the party, more than enough to suggest the match was well-made.

IN THE OLD DAYS, on the third day, the stage, in Van Gennep's terms, of incorporation, the nomad bride went to the tent of her natal family for a piteous goodbye. Now the bride goes instead to the party given by her natal family. At this Adams/Yovanovich wedding in 1999, the bride's hair was bound up and covered with the customary red *diklo*. In keeping with custom, the groom's red sash had disappeared. Instead he wore a red jacket, which I am at a loss to interpret; always before at weddings I attended, the groom wore a dark tux.

The hall, although smaller—a good share of the guests had gone home—was in the same hotel complex and, while the band played, the strobe lights flashed. The tables were circled by giant sprays of flowers. People wandered in and out. Some danced, some talked. There were announcements. The bride's father gave the groom three hundred dollars, "because I like him." The groom's father surprised the bride's parents with one thousand dollars "for coming all the way to Los Angeles" and giving up their right to insist the wedding be held near their northern California home. Everyone agreed the wedding was a great success. The dancing had been nearly continuous, the music never let up, and, for two nights, the young people stayed up until dawn.

About noon, day three, in keeping with the usual Machvaia female role, the bride was called upon to dance. Mouthing the words, she sang and danced to Whitney Houston's "I'm Every Woman." She performed the number perfectly, with considerable charm, and it was obvious she had practiced.

## "Weddings Just Got Out of Hand"

Over the last two decades, rituals became more intermittent and modest. Weddings have escalated in cost; Machvaia earnings have not. Only the relatively wealthy can now afford to live up to the opulence of the heyday wedding standard.

> Fatima (2000): Nowadays, weddings just got out of hand. Way, way out of hand with trying to impress everybody with what this one did, that one did. They try to do so much, it could put me in the poorhouse. It's not like it used to be when you'd spend a couple hundred dollars, put a little table, buy whatever you needed. Now it's a big expense. Girls don't cost what they did. Now they get a big price on them. Only $5,000 [brideprice] if you have a wedding. But you have to get halls because people don't want to ruin their houses. They spend thousands on halls—and you know it gets beyond you, spending that kind of money all the time. That's why they hardly have any more weddings. That's why the kids all run away. No one can afford weddings.

Weddings cost $25,000. It's crazy. I mean, it's all right for the few that are rich.

Even when they run away, without a wedding, it costs an arm and a leg. And believe me, I would rather give an arm and a leg. [Laugh.] 'Cause I could never come up with that amount, $15,000 [penalty by *krisa*]. It's out of hand! Another thing. Used to be you'd give five dollar *dahro* (brideswealth). Maybe twenty five. You give that now and they want to kill you. Because it cost them so much. You have to give at least $100 or a couple of hundred in order for that person [giving the wedding] to come out even a bit. And then, if the couple breaks up, they [bride's family] only gives back $2,500.

Now, you look at a girl you like and she says, No, I can't marry him because I am seeing somebody. If a girl said that thirty years ago, she'd be blackballed all over the place.

*Chapter 12*

# BORIA (DAUGHTERS-IN-LAW)

## Daughters-in-law

In Lola's day, the Machvanka *bori* had the lowest status in the family. She was treated much like a *bahū*, a daughter-in law in Karimpur (Wadley,1994, pg.56). Both terms, *bori* and *bahū*, allow the speaker to avoid the given name and show a considerable disregard for personhood, a situation persisting into the daughter-in-law's old age.

Daughters-in-law, an underclass whose devoted services kept elaborate rituals and the party going, have since been replaced by caterers, party planners, cleaning services, babysitters, nurses, and cabs. Once incredibly naïve and susceptible to direction, until married, girls were expected to know nothing about life or sex, a forbidden subject. The new *bori* got up early—"before anyone"—swept, cooked, cared for the children, and was the last to bed. One of the first things Lola's daughters wanted me to know was the challenge of their young lives, as servant and slave, when "everything was expected," and the difficulty of satisfying a militantly strict mother-in-law. Despite their grievances, I got the impression that they were proud to have stuck it out, and survived. Their complaints were laced with a wry braggadocio, suggesting they felt more able as consequence of their Spartan training.

Although separation of the sexes still pertains at ritual events, men with men, women with women, in earlier times the separation represented belief, interest, experience, and culture. Contact between the sexes was minimal; each had their own, male or female, spheres of influence. Women always had power, but it was not openly acknowledged until they had grandchildren. Most of

**145**

this past century, the husband was expected to put his mother's wishes before his wife's, and his wife was duty bound to satisfy his mother.

Once, the new *bori* gave her mother-in-law a few welcome years of leisure, encased in obedient offerings of respect. Women worked together, cooking, caring for children, telling fortunes, and, for this reason, the new bride's relationship with her *sokra* (mother-in-law) was more critical to marital success than her relationship with her husband. Girls became brides, mothers, grandmothers, and never abandoned a marital situation in which the relationship with the mother-in-law was agreeable.

When we were having coffee, Lola often mentioned a sister "back East" whose sons were trash and whose daughters-in-law were all like gold. Why, I once asked, do the gold daughters stay with the no-good sons? Lola stopped trying to thread her needle— she refused to wear glasses so it took her several minutes—and looked at me reflectively. "Well, if your husband had had a good mother and a lot of cousins and sisters and sisters-in-law, maybe you wouldn't have needed a divorce." Then, seeing her efforts had missed their mark, she explained further. "They love her. They love my sister. She is their luck." This made sense to me. I could well imagine that a family of women with a houseful of responsibilities, including childcare and entertaining guests, might resent serving men who were "trash" and find considerable comfort in their own company.

Not that a mother-in-law was expected to be especially kind; in training for an important post, the newcomer needed, it was presumed, considerable guidance. Gossip rated the mother-in-law in terms of the public and domestic performance of her daughter-in-law. The report of a sloppy and careless daughter-in-law could shatter the goodness of family and lineage reputation.

IN THOSE DAYS, while giving their clients practical advice about lost-cause men and broken hearts, the Machvanki readers seldom considered the men in their lives of a similar importance. For them, children, their difficulties with their children, the traumas experienced by their children, were what broke their hearts. I was assured in the Sixties that mothers were invariably "for you," on your side, the certainty of never being alone or without friends. Katy's oldest son, as a young man with a child, no wife, no job, and no money, once told me he didn't worry about his future. He could always go home to his mother.

But home was not always an option. During Lola's early days of traveling, the people were on the move. Changing addresses, phone numbers, even identities, meant finding and getting in touch involved delay. As a naïve seventeen-year-old bride, Lola didn't know where her mother was or how to find her. She was in her thirties when she finally went home to her aging mother, Stanya, in San Diego, and her mother immediately insisted Lola return to her family of marriage. A woman, Stanya said, can never leave her children. "That's right," Lola told me, nodding her head emphatically and repeatedly assuring me, "The mother is always for the children."

Nor were parents likely to be aware of how their married daughters were faring. It may well have been a tragic incident like the following that encouraged them to assume a more protective role. Lola described it as "the saddest thing that happened in my life." I know the memory kept her from ever returning to Los Angeles. This is what she said in 1969:

> I hate that town. My daughter Diane died there. She was married to my first cousin's son and they didn't give her good living. Only married a year and she got sick and died. They said it was pneumonia. But I don't know. Erusha [Lola's oldest daughter] went to see her and they said she was working [telling fortunes in her business place]. She wasn't; she was sick in the bedroom. I think they worked her too hard. They put her *ofisa* on the seashore where the wind is cold. She had to take three, four buses to get there. Then she had to work at home all night. She had a cold when I talked to her on the phone. I told them to take her to the doctor. When I saw her in the box, so beautiful, so young, I tried to lift her out. But the [undertaker] got in the way. I pushed him into the wall and hollered for him to put the father-in-law in the box instead and give me Diane back. I cried so much, my tears wouldn't stop; they were making the floor slippery.

Lola paused, and a tear streaked her mascara. As she stood to open the living room drapes to the motion of the passing cars, she continued:

> I knew she wanted to see me before she died. I know that 'cause I'm her mother. And I didn't make it.
> The next morning the father-in-law came over. I hollered and chased him out. I told him, "You won't get away with this. The God won't let you." I told him he couldn't escape until he died. And he would have to die for me to be satisfied.

When I asked if what she said constituted a curse, Lola fell silent. But, in another context she had already explained that strong thoughts, wishes, or words "only work with God's help."

> After a year, the God was good. The man's wife got sick and died. Their family got sick. They had trouble. They were pretty much destroyed. Then he died. They are buried next to Diane.
> That's the saddest thing that happened in my life. Nothing is worse than you lose your children. A mother is always for her children.

Today's young women say they would never put up with the hardships endured by their mothers. Instead of "sticking" with a marital situation they don't like, Machvaia brides call for help on their personal cell phones and their parents immediately send them airfare. Their new self-interest was probably encouraged by what they see of American women's roles and modern life on their television screens, what they learn while giving readings, and, in part, because chatting with each other on the phone, and online, has built a group of same age/sex peers who have a less sacrificial agenda. Sex is no longer the mystery it was. Elders lost a large measure of power when they lost control of all channels of information and communication, and likely means of transport. In 1999, Machvano Barney bitterly complained about these changes.

Computers are ruining the Gypsies. And telephones. And television. The kids know about matters they shouldn't. They know what is going on in the other households, all the gossip. Before, the older people were the only ones who knew anything at all.

Now, the husband/wife bond is acknowledged as critical to marital success—it took years of failed marriages and many girls going home to their parents for the people to arrive at this novel insight. The modern bride will insist on her own living quarters and her own *ofisa* (business place) as part of the wedding settlement. The young couple, living more or less independently, must depend on each other. Seldom reminded about the rules of respect, they are described by their elders as becoming "no respect."

Earlier, the choice of whom to marry was primarily based on family reputation. This is still credited as all manner of personal characteristics, including the lion's share of luck, is believed to be inherited by bloodline; and marriage creates new bloodline combinations. But current marital picks take account of individual qualities, maturity, what abilities each young person brings to the union, as well as the degree of empathy between the pair.

The relationship of bride and mother-in-law is no longer critical to the success of a Machvaia marriage. Without a willing *bori/* student/slave, the once important role of the mother-in-law has lost both purpose and status. The unlimited household service and elaborate hospitality that could be offered guests by several energetic daughters-in-law is little more than a memory. With the *boria* revolution, it has become apparent that respect practice owed much to the docility, obedience, and service efforts of young Machvaia women.

## Running Away

When I began my study in 1966, fear and dismay concerning young people who "ran away" was the awesome topic of gossip. The women gasped and their eyes grew big whenever *nashlimos* was mentioned! Once every two or three months, some family of note endured the

149

scandal and heartbreak of losing a beloved child to America. Runaways were grievous proof of a parent's failure to raise a child according to Machvaia custom. Running away cast doubt on the inborn strength of the bloodline and the people's belief in the superiority of the Machvaia way of life.

At first, before I knew all the implications, I found the reaction to *nashlimos* dramatically overblown. For one thing, the majority of young Machvaia who ran away to America didn't stay away. They returned, often within the week, after spending whatever money they had saved and satisfying their curiosity about the "freedom" available in America. (Ironically, Gypsies tend to think Americans are free, while Americans think of Gypsies as free.) Runaways discovered there were rules in American society as well and, accustomed to living corporately in the bosom of family, solicitously supported by kinsmen and like-minded peers, they were unprepared for the isolation and independence required by their newly adopted lifestyle. The American tendency to impersonality in business situations appalled them. Americans, they discovered, don't advocate generosity and trust.

The *nashlimos* trend may have begun in the Forties when Hollywood movies, I am told, tempted teen-aged Katy, her younger sister Boba, and two cousins to run away, disgrace their parents, offend their ancestors, and damage the value of lineage reputation. Katy candidly assured me that that's what people with ambition did back then. They "ran away to Hollywood and got discovered."

But when Katy got sick, Boba sent their parents a telegram: "Katy's sick!" Upon their return and in keeping with penalties of the time, Boba went on the cheap to a Machvaia family notorious for men with violent tempers, and Katy was given to a remote Kalderasha family. No one today, the Machvaia now assure me, would be so inconsiderate of their children's future.

IN THE DAYS OF TRAVELING, "marriage lasted forever"—that's what Lola claimed, the exception to this blanket statement being hers, which ended in divorce sometime in the Forties. But, by the Sixties, marriages often seemed quite fragile. Survival was no longer the young Machvaia couple's focus and romantic pairings were beginning to catch on.

Over this century, *nashlimos* (running away) has evolved two meanings, running away to America and eloping. More than half of current Machvais marriages are elopements. Without the notice of the three-day wedding ritual, these marriages are legalized with a mandatory $15,000 in fine/brideprice. Elopement can be the most economically feasible ploy for the groom's family because, in any case, brideprice is only a minor amount relative to the cost of the three-day wedding. Weddings are an expense for both families involved, those who are giving—who are losing a daughter's income as a reader and must pay for the third day expenses of the three-day wedding—and those who are getting.

In the case of the runaway to Outsider America, if a Machvaia girl and an Outsider boyfriend are involved, the family might, upon her return, show respect for Roma law by withdrawing from community events for several months. If the runaway is a boy, no one pays much attention. But for the most part, running away to escape Machvaia rule has lost allure. Young people have a much more realistic assessment of their survival possibilities in America. For example, when naïve Anastasia ran away in the Sixties, the dancing teenybopper television series "American Bandstand" cued her expectations. As it turned out, her effort at becoming American—for Anastasia never went back to her Machvaia *vitsa*—has been difficult and disillusioning. Not only did the parties and dancing disappoint her, but Anastasia had no luck finding the industrious American man who would be her financial support, ala the televised programs "Father Knows Best" and "Leave It to Beaver." As the errant offspring of a high-class family, to avoid shaming her family further, she has generally tried to remain out of Machvaia notice by never advertising as a reader. During this past half century, only occasionally did she manage to give readings at occult shops like the Mystic Eye. But most of her American jobs have been unsatisfactory.

IT WAS THE LATE SIXTIES when I met my first runaway, Patsy, Lola's granddaughter who had married a Latino engineer. Lola insisted we drive to Everett, north of Seattle, to see how her runaway relative was doing. "But don't tell anyone," she ordered. "'Cause we shouldn't." Patsy, as I recall, was overwhelmed by the unexpected visit from her illustrious grandmother, nervously popping out of

**151**

her chair, not knowing whether or not, considering her shameful situation, to serve us the standard coffee and donuts. We didn't stay long and, on the way back, Lola candidly assessed the situation in her no-nonsense fashion: "She'll be back."

Lola was right; three decades later, her children raised and married, Patsy returned to the fold by marrying a Rom who, like her, had spent most of his life as a runaway. But apparently Patsy hasn't been forgiven. I recently ran into her at a *capella* (funeral chapel lying-in) and we talked briefly. After that, some of the other Machvanki cold-shouldered me, turning away when I approached, and no one respectfully served me fruit juice, coffee, or the water of grief. I went back to my motel early.

Obedience to the law Romanes is apparently still in effect.

# Chapter 13

# RESPECT AND PURITY

## *Vužo* (Pure)

Perhaps nothing refers more obviously to the Eastern origin of the Machvaia than their purity and defilement rituals. Hindu rituals appear designed, in part, to maintain purity of caste by avoiding inappropriate contact with lower castes. Machvaia have no castes; their purity/defilement rituals provide defense against the contamination and danger of the Outside world. The Machvaia obsess about contact—nearly everything is vulnerable to contact. They rank their contacts in terms of the upwards and more spiritual direction.

> To quote from an earlier article on the subject (Miller,1975): The ideology of defilement, or *marimé* as the defiled are called in Romanes, is pervasive to Roma categories of belief and thought, and extends to all areas of Roma life in some way, underwriting a hygienic attitude towards the world, themselves, and others. Pollution ideas work on the life of Roma society, especially in the sense of symbolizing certain dangers and expressing a general view of the social order. Lines are drawn between the Gypsy and the non-Gypsy, the clean and unclean, health and disease, the good and the bad which are made obvious and visible through the offices of ritual avoidance. (41)

The map upon which these lines of separation are portrayed is the adult human body, the upper half of which is considered relatively *vužo* (pure), and the lower half relatively *bi-vužo* (without

**153**

purity). The mouth and head area are the most pure and "up" in the spiritual sense, the area of the anus and genitals the least so, and items contacting upper body areas are segregated from items contacting the lower half. Rites of purification and separation involving special soaps, clean running water, two sets of towels, and separate apparel protect the upper region. Upper body items such as shirts, blouses, and headscarves, are washed in a *latchi* (good) container, pail, or washer. Upper body items that drop to the floor where people walk are ideally tossed in the garbage or used, thereafter, to treat the lower body areas. Permitted the task of ministering to both body areas, the hands have a transitional status and washing them with the face soap and towels brings them into consonance with the upper body status. Hand washing is particularly important after defecation, before preparing food, or when approaching the saints.

ECHOING THE DANGER to the inner from the outer, or Machvaia from Outsider, the inner orifice of the mouth and digestion is especially sensitive to pollution. Food must be fresh and, preferably, bought the same day from a "nice" grocery and prepared in the Machvaia kitchen. Those things that can be washed are subject to a thorough cleansing; meat is most notable in this regard. Cooked food is especially sensitive to pollution. No one should serve family or guests leftovers; leftovers go in the trash.

What is eaten is ingested, taken into the body—it becomes the body—and at an elemental level, ingestion suggests the process of political incorporation. Any meal, taken in unison, is a positive statement of consensual approval. Eating together signifies that those participating are equal in respect, morality, and purity practice; they are one.

FOR CENTURIES, Gypsies have been small and vulnerable groups in the milieu of larger host societies. In Europe, they are generally treated like the lowest in status. In reference to the body as a symbol of society, Mary Douglas (1966) suggests "that food is not likely to be polluting at all unless the external boundaries of the system are under pressure" (128) and that "when rituals express anxiety about the body's orifices the sociological counterpart of this anxi-

ety is a care to protect the political and cultural unity of a minority group"(125). In an article published in 1975, Douglas states:

> By believing in the protection of a power that is equivalent,
> or greater, the Roma make symbolic defense against the
> inroads of the larger and politically more powerful society.
> The smaller is permitted to nourish confidence in its own
> systems of belief and values by avoiding challenge. The result
> is that despite demeaning life circumstances, which include
> frequent and irritating inequities, morale is maintained at a
> favorable level. (46)

The Machvaia pioneers to America considered it bad luck, an invitation to disease, to eat in the restaurants of Outsiders. But that was
changing when I knew Lola; she adored shopping at the stores in
mid-town Seattle and ordering lunch at the Woolworth's soda foun-
tain. I was seated next to her there when she was served a root beer
float with froth running down the side of the glass. She sent it back
in a fury: "You see that? No respect. That waitress made a mess."

Largely by observing, I learned to leave my napkin on the table;
if it landed on my lap, it lost all goodness. Both hands available on
the table was advisable, and I must wash them carefully, and preferably publicly, before cutting and slicing, before cooking, before
serving, before helping out in the kitchen. Certain topics were forbidden to mention, particularly anything suggesting sex. When the
dishes were passed around, it was polite to take a little, but not too
much, so that all might be served according to their needs. This behavior was best accompanied with a silent wish for the good health
and appetite of all those in attendance, thereby increasing the "up"
dimension of the occasion.

## Health and Right Living

In the past, purity/defilement practices and beliefs were underwritten by the Machvaia understanding of *sastimos* (good health). At
one time, most disease (*nasvalimos)* and disability was conceived as
communicable, and blamed on the Devil or Outsiders. A salient

reason for the latter was the Outsiders' failure to keep the separations. Ignorant of purity ritual, they were, of course, dirty all over, disease-susceptible, and disease spreaders.

Minimal contact with Outsiders was the ideal. Working an eight-to-five job in the company of Outsiders lowered the Machvano's social status. Besides the threat of disease, there was the contagion of thoughts and ideas, and these have a pervasive power. Eating and drinking with Outsiders involves the intimacy of ingestion and sharing, suggesting political incorporation, which is the abomination these lines of separation are designed to prevent. Bibi, Lola's sister-in-law, sometimes described my darling Lola—for so she became to me—as "*dihli*" (crazy), citing her predilection, when she was younger, for drinking in cocktail lounges and bars with "strangers" (Outsiders).

The new and not overly used is associated with purity, and the Machvaia ideal, the royal road to health and good luck, is for couples to marry early and only once. This was easier to achieve a century ago when life was hard and survival, of necessity, a couple's primary focus. Raising children in keeping with custom and getting them married to Roma, preferably Machvaia, was, and still is, the married couple's given mission. But by the Seventies, a growing number of teenagers had run away to try their luck in Outsider America and proved their parent's failure in these regards.

Even today, as it was in the past, good health and prosperity are presumed locked into moral family living. But illness, unhappiness, and even insanity, is no longer considered inevitable if couples don't live in the family *vorta* (right), don't raise their children "right," or fail to pay attention to business and take care of each other.

MY FIRST YEARS WITH THE MACHVAIA, I watched bad health follow marital disaster. As Katy's husband chased around with Outsider women, and spent all her savings, Katy stopped telling fortunes—"How can I tell my customers how to live when my own life is a mess?" Required to resort to the humiliation of Public Assistance, she suffered a series of mishaps, wrecking a borrowed car, singeing her eyelashes when the gas heater exploded. Then her favorite daughter ran away with a Rom of lesser status and Katy was sick in bed for weeks.

## Purity, Shame, and Outsiders

The life stages baby, child, adult, and elder are associated with appropriate powers, interests, and behaviors. Neither capable of polluting nor being polluted, children are believed innocent, good, pure, and pre-sexual, whereas the *phurotem* (elders) are wise, good, pure, and presumably post-sexual—or at least no longer likely to become parents. Matters of pollution become relevant with sexual contact and marriage, which is the ritual transition to adulthood, the transformation of boy to man (Rom, husband, and Machvano) and the girl to a woman (Romni, wife, and Machvanka). Marriage, publicly acknowledged and coupled with the combining powers of sexual contact, is believed to awaken consciousness of shame and respect, as well as an aptitude for thinking good thoughts and having a kind, empathetic heart, the recommended ideals for adult behavior.

Becoming an adult is to become responsible. The respectable and mature are expected to understand themselves and, unlike *dihlia* (crazy people), to appear reasonable and understandable to other Machvaia. Until these past several decades, raising children in keeping with Machvaia standards was believed to require authority: "You have to make them afraid." Respect is locked into the comprehension of shame—without a sense of shame, there is no possibility of respect. Within the family, failure to show respect is met with *"Nai tuchi ladjav?"* (Don't you have any shame?). Those Machvaia who never marry are few; they possess limited social and political powers, and are regarded as unnatural curiosities.

Shame/respect awareness is also associated with purity containment. With marriage, the two areas, the mouth and the genitals, particularly the female genitalia, another area of incorporation, come under a symbolic and political control. The adult political powers of the two sexes are assumed, the men to participate in the *krisa* court system and a woman's ability to defile a Rom, an ability lost by *krisa* order during the late Sixties. Adult ritual obligations commence; these include hospitality service, holidays, celebrations, commemorations, fasts which may be added, and the lineal *slava* that the father passes along to his married son. Those just married have the opportunity to negotiate as adults in the public arena, to begin to build their reputations and assess that of others, to prove themselves worthy or not, and to give and be offered adult respect.

Sexual relationships with Outsiders can be a potential threat to a small society. Although currently the Machvaia Rom seems able, without a significant loss of status, to enjoy extra-marital relationships with Outsider women, marriage to an Outsider is, even now, not ritually acceptable. Early in the last century, Iera Lee married Indiananka, an Outsider who learned to tell fortunes, speak Romanes, and make *slava*. The pair settled in a Kalderasha territory where mixed marriage arrangements were apparently not stigmatized and raised their children. These, now grown, have been treated the same as all Machvaia in good standing and had no difficulty getting married in *abéav* (wedding ritual) to other Machvaia.

AN OUTSIDER CHILD IS, in fact, labeled good and pure, much like all Machvaia children, and judged suitable adoption material without penalty of any kind. I know several childless Machvanki who were able to find pregnant non-Gypsy girls willing to part with their newborns in return for several months of solicitous prenatal care. Adoption has historic value: the estimable Zhurka, the first pioneer to America from Machva, adopted and raised an American boy, GadzoRo; his descendants continue the Zhurka/GadzoRo bloodline. Although the people keep no written records and tend to forget the past, the blue eyes evident in the Machvaia group as a whole suggest that this relaxed attitude towards adoption has been in place for some time.

Despite a penchant for adoption, and despite the tragic myth about Gypsies stealing children that pervades Western society, I can't imagine a Machvanka would ever steal an Outsider child. Lola assured me that the stolen baby's mother would undoubtedly die of a broken heart—"Mothers are always for their children." After that, the ghost-mother would likely wreak some terrible revenge, and haunt the thief's bloodline "forever."

At first, the easy Machvaia attitude towards Outsider adoption struck me as curious, given that bloodline inheritance is critical to the nature of Machvaia luck, to the backing of ancestors, and the people's inherent adaptability to custom. But contact has power and, perhaps the Machvaia triumph by absorbing apparent characteristics of the larger society via Outsider children without losing any of their own characteristics. At any rate, it seems the pollution rules regarding female dangers are more relevant to the protection of Machvaia society as a whole, and to male ascendancy and keeping women in line, than to keeping bloodlines pure.

## Females and Containment

Women are believed more polluting than men owing, in part, to the character of adult female genitalia and the inner orifice of the female womb, hidden areas associated with the mysteries of blood and birth. In the past, as a woman became a *phuri* (old woman)— no longer fertile, no longer able to pollute men, yet still a productive asset—she was accorded some of the same status and respect as a man.

Polluting power requires that adult females take a particular care in personal maintenance, in purifying and separating, and creating a hygienic environment in the home. Menstruating women cannot light the Saint candle or cook the special *baX* foods. In the past, because of point of origin, a newborn was considered polluting, and both postnatal mother and child were isolated for several weeks. Now babies are born in hospitals and, although their point of origin is the same, they are no longer treated as a danger.

During the years of my research, sexual intimacy with Outsiders was a serious offense and, for a woman, considered "the worst" that might happen. Because women bear the children and are said to "make the home," the crime of running away was read as a threat to the *vitsa*, an ominous foreboding of the group's absorption into the larger society. In those days, sexual intimacy was presumed in every case of *nashlimos* (running away); nowadays, male runaways are ignored. Early in the last century, a girl who ran away and returned was penalized by being "thrown away" cheaply to the first family that asked for her hand in marriage. Both Katy and her younger sister suffered what are described as "hard lives" for this reason. Males are held responsible for any female error and, by throwing his daughters away in this manner, Katy's father effectively demonstrated his sensitivity to the moral code. When they returned, the runaways were checked for venereal disease by an

**159**

Outside doctor, and the medical results announced to the community-at-large. Even with a clean bill of health, however, Katy's *famil-
ia* observed several months of isolation from public gatherings, and
the shame became part of their reputation story.

REGARDING THE HAVIK BRAHMINS of South India, Ed Harper
(1969:81) has the interesting thesis that those "who lack power and
prestige, who generally do the bidding of others, and who have
minimal control over their own social environment are likely to be
portrayed as dangerous or malevolent . . . even though there may
be in fact little realistic basis for such fear." Until recently, elderly
Machvanki were often suspected of witchcraft, of cursing and making someone sick, or unable to talk, or causing accidents. Like a
force of nature, they were unaware of their power, however, and
therefore considered blameless. Indeed, the curse of the *phuri* (old
Machvanka) was presumed to be even more powerful than the
curse of a Machvano, and there were occasions during my fieldwork when an angry *phuri* played with this power.

For example, Boba, one of Lola's daughters, had a drug-
addicted son. As he lay dying, she was forced to endure the addi-
tional pain of public criticism. In retaliation, she took some pleasure
in playing the witch, staring over our heads, muttering to herself.
Although her sisters found this funny, there were those who were
appalled. At Duke's six-week *pomana*, Boba, half crazed with loss,
cursed the people attending, some of whom stood up and left. Poor
witchy Boba had a very hard and short life. Later, as she was dying,
only Katy and I were at her bedside.

Fear of the Machvanka's power to curse is falling out of fashion, but not entirely. Sabrina, now in her forties, has had trouble
making a living and must keep moving to find a suitable place to
give readings. She allows that her difficulties might be attributed
to an unknown disgruntled witch.

ONCE, THERE WERE OTHER FEMALE powers as well. The power
to pollute was, at one time, complemented by the Machvano's susceptibility to rejection (see Chapter 14) and gave women a considerable political clout. Until early in the past century, healing and
making medicines was the business of respected older women who

knew about the plant world. It is interesting to note that, in Romanes, *drab* is medicine and/or herbs; *drabarimos* glosses as fortune telling.

## Males, Prestige, and Authority

As Mary Douglas points out, "sexual dangers are better interpreted as symbols of the relations between parts of society, as mirroring designs of hierarchy. . . " (4). Machvaia male prestige and authority is ostensibly superior to that of female prestige and authority, and rests, in part, on the advantage of the more outward character of the male genitalia. A man's body parts, less mysterious, less involved in the future of the *vitsa*, are, according to one comical Rom, "easier to wash." Raised as little kings, Machvaia males, being "boss," being more prestigious and less at risk in the world-at-large, have greater freedoms of activity and choice than Machvaia females.

A century back, when the people arrived from Serbia, the joint family was still a functioning unit of grandparents, father, sons and their families living together. Obedience by age and sexual status was the rule. The eldest male, the final authority in the family, decided when the family would stop, where they would winter, how they might avoid police harassment. Then, the Machvanka presumably deferred to the Machvano; today, she remains likely to do so only in public.

When I began my study, in part because family harmony is believed to create luck, Machvaia women ordinarily behaved, despite their complaints among themselves about male privilege, as if men were indeed the boss. Married into the lineage of their husbands, identified, over time, as permanent newcomers in their family of marriage, they were certainly at some power disadvantage. Husbands and fathers normally drove the women to stores and to rituals, set them up in business, provided protection from the unwanted attentions of other men, and represented their interests in the Roma court of law. Husbands were dependent upon wives for a properly *vužo* (pure) home environment, the children that would continue the lineage, the money to live on, and the money to entertain and build the goodness of reputation.

The gift of respect—and, to the Machvaia, respect is always a gift—from women to men reflects the man's greater accountability in the public arena and the mutual dependence of both sexes on the message of reputation. Adult males are the public and ritual persons. The Machvano lights the devotional saint's-day candle; he cooks, with other men, certain ritual dishes; he gives and collects the brideswealth at weddings; he is predominant in most ritual affairs. As mentioned, Machvaia men are responsible to law and moral code for the behavior of their families. They arrange the marriages. They meet in *krisa* to make the laws, and must see the law is obeyed. Men are responsible for fostering friendships with others in the community by the generosity of their gifts, their entertainments, their sociability. As Ortner and Whitehead (1981) point out, "there are certain oppositions that recur with some frequency in gender ideologies cross-culturally," nature/culture, the tendency to align the male with culture and to see the female as closer to nature, the male with the social good and the female with self-interest, the male with the public domain, which is, of course, prestigious, the female with the domestic (7).

In an ideal world, the Machvanki earn the money and earn enough to happily sponsor their husbands' many social activities. But even in good times, legend and belief can be hard to realize. Traveling with Lola's son Miller and his wife to and from ritual events, I was cozy between the pillows and bedding in the back seat and could overhear half-humorous debates as Miller demanded money for gambling and entertaining, and Duda insisted on holding enough aside for the bills. Indeed, among the Machvanki, a woman who doesn't hide enough cash from her husband for financial emergencies and her children's welfare isn't considered much of a woman by the other women.

## The More and the Less Estimable

Machvaia consider they are, as a whole, less mixed than other Roma. Respect is their *baX*, good luck, in the sense of a preordained fate. Respect behaviors are believed to come naturally to them, to be the preferred action that will lead to successful results. As in Hindu India, rank is conceptualized in terms of purity and singularity of kind, which is expected to pair with other estimable and lucky qualities, being rich, healthy, handsome, generous, and otherwise well favored. After six or seven generations of preferential intermarriage, Machvaia to Machvaia, the people are nearly all related by blood and "cousins." It was a Kalderash Rom who told me there was only one class of Machvaia; "Machvaia are all high-class."

Nevertheless, Machvaia respect is an institution in process and those Machvaia to whom I presently talk admit, "The younger generation is losing it."

DURING MY YEARS AMONG THE PEOPLE, differences of status were continually assessed and reassessed. In deciding how to offer respect, Machvaia rank one another according age, sex, lineage reputation, wealth, and the moral code. High rank and glory is attained through right living and heart-felt generosity.

Even today, earmarked for special demonstrations of respect would be the Latchivalo Rom (Good Rom), and those who have given favors, the Chivréa (godparents) who assume the lifetime responsibility for the godchild's good health, the man or woman proxy who takes the suit at *pomana*, the bride's family—a bride is a most estimable gift. Machvaia elders, particularly those who demonstrate wisdom and goodness, are said to be "close to God" and as near as the people come to priests; they were offered exemplary respect. A Machvano who attends many public events, crossing many family and *vitsi* lines might become known as an Ashundo Rom (literally, "Heard-About Man," i.e. heard about for all the right reasons). Lola's son Miller listed the Dead Ones PunRoRo Uwanovich and Yasha Lee of Los Angeles, Blenci Adams of Palo Alto, and Atarino (Miller's grandfather) of Sacramento. Every one, every family, might make a different list. But Zhurka, the first pioneer to American from Serbia, was most certainly Ashundo (see Conclusion).

The politically powerful Machvano who controls a territory, who can mete out *ofisuria* (business places) to other Machvaia and offer his constituents some form of police protection is described as Baro (Big Man); Big George Adams, who "ran" part of Los Angeles in the Fifties and Sixties, was Baro. Jolé Merino of San Jose/ Los Angeles and Nino of New York were also Big Men. In truth, an extra bit of respect is owed anyone considered particularly lucky and successful. Wealth is considered praiseworthy and powerful. At the moment, no one is Baro, but there are a number who might be considered Barvalo (Rich Man).

Men, as mentioned, are the public persons and, during my research in northern California, nearly all those estimably ranked have been men. Only after her husband had died did popular opinion accord the elderly Luia the title of Barvali, reputedly rich and admired. The notorious Barbara Miller is a more exceptional case; no one I talked to could remember another female Bari (Big Woman).

For several decades, Bari Barbara and her daughters were the only fortune tellers in San Francisco. When her husband, who was described as "beautiful as a matinee idol," went crazy, Bari Barbara fearlessly took over his territory and "ran," as the people tell it, "all of San Francisco." Her connections with the San Francisco police seem to have been more successful than her connections in Los Angeles. In the Sixties, in an effort to help her daughter's husband, the son of the former Baro of Los Angeles, she was jailed with him for attempting to bribe the LA police.

## Giving Respect

According to Goffman (1963:6–7), in the opinion of the larger society the social identity of American Gypsies bears a stigma. Yet Gypsies, he writes, remain relatively untouched by their "failure" and protected from despair. Insulated by their alienation, protected by identity beliefs of their own, they take refuge in "a separate system of honor."

Gjerdman and Ljungberg gloss the Romani term *patchiv* as respect, reverence, honor, to treat with honor, to esteem. They point out respect is usually accompanied by *dav* (to give), for respect is honor given. "Respect," the English word, is properly used to connote those matters of etiquette by which "a self that is worthy of deference" (Goffman,1967: 84) and "which must be treated with proper ritual care" (91) is presented. Machvaia translate the Romani term *patchiv* as both 'respect' and a party honoring a special person with extra measures of respect.

Respect, as the Machvaia use the term, includes obedience (*padja*) and trust (*padja ma*), both found in Gjerdman and Ljungberg

(1963:307), as well as respect, obedience, and trust, all of which are synonymous with the auspicious. When I asked Katy what trust had to do with obedience, and obedience with respect, she answered, "Who would you respect? Your parents because they gave you life, your grandparents who borned them, your godparents because they are 'like God.' These are the main ones. But anyone you trust and would obey is respected."

But when I asked Machvano Stévo the same question, he answered, in the Goffmanesque manner of backstage aside that Meyrowitz (1990, pg. 68–71) mentions, "Of course, who can you trust? No one. Everyone has to cheat, to lie, to survive." Reflectively studying the ring on his hand, he added, "Sometimes I just believe a little—because I have to."

Respect underwrites the smooth interaction of family, lineage, and *vitsa* (named lineage group), particularly at the public events. Respect is the right kind of action. Respect behaviors involve separation, women and girls together, boys with men, and verbal avoidance of anything relating to the bathroom. Respect behaviors involve discretion regarding approach—those entering a room should not interrupt the proceedings—seating, physical movements, facial expressions, the appropriate attire, and the way the different sexes pass and circle each other without mishap, the women ably negotiating their flowing skirts (which were once a problem), the men making minor adjustments to their chairs so that no one, except as intended insult, presents a back.

Respect relates to authority and ascendancy, and the way men should move through the doorway first, eat first, be served first, or in conjunction with separate food service to the older women. Staring is avoided; it implies excessive interest in the other person. Smoking is disrespectful, except with those of like gender and age. Contradicting anyone or the direct refusal of an order is considered bad form; silence or an indirect response is better.

Respect betrays sensitivity to the thoughts and feelings of others. Failure to show respect is conceived as discourteous and unkind. Repeated neglect can be read as an insult. There is, in fact, a point at which, "if you don't give respect, you won't get it. If you don't mind your parents, right or wrong, then people won't think your family is good." In an earlier time, the people believed that to fail

**165**

to give respect damaged the luck of the giver. When Old Lola didn't like the hospitality offered or the topic of conversation, she would say, "*Me sem respect* (I am respect)" to indicate her displeasure. If the situation didn't improve, she would leave.

Giving respect, deserving respect, accumulates merit. In Romani, *sevapo*, a good deed (Serbo-Croatian sevap) is a gift of respect. The favor of "taking the suit" on behalf of the deceased at *pomana* has elements of risk, and puts the giver "up"—it is said to be a "help" *sevapo*. Giving the favor, the *sevapo*, of baptizing for another family, is a gift of "mercy." A *sevapo* that goes out of the way to help those in considerable trouble is a gift of "salvage." The latter is humiliating to those who require it, a deathblow to reputation, implying poverty, stupidity, bad luck, and inferior bloodlines. Whenever a Machvaia family requires aid that relatives are unable or unwilling to give, the family tries to maintain an honorable status within the community by secretly seeking Outsider assistance.

Respect in the day-to-day is shown by attending and helping at rituals, visiting *capella*, the chapel for the Dead One, and traveling with the mourners to the cemetery for the final goodbye. Respect is accompanying the sick to the hospital for surgery, and waiting with the worried family to provide them comfort and support. To be liked, admired, and shown respect, it is best to be generous, giving good advice and service, giving financial help to the needy. Daughters-in-law are still inclined to offer respect to their elders at ritual events with singing and dancing performances and the tribute "*Patchiv tuchi*" (Respect to you). More often, they will say "*Pachiv tumenge*" (Respect to everyone). Regarding shames, sanction is still observed by those middle-aged, older, and respected. When, in 2006, young David ran away with a girl from the Johns lineage, David's father insisted on thirty days of isolation from public events for the pair. As he explained, "No one bothers anymore. I do it for my own respect."

RESPECT AS A CENTRAL MACHVAIA PRECEPT relates to ideas about inborn aptitudes for purity, luck, and rank, ideas closer to South Asian lines of thought than those of the West and somewhat like Inden found in Bengali texts (1976:2), in which genera (kinds) are coded for certain elements, characters, predispositions, etc.

Machvaia believe Outsiders are not born with this incipient respect/
shame awareness; they are not expected to know anything about respect, how it is merited and given. As a consequence, Outsiders are
not necessarily owed respect; they are neither to be obeyed nor
trusted. A few Outsiders, however, President Franklin Roosevelt and
John Kennedy, have apparently been offered reverence by some
Machvaia. I have found their pictures hanging near the household
shrine area.

## Beware the Difference

In the past, the Machvaia considered males and females of two vari-
ant "kinds," something like two species, so different by temperament,
interest, and understanding that any competition between them
was impossible to imagine. On the other hand, their complemen-
tary and incendiary nature, yin to yang, was a power not denied. If
two people, male and female, were in the same room without supervision, sexual congress was presumed inevitable.

That's why, Ephram told me, he could never be alone in the
house with his seventy-year-old mother-in-law, Old Lola: "We can't
tell what might happen," suggestively sly. I got the impression that,
in such an unlikely event, he would feel duty bound by the urgency
of his masculinity to at least make a pass. But I reminded myself that
Ephram was a playboy—that's what Lola called him—and not particularly known for respect.

This presumed difference between Machvaia men and women
seemed a monument raised to false gods to me. Having grown up
in a mixed-sex, somewhat competitive school, home, work environment, I couldn't accord "the difference" much significance. Nevertheless, I learned to show respect, to become aware of where and
how I was sitting, to avoid the bathroom unless the party was large
and I could slip away without being noticed. I monitored my facial
expressions with care, and particularly my eyes after the time, when
serving the men in the front room of a tiny house in Los Angeles,
I made the mistake of looking directly, out of curiosity, at Sailor, a
visiting Machvano from New York, and found myself so unnerved
by his invasive stare that the coffee I was pouring landed on his
trousers.

Over the years, most Machvaia men became somewhat like exotic zoo animals to me, especially at a party (Lola's male relatives being the notable exception). I began to feel more intensely female than I ever had before, the result, no doubt, of my earnest efforts at the culturally correct deportment. Staring is actually considered rude and I never again was caught unaware. But I became sensitized to the primeval power of "the difference."

Beware of emulation for, as you act, so you will become. By the time I got to California where the gatherings were in the hundreds and, for several years, people I didn't know at all, I found it a considerable gift when, on arriving at a celebration, I could quickly head for one of the women's groups, and avoid the constraint of respect required in the company of men. I acted as Machvanka as I could, and the fact that all women tend to be considered essentially of the same female nature proved to my advantage. With the women, I felt immediately relaxed—"safety safe," as Rose likes to say—and relieved to be defensively surrounded by my own kind.

# Out of Respect, 1970

SEVERAL YEARS AFTER I began fieldwork in Seattle, I was traveling down the coast every summer, looking for Machvaia. I was, in fact, in Oakland when an emergency took the extended family I was staying with, other than their two ten-year old boys, out of town. One of the boys had never been to school, not even one day. As his mother explained, "We have never lived in a good and lucky enough neighborhood." What an opportunity, I thought, to broaden the boys' horizons and show them the city only a bridge away!

THE DAY WAS BRIGHT, the sky and sea were blue, and our Sunday outing in San Francisco began well enough; the boys liked the cable cars. The streets, they agreed, were certainly hilly. But, forgetting all about the shameless painted and sculpted portrayals of nude men and women, I made the mistake of including Golden Gate Park's de Young museum in our itinerary.

The pair tried to avoid looking, they giggled at a naked lady, they got red with embarrassment when we hurried by a marble statue. One of them began to peer around the corner into the next room before we entered, and then he insisted on walking in backwards!

I searched desperately for paintings with people wearing clothes.

Neither wanted to use the Men's bathroom when I pointed one out—what was I thinking? "No, thank you," Fonzie politely said. "They probably just have some antiques in there." That's when we left.

I had forgotten the people's comprehensive investment in the new and that, for Machvaia, age and use decreases value. I hadn't realized modesty etiquette, sexual differences, and the requirements of respect apply to children, as well as adults. But I did learn that art is not universal. Art is historical.

# Chapter 14

# KRISA AND CONCILIATION

## Marimé (Defiled)

In the Sixties, I would overhear exciting news like, "The Snakes are out. And so are the Spokane Marx families," and ask what that meant. "*Marimé*," the people would answer. Ritually defiled. Or, "Blackball." In either case, "We can't eat with them."

Defilement is a shame—shames join what should not be joined. Throwing a skirt, a shoe, a petticoat, (approximating something from the female lower body) at, or over, the head of a Machvano immediately transformed him into the outcast condition. Lola said she couldn't imagine treating anyone in such a terrible fashion. "All my life, nobody did that. You'd have to have real hate. The man would be 'out' forever."

In the past, a man pronounced *marimé* was avoided by all others of good standing, at least until he had arranged, paid for, and been cleared by *krisa*. *Marimé* gave an aggrieved woman the power to confront her victim and state her complaint in a Machvaia court of law. But when the defiled faced the *krisa* and promised never to do what he had done again, she removed the stigma by admitting she had not actually defiled him.

I was once told a story about a Romni (Roma woman) who claimed to have polluted a man by placing one of her pubic hairs on his head. Called to testify at his *krisa*, she slowly and solemnly unwrapped layers of paper until she came up with a black hair several feet long. That was the end of the story. But I like to imagine the men seated at the table were amused.

**171**

IN OLD DAYS, the rules concerning rejection were undeniably strict. Bibi, who was born near the beginning of the last century, wanted me to know:

> Once, rejection was a very big thing. It had a big power. Like, if you invited Outsiders to anything, a wedding, a *slava*, a Roma party, you were out, an outcast. In those days, Outsiders were strangers and no one, no one that I knew, was crazy enough to ever run away, *nashlimos*, to America.

By 1968, very soon after I had finished my thesis on the subject, the penalty of ritual defilement was losing teeth and, within a year or two, *marimé* had officially changed. The Roma of California agreed that matters of *marimé* would no longer involve *krisa* adjudication. When I asked Lola's son Miller why a man's dramatic loss of ritual purity was no longer considered criminal, he explained that "too many women were doing it, so many that the *krisa* (courts) couldn't keep up." As a result, women lost an ancient legal power. Now whenever it is necessary to punish a wrongdoer and family, the men at court stipulate, like before, a period of isolation; one to three months is average. But, instead of *marimé*, they call the penalty "blackball."

## Conciliation

Rena Gropper has studied both Machvaia and Kalderasha in the Manhattan area. She writes (1967:1052) that the Romani term *krisa* glosses as "justice . . . encompassing (1) the personnel required for court trials, (2) the body of pertinent customary law, (3) the prescribed ritual for holding the trial, and (4) the underlying value system." The people have, of course, always been subject to the laws of whatever country they were in, but *krisa* is intended to resolve intra-Roma conflict.

*Krisa* and courts are the business of the Machvano. He is the one responsible to the community-at-large for the moral behavior of his entire extended family and can be held responsible for any fines incurred by his family and lineage. As the political person, the ideal characteristics of the male are an even and fair-minded temperament, and concern for the general welfare. "Being good with each other" is a Machvaia value and *krisa* works by consensus. Ideally, a *krisa* must continue until all those present agree on the verdict.

Ideally, the men meet as equals in respect and privilege, none to have more power and influence than any other—except by the increased spirituality associated with age. One or several elderly Roma statesmen, men considered just and knowledgeable in *krisa* practices, are usually solicited to monitor the legal proceedings. As children, boys will play at make-believe court, taking opposing sides, wielding the penalties of fining and shunning, the only coercive *krisa* powers. Although previous judgments serve as guidelines, the rules of *krisa* can be remade according to the temper of the changing times.

WOMEN BEING BANNED FROM THE COURT SYSTEM, I, of course, have never attended *krisa*. I learned about them largely through the usual channels of gossip, the reports of Miller's lively wife, zippity Duda, and the *krisa* experiences of Old Chally. A century ago when the people arrived in the States, *krisa* was a job for both men and women.

> Duda: It used to be everyone got together for *krisa*, the women, too, if they were involved. Now it's mostly the men, and it's mostly by phone. The women don't care to *krishel.* The men call all over and the bills are big. But it's pretty fast, faster than getting everyone together.
>
> Daughter Sabrina added this salient point: "They (men) need *something* to do."

But, community morality and judging the errors of others and sensing subtle shifts of public opinion are everyone's business. Machvaia are quick to condemn shameful behaviors, and believe a fulsome expression of feelings leads to good health: "You will get sick if you hold it [emotions and feelings] in." Gossip, once conveyed in person and by phone, and now by phone and electronic media, brings the deed in question to a general attention. Indeed, most issues, with a little public airing, are settled without resort to *krisa*. People tend to move away or turn their backs; friends caution about the cost to reputation of a public shame; a senior member of the extended family threatens or pleads to good effect.

Also, if the culprit is from a popular and "good" family, there is a tendency to wait and see how the situation resolves. "We don't like to talk about that," the women might say when queried. This can keep the gossip localized. Popularity is a power and shames are only penalized when the larger Machvaia community gets involved.

ONE REASON TO KEEP A SCANDAL low key is that it affects not only family, but also community and *vitsa* (named lineage group) reputation. The Machvaia like to think of themselves as a matched assortment of high status kind. They describe some of the other *vitsi* as "killers" or "bad." The Lucky Brothers *vitsa* is, of course, "lucky." The Johnsons in Florida, for example, are "rich" and fun to visit. Although Machvaia live among other Roma, compete with them for territories and share many of the same problems owing to similar lifestyles, they concur that no other Roma can be trusted. Sometimes they inter-marry; indeed, as elders lose the power to arrange all aspects of Machvaia marriage, intermarriage is on the rise. And yet most Machvaia families have more contact with Outsiders than they have with Kalderasha.

Meeting in *krisa*, different *vitsi* tend to become warring factions; the blood and kinship ties that encourage harmonious negotiations are absent. In addition, belief and custom differ somewhat from one *vitsa* to another. Conflicts with other "kinds" of Roma over fortune telling territories are seldom settled to anyone's complete satisfaction. In the event of divorce, a Machvanka married to a Kalderash Rom is likely to lose all custody of her children.

When Machvaia meet Machvaia in *krisa*, however, a therapeutic airing of all grievances tends to clear the way for compromise. Relatives push both sides for a settlement. If the conflict isn't cleared, neither side can go to the same gathering in case the other family might be there, and fighting might ensue. Conflict, as mentioned, is anathema to the good will, and good luck of a public event.

As Weyrauch and Bell (2001:79) point out in Gypsy Law, the idea is not so much vindication of individual rights, "eye for an eye," as to reestablish peace within the group. After a Machvaia/ Machvaia settlement, any remaining dissatisfaction is released to a higher authority. Whatever the *krisa* decision, an element of fatefulness prevails, the sense that The God and the legacy of the ancestors' *baX*, whether good or bad, is in the details. Machvaia believe that everyone, in some fashion, will get exactly what he deserves, either in *krisa*, or through a supernatural justice that can involve the extended family—and even descendants at some future date.

## The Old Culture

In 2001, the estimable elder, Phuro Chally (Old Father-Gentleman Chally) told me that in earlier times, the *krisa* dealt mostly with the business of *dahro*, donations of money promised by the men assembled at weddings and not yet conveyed to the groom's family. Now, as territories become scarce, expensive and so often must be purchased from the owner, it is *ofisuria* (fortune telling offices) and contests over territory. Or it's the money or fines somebody owes and hasn't paid. Or who gets the children after a divorce.

Until the recent past, any property and all the offspring of the divorcing couple belonged to the groom's family. In the Thirties, Marko's son died and Marko sent his daughter-in-law back to her parents, keeping all five of her children. Nowadays, child custody is negotiated as peaceably as possible by the two families. Now, both sides have equal rights—although some families claim to adhere to the old ways when it suits their purpose. If the child is a girl, the bride's family may be given first consideration. If the one child is a boy, he may go to the groom's family.

Once, both families wanted, and fought for, the children. Grandparents considered their lives richly enhanced by the grandchildren they raised, indulged, and who would, it was expected, care for them in their old age. When their son's first marriage ended, Duda and Miller kept their two-year-old grandson and sent the new baby home with her mother.

More and more often, however, as the extended family loses the function of sharing and aid, children become a financial burden instead of an old-age investment and the groom's family is usually content to opt out of the childcare responsibility. The people now agree that the mother is more involved with her children. Chally says it is "sad," but not wrong, perhaps because it was right most of his life, "to take them all away from her."

175

IN 2001, the estimable elder Chally had this to say:

> The way we are doing *krisa* now is like a vote and a little
> Americanized, a little more modern. You ask each person,
> one by one, so they don't all talk at once.
>
> We do it now with two groups. Each person tells his story
> to his group. That way, there isn't so much arguing. Each
> group analyzes the problem, and then the people involved
> with this guy talk to the other people. They negotiate.
>
> You know, Gypsies have changed in many ways. But the
> old culture is still there. We talk about the problem. And we
> agree.

# *Bibio*

WHEN FAIR HELEN RAN AWAY FROM HER MARRIAGE to Bari (Big) Barbara's grandson, she created quite a scandal. Last seen waiting at a bus stop, coiffed and fashionably attired, she was lured away —shame to tell!—by a notorious Rom gigolo. The problems of the rich and famous are hot topics of gossip, and Barbara's runaway *bori* (daughter-in-law) became the news of the day.

Perhaps in tribute to Barbara's former role as the powerful ruler of the San Francisco Roma, Good-Time Miller called to suggest that a *krisa* (Roma law/jury) of women hold their own court. Miller, who is Barbara Miller's nephew, assured her the men of her extended family would stand behind the verdict. Barbara began by consulting her two prestigious older daughters, Miller's wife, and possibly others, and they, of course, agreed she was the injured party. Barbara had paid the brideprice, paid for the three-day engagement, two days of the three-day wedding, and she had set young Helen up in business. Now, she would have to find another bride and do it all again.

Helen's family complained they had no money for the usual fines. Or they didn't want to pay. Eventually, years later, Helen came up with the money owed but, in the meantime, *krisa* settlement gave Barbara custody of Helen's boy, Baby Miller.

I mention this episode of Machvaia history because I never, before or since, heard of another all-female *krisa*.

BARBARA MILLER HAD MANY NAMES. Barbara Miller was one of her "American" names and, no doubt, the least popular.

**177**

I called her Bibi in reference, or Bibio to her face. A term of respect, Bibi translates as "Auntie."

Lola, my dear Machvanka friend, always held her sister-in-law in the highest esteem; indeed, she named several of her children for Bibi and Bibi's family. I can't say Bibi returned the favor. When they were young parents, Lola and Bahto set up an *ofisa* on Montgomery Street in Bibi's city. As Bibi's older brother, Bahto may have believed he had that right; according to custom, elder siblings did. But, by the third day, two "nice polite policemen came by" and told Lola she would have to pack and leave the city "by noon tomorrow." Interestingly, Lola never held this quick eviction against Bibi. It is a female thing, Lola said. She believed "Machvanki should stick together."

THE BIBI I KNEW WAS NO STRANGER to courts of law. Decades earlier, when the renowned Baro (Big) George of Los Angeles died, his son Lynwood John, who had married Bibi's second daughter, tried to assume his father's role. Machvaia remember their "like gold" leader George Adams nostalgically; he generously doled out fortune telling territories, and he protected his clients from arrest. Bibi, then Barbara Miller, Bari of San Francisco and familiar with pay-offs, was persuaded to help George's son. But their efforts failed; Bibi and John were convicted and sent to jail. John blamed Bibi; he had warned her not to mention the extent of her wealth, but she had to be a big shot and brag. That riled the police, making them green, John supposed, with envy.

One time I asked Bibi what jail had been like. She swore it wasn't half as bad as being married to Duiyo. During her year or so in prison, husband Duiyo sold their elegant house, all the furnishings, the satin sheets, the carved headboard with the crown, the baby grand, Bibi's valuable jewelry, and spent all her savings. Bibi hated him for that and always blamed Duiyo for "squealing." Duiyo was jealous," she assured me many times. "He was jealous of me, jealous of my money. He kept trying to ruin my customers." Although technically, she had been found guilty of bribery in Los Angeles, long miles from Duiyo's threats, she claimed he turned her in so he could rob her. "I don't know what he was thinking, putting me in jail, wiping me out."

178

So Bibi blamed Duiyo and John blamed Bibi. It is the nature of the people, as I have learned, to project. How much of these stories are true, I cannot say; John may not have any more idea of the illegalities involved that led to their arrest than Bibi. Bribery was then regarded as acceptable Machvaia practice, effective, at least on occasion, here as in Europe.

But I do know the Roma men found it hard to believe a mere woman could run a city. Even Bibi's blood relatives had trouble with the idea of a woman leader. Men are supposed to be 'boss' and Duiyo felt "less than a man," no doubt, married to a woman who insisted on her own decisions. Before he became obsessed with a blonde Fox Theater usherette and went "crazy for love," Bibi's gorgeous first husband set up the royal system of influence that Bibi inherited. But, although he shared her reign and her money, Bibi's second husband Duiyo never advanced to Baro status.

UPON HER RELEASE FROM JAIL, Bibi had no income and no property.

> My youngest daughter was living in garbage up to the neck and no money. She only had two dollars. I took it to Safeway to get milk for the baby and caught a customer for twenty- seven dollars. A few more trips to the grocery, and I had six hundred. I had been warned never to fortune tell again, but I thought—what could I lose? I am better off in jail if can't *drabares*. So I went to the police station and told them I had incriminating tapes and they better not give me any trouble.
>
> I didn't know anything else. I had to tell fortunes.

Over the years, Bibi recouped her good fortune. Although forbidden to work, the police never bothered her again. Perhaps they had no grounds. An enterprising Stevens family in Los Angeles hired Attorney Barry Fisher and, by the mid-Eighties, fortune telling was legal in California.

I have heard Bibi described as the first Machvanka to appear in public without her headscarf, the token of marital affinity and obedience. Married, I can imagine she enjoyed

**179**

showing Duiyo this disrespect; marriage had devolved into a competition. Divorced, she longed to get even.

My impression, seeing him at parties, is that diabetes never deterred Duiyo from serious drinking, and, two decades after he stole all her money, Duiyo was sick, broke, and in a wheelchair, having lost both legs from the long-term effects of disease. He came by her ofisa with an attendant to plead for money, "only five hundred dollars." Bibi refused to let him in, and, with considerable satisfaction, I would imagine, she cursed him, explaining he was already victim of her former curse. "Remember when I called on the power of The God that you have no legs to walk on."

When Duiyo died, however, Bibi sent six thousand for his *pomana*. Perhaps it was a matter of pride; everyone knew that Duiyo had once been her husband. But death changes all relationships, and even the feckless Bibi understood that a ghost has unpredictable and disturbing powers.

BIBI WANTED ME TO UNDERSTAND that big-time leaders are required to be mean and tough. She only shared her territory with her children. Several Ginershti families were allowed in her city because, as she explained, the men sold cars for income. Fearing their male relatives might try to take over, she refused to tolerate any other fortune tellers.

Whenever her rule was challenged, she always won, with the help of the local police. A Rom was locked in a funeral home overnight as punishment for sending a hearse to pick her up; a sense of humor was never Bibi's forté. She made another, the infamous or famous, depending on your point of view, Tinya Bimbo, sweep the sidewalk in front of her storefront. Bibi seemed quite pleased with herself, even smug, as she explained to me how she had mailed snapshots of Tinya's humiliating clean-up back to his Chicago constituency.

Most leaders are charismatic, charming, and generous. But how could Bibi be generous with her territory, given that a female Bari was an anomaly and the male half of the Machvaia population believed they had the right to rectify the situation? Bibi was not known for her soft heart. She seldom gave people reason to like her. Even her children don't describe her as warm. I suspect she never had much faith in affairs of the heart, after her first marriage to the Miller [yes, another Miller] Uwanovich, "the most beautiful of all the Machvaia men" according to sister-in-law Lola, and the second, to greedy Duiyo. Happiness, she assured me, comes only with money.

Normally, in keeping with *krisa* law, jail time will trash any possibility of luck, the sanctity of respect, and Machvaia social status. But Old Bibi was a woman of enterprise and courage. Unbeatable at business, the most popular fortune teller at the local fairs, a former female leader, indeed the only one in existence, she managed to survive her disgrace. She aged well and lived into her mid-nineties. Long life is a triumph of sorts, the visible evidence of good luck. Bejeweled and glamorous, for years she lent the spiritual importance of her advancing age, good health, and wealth to the many Machvaia events she graced.

IN THE LATE SIXTIES WHEN BIBI was in jail, I would walk by her business place on Market and find the storefront dark, the astrology chart in the window dusty. By the Seventies, the lights were on and she was open for business. In the Eighties, when her sister-in-law Luia BaXali (Rich Woman) of Reno died, Bibi complained there was no one left with whom to share the old days. At least I was an interested audience.

We were sitting in her closet-sized business place when she beckoned an elderly man in from the street. Bibi had a genius for smelling money. Pinning a straying lock of white hair back into her bun, she whispered that despite his homeless appearance, he had enough for a reading. While she began to tell the future, I went out for two paper cups of coffee.

When I returned, the man was gone. Bibi confided in a resigned, but matter-of-fact, tone,

"I was just a little girl when mother said I would have money luck and no luck in love."

[Long pause as she folds the bills and stuffs them into her bra.]

# Chapter 15

## LEAVING THE GYPSIES: MILANO'S STORY

*I*'VE KNOWN MILANO since he was a lad of seven. The middle child in a family of five rather somber siblings, his black eyes have always danced with a saucy humor. He made me laugh then; he can still make me laugh.

Like so many of the people, he has always been unconditionally generous. During a dark period of my life when I was "living poor," as the Gypsies say, and my luck seemed to have left in a panic, Milano, who was then in his late twenties, saved me. He invited me to celebrate Thanksgiving with him at a posh San Francisco hotel and spent hundreds of dollars on food and champagne. We spread the afternoon out in an easy fashion, returning to the buffet every few hours, exchanging stories—his were best, full of the irony of being a Gypsy in America and gay besides. That afternoon of hilarity and pleasure—who can say what changes our luck?—was a turning point for me, and my circumstances improved. That good-time lunch with Milano occurred shortly after he discovered he was HIV positive and, in retrospect, I have realized he was packing as much fun as he could into what he presumed were his last days on earth.

IN THE WORLD MACHVAIA, everyone *must* marry. Marrying bestows adult privileges and insures the continuity of the generations. There is no role for homosexuals in the Machvaia community, and most of them remain closeted, marrying, having children, and pretending to be straight. But gossip regulates, censors, and reveals, and the people know who is pretending.

**183**

Of all the runaways I know who stayed away to make it on their own, Milano is the most successful. Coming of age in San Francisco, Milano "ran away" into the arms of the lively local gay community. Famously gay-friendly San Francisco immediately furnished him an alternate identity and role.

Like most Machvaia, Milano had gone to school only when it was convenient, when he wasn't needed at home or sleeping in from a late-night before, and his reading and writing skills, of course, were sketchy. But, by age fifteen, he already possessed the self-confidence, panache, and gift for adaptive mimicry that marks so many of those born Roma—is it in the genes, I wonder? As soon as he left home, he was required to become self-supporting and he has managed very well financially. He claims his total avoidance of his Machvaia family is the reason for his luck. He tried for some time to straddle the two communities; he even told fortunes at the local Psychic Fair with his sister. But now he adamantly refuses any contact—"When you're out, you're out!"

Sadly, during these past decades, nearly all his same-age gay friends have died. Milano is one of those who are living long and fairly well with HIV. He and I keep in touch. When I moved to Seattle, he called from San Francisco and agreed to let me record his life story over the phone. Milano was then in his 40s.

## The High Wire Act

According to Milano in 1999:

I seem to make people laugh. To me it's natural to be funny. Because I tell it the way I see it and feel it. And it comes out that way. Funny. Not that I plan it to be funny. It's just my life. It's hysterical. A lot of the time I don't believe myself or this planet that I'm on.

My life has been a high wire act. A circus. It's like you're not prepared, no practice, and you have to perform perfectly the first time out. And you got to do it. It's just amazing what you can do when you have to. There have been some really bad times. And in my case I did it more than once—the high wire act. Really bad times. Unimaginable. How anybody could have that kind of life . . . I'm just glad it's over. [So he thought at the time. A decade later, he is still going strong.] There were the times I had no financial freedom. Had to keep trying to do everything. But I'm OK now. [Milano owns the condo he lives in and has achieved financial independence.] But, shit, I'm nowhere near where I'd like to be. I just have enough money to see me through.

I talked to my doctor today. They did find that the cause of my numb painful feet was all the medications. So I said, OK, that's good. Cause I quit taking them. But it's not good. Because it's been exactly one month now since I quit them and I'm not taking anything. For years, I've been on everything you can imagine. So I've got an appointment to go Friday and see what other new poisons they have available. Well, they said one month isn't that long. The medical condition that I'm in, it's what makes me do the things I do now. Like shopping.

Actually, today I had a pretty good time by myself. Once-a-year sales this week. The weather was beautiful. I bought the shoes to last me for the rest of my life. They went down to $399—they were $799. Alligator. Only one pair left in my size. Not like you're going to wear them every day for walking around or in the subway. They'll last forever. Now I don't want to buy more stuff. That's the end of Neiman Marcus. I got a silk shirt, a leather jacket, alligator shoes. You know what I mean?

I'm a lot more free with my money now. I used to be as tight as they come. You could hear me squeak. But I'm not squeaking now.

When I first left the Gypsies, I had to work from six in the morning until nine at night. I got to the salon early in the morning. I was the receptionist. Did shampoos, entertained, the whole thing. Seven days a week, I left there about one in the afternoon and had enough time to get home, change, take a twenty minute nap. Then I went to the restaurant downtown. I did everything, hostessing, bartending, waitressing.

That job answering phones—I think that was next. They really did me a favor. Even though I hated the job. That was rock and roll, baby. I had to learn to read, to spell, to write, to pronounce words I never heard of. You had to read, write, type, and you had to be fast. I was a bust in school and I had to work hard. Had to learn quick. Or else. Had to answer like I was the business, a doctor, a secretary, a bank, a brokerage. You had all these different personalities. Outrageous and irate people to deal with on the phone: psychiatrists, surgeons, dermatologists, detectives—you name it. Can you imagine handling a toll call on one ear and, on the other, a life-threatening emergency. Oh my God! And you're paging people and you're screening people. Oh, my God!

I don't know how I did it. I was young; I was ambitious; and I knew I had to do it because I needed the money. I only went [on a piecemeal basis] to the sophomore level in high school. And it wasn't easy. We went from switchboards to automatic, from plug-ins to automated. There were a lot of people who were fired because they couldn't keep up the pace. People were let go that had been with the company for years.

Didn't make much, but at one time I was living with a sugar daddy. I was very, very lucky. Without that, I would be dead. No rent, food, this, that. But I was living a high life. You know what I mean? Not being able to actually afford it myself. I had a car; I had valet parking, going to work, making $4.75 an hour. The people at the phone answering work had no idea what was going on. You know they were all in the poorhouse and I was walking in with suits, silk shirts, jewelry; and everybody knew I had valet parking. [He laughs.] It was hilarious. I did that for more than ten years. They'd pass me a bonus. Because, for the longest time, I was the one who took the most phone calls.

Then I went to work as a receptionist downtown—that way I got medical insurance. Several years.

Then I went to work for the medical society for about a year and a half. That was chilling. I just attended to the emergency calls for the doctors. I'll never forget one night I answered the phone and it was Raida, my in-law [through his sister's marriage]. She was calling. I said, 'Good evening, Dr.

Margolis' exchange.' She started to talk and I said, 'Raida?'
She said, 'What the hell are you doing there?'

I always wanted to save enough to buy my own apartment.
I made the money, but I don't know what the hell happened
to it. Don't know. The restaurant job was fun because the guy
next door owned a clothing store and dealt coke. I was always
wired. I was all of twenty and wired. You could do anything
then. I haven't touched any coke, any stuff, for ten years.
Because I know if I do, I might as well jump off the bridge.
Won't do me no good. [Laughs.]

I know it's possible to survive with HIV. To be a long
survivor. I know it's possible because I know guys who, like
me, are still alive. I expected to go ten, fifteen years ago. But
I didn't. [Laughs.] But all of my best friends have died.

### Resort Life

I'd like to sell one of my two apartments and go someplace
that has resort life. For men. Like we used to have right here
on the Russian River, one hour from San Francisco.
Everything on one property. But those places don't exist
anymore. So I'm checking things in Australia, Germany,
France.

Woods Resort [on the Russian River] was fabulous. From
the time I was twenty until I was thirty-two, there was this
private land, maybe thirty-five acres and so big, you know,
very wooded, cabins, disco, a pond, swimming pools, a
restaurant.And it was just for men. You know what I mean?

I used to hang out there a lot. Major drug scene. I used
to arrive with a case of champagne, two or three grams of
cocaine, and swimming suits to kill. I used to drink, laugh,
swim, barbeque, tea dance, nap—then get ready for the
night stuff and dance until four-thirty in the morning. I miss
that.

I'd always take care of the waiters. I brought my own
stock, but I still remembered to tip. I'd sit by the pool with
my CD, my Neiman Marcus towels, drinking the champagne
I brought. You know what I mean? Not only was it intense

and short-lived, but it was amazing the amount of money I spent in a short time. Half the time I was even minus in the dollar zone.

That was my champagne period. I drank nothing but Cristal, $100 a bottle. Or Dom Perignon. I was just spending money. Cocaine and stuff. At the resort, I was going back and forth to the room every ten minutes to do another massive line of cocaine and come back in a different bathing suit. [Laughs.] Then get ready to do the little tea dance. Then everybody would go to take a nap. Then dinner. Then hit the mirror again. Thousands of dollars going nowhere fast. But it was fun.

I was always very lucky to have this good friend who was a hairdresser. Especially someone like me, I would be a slave to my hairdresser. I was getting my hair done a lot. Like— sometimes we did it twice a day. I'm not kidding you. First thing in the morning before I went to work it took forty-five minutes to blow dry the damn hair. Because there's so much of it, it's so thick, it's so wet. So in order for the hair to come out right, it's gotta be blown-dried soaking wet. You can't just dry it. It's too curly, too frizzy, and you gotta tension it. And between those times, we used to relax it with conditioners. Forty-five minutes, my God! And when you get home, you wanta go out—whoops!—wash the hair again. This went on for years. No kidding!

One time I was at the resort, Woods Resort, and I called him. 'Listen here, you better come over, all expenses paid.' He did my hair and my friend gave him $120. And it was great. Talk about service. I called him to come from San Francisco, 100 miles. In each direction. [Laughs.]

### AIDS

After that, AIDS. Things started really chilling. A lot of people weren't around any more. Dying. It scared a lot of people. People weren't out socializing any more. The party was over. The volume was down.

When I found out I was HIV positive, I thought that was it, I was only going to have a year to live. That's when I really started spending. That's when I rented the penthouse. I figured this was it. So I was really living high. Even more than I was in the past. I didn't invest in anything, I was just spending. So there wasn't like a huge income coming in. It was all going out. I had made quite a bit, and it went out. Had I invested in condos then, I'd be much better off. I wasn't thinking about investments because I was HIV-positive and investments are usually long term. And if you don't got a term . . . [Laughs.] Like terms of endearment? No terms? That's it! I thought I would go. I was the best client at Fillmore and Sacramento, D & M Liquor Store. I never left there with only one bottle. Never.

About this time, I met this friend—the manager at a department store restaurant. Brand new. They served every top-of-the-line champagne. Dom Perignon wastwenty dollars a glass. We'd buy one glass and it was refilled again and again. We knew everybody there and they kept filling my glass up.

I'd give my friend a gram and he gave me a bottle of Cristal. He was coming by, like, every other day. Of course he didn't work there that long. [Laughs.] It so happens he was positive, too, and he died several years ago. You know what I mean? He was a gas! He was very funny! His name was Richard. This was before protease inhibitors. About that time people were buying life insurance policies at sixty to seventy percent of value. They were advertising—why leave your money to someone else when you can spend it yourself? They started making beaucoup bucks right away. So Rich saw the ad, gave them his $200,000 insurance policy, took his $120,000 and went and bought himself a Jaguar and then picked his mother up and they went around the world. It wasn't too long after that that he was c'est la vie. But he used to be at the disco every night. A good dancer, I guess you could say. That is hilarious. [Laughs.] I guess you could say.

After the good time was over, I hit the most rock-bottomest time that I ever hit in my life. Trauma and tragedy.

I had been on combinations for some time already—I was the first one at the door, even before they hit the pharmacy. I was part of the early unofficial research, a step ahead of the game. But I got really depressed. Had enough. It was kind of like it wasn't worth it. Not just that all my friends, except Tyrone, had died. There were several other reasons.

I had experiences that taught me I had better get a grip and I'd better get it fast. I wasn't getting any younger. I knew I needed money. There was only one way I knew to get it. Determination. Hard work. I worked hard when I was younger. But I took vacations. What I did throughout my life was work a couple of years and take a couple of years off. It always worked that way. So it wasn't like I'd work continuously. I saved some money for vacations and I found a sponsor. I had a lot of sponsors. I mean a lot. I have gotten every major company known on this planet to sponsor me. Big companies. [The businessmen who engaged him paid him in some fashion.] When you want to hire a movie star you gotta pay. [Laughs.]

*Businessman Milano*

That all changed when I went into business. I went in on a wing and a prayer, into business with Tyrone. I had to do whatever was necessary. Tyrone had the money. But it was fifty-fifty all the way—that's the way it had to be. If you didn't have your money, how could you be a partner? That's in any business. I understood that very clearly. It wasn't like, oh sure, I'm going to borrow some money from you and go half with you in this business. [Laughs.] It was not going to fly unless I put up half.

So then, of course, you know I opened the store [hair salon and cosmetics]. And I wasn't sure what the hell was going to happen. It was a make-it or break-it deal. Because I'd sunk everything I had into that shop. Basically. It was the second time I'd sunk everything—the first time was the apartment. This one [the one in which he is living at this time]. I sold my soul. I didn't have two nickels left after I closed the deal. I sold every piece of jewelry that I had and every piece of jewelry that I didn't have. [Laughs.] I got the apartment before I got the store. Now I have two apartments in the same building. The store came next. After the store, the condo in Hawaii. So I was moving it and doing it. And, on top of that, we went with check in hand to buy the restaurant I wanted. The deal fell through because the guy didn't want to give me a good enough lease. I told Tyrone, 'We're out of here, baby. I'm not putting my life on the line for a lousy four- or five-year lease.' I wanted ten or nothing. Cause I was putting the apartment, everything, behind it. The first apartment was a court probate. All someone had to do was bid twenty-five cents more than me and I would have lost it. When I got there, I saw the place was full, and I thought they had all come to bid on my apartment. [Laughs.] They didn't even know it existed. Nobody wanted studios then, I guess. [Laughs.] The gavel went down and it was like sold for $54,000 and I said 'Yesssss!' I walked out of that courtroom with tears running down my face. Because I knew at that moment that I did something right.

Two apartments, the store, the condo in Hawaii, and we were just about to get another in Hawaii, a cute penthouse with an ocean view. For $40,000. But that's just when things started to fall apart. It was too late. It didn't happen. That was right when I took him [Tyrone] to the hospital, that first night. Shit. But it was hilarious, too. He was laying there in total pain, and I was by his side with pen and paper in hand. [Laughs.] He looked at me and said, 'I know what you're thinking.' I said, 'Don't think like that.' He said, 'This is not the time.' I said, 'No? I can't think of any better.' [Laughs.] Oh, that was wild. And then the female doctor comes out and says 'It's fifty-fifty.' It was heavy. I had known. Because, HIV-positive, all he did was smoke cigarettes and drink alcohol. I am totally convinced about the danger of cigarettes. I only smoked when I was drinking. But I'm convinced that, if I had kept smoking, I wouldn't be here talking to you. Cigarettes, that's the most illegal thing on earth. But you can get it anywhere, any time. So what the

fuck—excuse my French—is going on? In London, they
smoke and eat at the same time.

He speaks from experience. He has taken several trips to Europe
and, more recently, a cruise around the world.

I used to spend $300 for three hours of coke. Finally, one
day, I stopped. It wasn't the money situation. It was the
health situation. I was fortunate.
    Somehow, today, I am celebrating. Celebrating the
bargain of the alligator shoes. My feet feel better. Still like ice
and numb. But I want that to go away now. Without the
medication, I feel better already.

## Life Is a School

Milano says that the only way to become American, and to succeed
as an American, is to leave the Gypsy past behind completely. Of
course, doing this has protected him from the shame associated with
runaways and any pressure from his family to return. Also, given the
Machvaia tendency to a "soft heart," Milano, in all likelihood,
wouldn't have been able to refuse those insistently needy kinsmen
who asked for his financial help. It seems doubtful he would have
become economically self-sufficient, owned several apartments, or
had the money to further his education with trips around the
world.
    I asked him if he ever regretted leaving the Gypsies and what
gave him the courage to do so.

How did I leave the Gypsies in the first place? I was lucky in
the transition. When I started at the disco, I thought I had
arrived—do you hear me? Little did I know.
    Well, when I look back at it, I realize I was happening.
Young, and I'd walk up to the bar and get free drinks all over
the place. Listen to this. I'd leave home with ten cents; the
train was a nickel in one direction and a nickel in the other.
I'd get back at three in the morning and all I'd spent was ten
cents. And a lot of time I took a cab home or somebody else

dropped me off and I saved that nickel. [Laughs.] It was hilarious.

I was nowhere near twenty-one when I used to sneak into the Cabaret Disco. I'd slip through the kitchen where all the illegal aliens were cooking, and they'd look at me like I was an extraterrestrial. I'd be dressed up in—God if I even looked at clothes like that these days I might as well curl up and die. Super flashy sequined outfits. Malcolm Hall was the biggest designer at that time. I'd run through the kitchen and up the stairs where everybody was jumping up and down and nobody was paying attention to me. You know what I mean? I was all of fifteen. Fifteen and drinking up a storm. I'd get a cab or a trolley from home and never be sure if the door to the kitchen was open. Most Saturday nights it was wide open, cooling the kitchen workers off. I met a lot of people from all over the world. The only thing I was interested in was disco, disco, disco. I didn't care if anyone else lived or died. It was great, everyone dressed up, all enjoying themselves. It was very different. I didn't know what I was going to do next. Way before John Travolta was out, I was wearing the beautiful white suit, those alligator shoes. I did it in `74. Travolta's movie didn't come out until `79. By then I was nearly twenty.

I'll never forget the time I didn't go home until six in the morning. My parents were in Stockton, and I left home at one. I thought, they aren't coming back. Right? So I took off. And when I saw the car out in front, I thought, uh, oh. All the lights went on, and I was walking up the stairs in this screaming orange velvet blazer that was trimmed—lapels and all the way around—in sparkling sequins. And a floral shirt. I looked like something out of Austin Powers. Only more so. Unbelievable. Big platform shoes, too. And I had two hickies. One on the right and one on the left side of my neck. Yeh! I looked worked over. And I was.

I don't know how people raise children nowadays. The cartoons have language we would have gotten beaten up for when we were young. What happened to the censors? They aren't censing. They have all been bought off. [Laughs.] The language! It teaches ugliness and disrespect. I think you have to grow up with some respect. If you grow up without respect, then you don't respect yourself. And you become a disrespectable person. [Laughs.]

I guess if I had children, I would understand about protection. But life is so short, I would have had trouble denying my child the right to experience. You know? My parents couldn't have prepared me for my life. They didn't know anything about my life. I was thrown to the dogs. I learned everything in the street. And in the bars. And what have you. How to dress. Everything. I had to learn everything by myself.

I'll never forget the time I went to a restaurant in town, and I was afraid because I didn't know what fork to use; there were too many on the table. We're going to do about four courses, you know? I didn't know about escargot or pâté foie gras. In our home, everything came to the table at the same time, like a Chinese restaurant. [Laughs.] You know what I mean? No first course, second course . . . One course and that was it, baby.

Life is a school, without a doubt. I just hope we go to a better one when we leave this school.

When you leave the Gypsies you have to sever all the ties. You really have to completely make a 100-degree turn. The Gypsy life can be very good for some. But those who aren't into it, you just have to move out. You really have to sever the ties that bind in order to continue your life with some form of happiness. You just got to go. Until then, you won't go and you won't make it.

I had a lot of support. It was fun and funny. I had a lot of laughs. And the time just went by so fast. You know, I'll never forget my first hit of acid. It was like the greatest thing that ever happened to me in my life. It was like—wow! I was alive. I felt like I was alive.

*Friends*

Sylvester. It's spelled just like the cartoon. He was amazing. The first time I laid eyes on him was at a place called The

Elephant Walk. That's a bar/cabaret right on the corner of eighteenth and Castro. And I was all of fifteen years old and I never knew what a drag queen was. The show started, and I was drinking a cocktail and—oh, my God!—I thought it was this big heavy black woman. But it was this big heavy drag queen. That was Sylvester. He sang terrifically. You know. After the show we talked a little bit. And the rest is history. He was on welfare and food stamps. I'm talking about hardship times. But you know what? Everybody else was on the same thing. Including myself. In those times, you could get by on welfare.

Sylvester got really, really lucky. He met a record producer and he cut a record. He made "Disco Heat." It sold well. He got off welfare. He got tickets to perform all over the world. He was on the rise. Not a star, yet. But making a good living. Really big in Europe. Number one. And when he came back, he was just about to hit a major contract deal and he was doing a benefit in Boston. For AIDS. As he was getting ready to go on stage, he got a phone call that his lover just died of AIDS. But the show had to go on. After that he didn't do any more benefits. In less than a year, he was dead, too.

He knew he was dying. Everybody did. I tried to make him feel more comfortable. I told him my life was shit, and I could go any day, Arrivederci, Baby. We got into a conversation and he said, 'Listen. You got to live like you're gonna live. Because if you live like you're gonna die, you're gonna die.' I never forgot that, what he said.

I've had a lot of friends, a lot of friends. All those people that I grew up with then are ninety percent dead. And the few that are left are barely left. So, to me, there are none. And now I'm feeling like, oh my God, they were my family! That's why I don't feel anything for anyone any more. And nothing could touch me. Whatever tragedy won't faze me. Because I've already felt everything. Tyrone was the last one. There couldn't be anyone that could touch me again. I knew him for twenty years. Twenty years we were friends. And friendships like that don't come along every day.

**195**

Those were the good old days. But there are still more good days to come. Still more memories.

## After the Gay Parade

The next time Milano called, he had exciting news:

Everybody in this town was there [to see the parade]. I mean the whole town. Must have been pretty close to a million people [600,000 according to the media], from the Embarcadero to Civic Center and jammed in all areas. You could not move. The weather was impeccable; it was eighty. I was in my silk polo shorts and shirt—beachwear. And I was with some really neat friends. A guy I knew came from Las Vegas and he got a fabulous suite overlooking the parade. We started up there and had Bloody Mary's. We decided to hit the street and watch the parade. Smoked a little weed. Drank a beer. After that, chicken-on-the-stick with garlic fries. Watched the show. Joan Baez was singing. She was really, really great. Other top entertainment. And Sweet Pussy Paulette. And she was VERYgood. Very good. Dressed very hot. There were naked people there and good-looking people there and very unattractive people there. Everybody.

These new friends I met invited me to a cruise. Really soon, I'm gonna hit the road. I'm leaving July the tenth for one trip. Las Vegas next weekend. After that, I'm going to meet another friend in Florida, in South Beach, for a couple of days. Then the friend in Las Vegas is having a party. So I am going back to Las Vegas. A five-month cruise around the world, leaving from Greece. That's in November. I'd better start putting the money together really fast. Well, this opportunity isn't going to come again in my lifetime. I might sell all the investment pieces [jewelry and antiques] that I bought really low. I know I could probably make two or three grand on each piece. I was thinking that if I did that, like tomorrow, I could pay off the last unit in this building. But I don't really need to do that. Or I can get the money for the cruise in the hock shop. I'm pretty good at doing whatever.

You know, doing whatever it takes. I figure, with these people, with these quality-type friends, from what I've learned in the past, luck is knocking at my door and it may not be knocking in a year. It's a rare opportunity for me. Because all my old friends are dead. I need new friends.

# Balloons at the Fair

WHEN KATY AND I ARRIVED at the Pleasanton Fair, I wasn't surprised to find that Maneia, a Kalderashitza who I had never met, knew nothing about my new apprenticeship. It had been Katy's idea to go. "Come with me," she had insisted, "We'll go to the Fair this weekend and help Maneia with her balloon booth. Last week my Butch and Lady (Katy's son and daughter-in-law) made two thousand. It's what Butch does for money. You know I never get to see Butch and he's only in the area for a week."

Incurably optimistic, I was anticipating a bit of cash to beef up my Unemployment income and agreed to drive us in my aging Volvo. We left before dawn the next morning.

MANEIA WAS ALREADY WORKING the balloon concession. She quickly relegated me to the air pump in the back with several young boys. My job was to tie until my fingers got numb and then hang the filled balloons on reversible dart boards. I could hear Katy and Maneia calling for customers in the front and glumly wondered how my elementary tying and hanging skills would be paid.

The afternoon was hot. We drank pop, but there was little time for conversation. By mid-afternoon, I had ingratiated my way into the actual booth, and was industriously fielding the darts that whizzed by my ears. We didn't pause to eat; we were too busy.

199

WHEN I COULD, I STUDIED MANEIA, a short, placidly stoic
woman with a heavy, rich vibrato that she used to advantage.
Over and over, the marketing prose was sung:

> *Break the balloon and win a prize.*
> *One balloon gets a prize.*
> *Here, there, break the balloon.*
> *Let's try again, one more time.*
> *Break another, you get a better prize.*

The voice never rose in question. It reassured; it rang with con-
viction. She stood like a flightless bird on five-inch heels, her
heavy breasts resting on the belly of her canvas pocketed
money apron, her head drooping forward from the premature
hump in her upper back. Economizing on movements as well
as words, shifting her weight from one shoe to the other with
deliberation, she refused to sit down until the sun had colored
the west and the fair-going crowds had thinned to a trickle.

The only sight that broke the spell and made her come
alive was her son, six-year-old, grossly overweight, Danilo who
approached her periodically with food money requests. She
never refused him. Once she reprimanded him for playing
with non-Gypsy children, although Outsiders were the only
children available. She changed his light shirt to a woolen un-
dershirt with sleeves and, as evening began, added a heavy
jacket explaining to Katy, who protested the weight of the
clothing, that Danilo was delicate, "he keeps getting colds."
Danilo was the prize of Maneia's life, her baby.

OUR FOURTEEN-HOUR DAY ENDED AT MIDNIGHT. Carrying our shoes, pale with fatigue, hunger pangs, and indiges-
tion, we paid the balloon boys a few dollars each and sent
them home.

I slept with Katy in one twin bed; her son Butch, daughter-
in-law, and a grandchild in the other. The baby, they told me,
cried all night. I didn't notice. Morning came too soon. Mus-
cles stiff, feet swollen and blistered, fingernails broken, eyes
sore, my mind floating in some far away, I found my reflection
in the bathroom mirror hostile and spooky.

While packing, I explained to Katy I couldn't stay another day, that Maneia didn't need me, and I was going home. She objected. I was indispensable, she said, adding that her husband couldn't come and pick her up without me, she couldn't get home. I paused and turned this over in my mind, deciding it was untrue. Someone was always driving from the fairground to San Francisco.

Maneia's relatives, brothers, daughter, and in-laws, none of whom I knew, dropped by as we drank our instant coffee. They said good morning, discussed the business of the day before, and suggested that I stay. One person was on my side, however-when Maneia entered, she accepted my decision without protest.

I had learned the previous evening that the reports of large sums of "*but lové* (big money)" were true. They were the totals for the entire traveling extended family, green and silver heaps on the motel bed to be divided each night among many adults, the six months earnings that had to stretch over the expense of twelve and that were not, I knew now from direct experience, made easily. There were no free and easy pots of gold in Pleasanton.

The sum of $250 collected in Katy's pockets was turned over to Maneia; Katy received $60 back. I, being no relation and certainly no particular asset, was lucky to get $15. Even Katy looked a little tentative as she asked me again, "Stay. Please!"

SEEKING PRIVACY, I took Katy to a coffee shop nearby. Among Machvaia, friendship is kinship, and requires unending support, generosity without measure, nothing refused. It was up to me to discover Katy's motives, her needs, and to read her mind. We sat in a stubborn and companionable silence. I thought about her anticipation, her promises to me and her husband King, about how the day had gone and I realized my leaving would confirm her failure. Perhaps she would add a hundred from her reserve so she could return like a conqueror. But what about her business partner who abandoned ship?

Katy's had been a difficult, hard luck life. Married for years into the Kalderasha and estranged from her family of birth, when she returned, she had, in a sense, lost her Kalderasha-raised children. The marriage to her first husband, Playboy, had been disastrous; her marriage to King wasn't working. Then I remembered what Katy's mother, the indomitable Lola, had said about free enterprise; "If you don't try anything, you don't know nothing, you can't have nothing, you're never lucky."

I did what I could to save Katy's face:

Katy, the carnival business is not for me. I came and I tried, and I know that now. But I'm glad you asked me. I'm glad I came because I wouldn't know if I didn't try. It is something you and I can enjoy together when we are too old and tired to look for our money luck. It will be part of our history, our day at Maneia's fair, you and me, working the balloon game.

# Chapter 16

# THE NEW CHURCH OF CHEESE

## Keeping to Themselves and Slowing Down

The rituals described in this manuscript refer primarily to what I call the Machvaia ritual heyday, the 1970s and 1980s, when money was readily come by and the parties got bigger and better. "The more money you got, the more you show," according to Anastasia, Lola's niece.

Since then, the cost of housing in the States has escalated; the San Francisco studio I rented for $85 in 1973 currently costs $1,700 a month. To add to the difficulty of making ends meet, Americans, the Machvaia tell me, are not as free with money for readings as they were.

Machvaia also complain that—despite the fact that it isn't part of their inborn luck!—Outsiders have begun telling fortunes. Even worse, a great many other kinds of Roma have copied the Machvaia style of giving readings, adding to the general competition. California is now carved into business territories and the competition for territories is manic. Whenever an established California *ofisa* (office) becomes available, it is sold to other Roma. Lola's daughter-in-law died a few years back, and her office cost another Machvanka $75,000 for the privilege of taking over the rental. Part of the expense, in keeping with purity/defilement standards, were the new kitchen and bathroom sinks, the new toilets and tubs that had been installed to create a home suitable for Machvaia living.

Establishing a new *ofisa* usually involves the help of Outsiders in some fashion, the approval of a city council, the expense of a lawyer, possibly notifying the police. What Sutherland (1975:65) wrote about the Roma is still generally true, ". . . the *gadje* are the source of all livelihood and a certain amount of political power . . ." Any hope of a getting and keeping a territory requires the clout of Outsider backing. Otherwise, another fortune-teller, usually from another *vitsa*, can come along, open an *ofisa* nearby, steal the reader's clients, or employ some dastardly means to get their competition evicted.

Many of the Machvanki now do business online, working in their homes at pittance wages for one of the psychic agencies advertised on television. This impersonal mode of work makes it impossible to enlist a client's loyalty and long-term financial support, formerly a reader's back-up money in the bank. In these more difficult times when "everything costs money," the generous communal sharing and giving that once characterized the extended Machvaia family has become nearly impossible. Now each household tries to pay its bills and maintain a decent credit rating, a matter of little concern in the past when a new identity was easily come by and the paper trails of debt not computer-assessable.

The problem of scarce resources is one that wars with the people's ideas about luck; good luck presumes unlimited material goods and unlimited favorable outcomes. Luck *po drom* (on the road), for example, depends on the possibility of more fortuitous outcomes just around the bend. The current environmental situation, with increased costs for energy, food, and travel, with escalating challenges on a global scale, strains Machvaia beliefs about unlimited luck and unlimited generosity.

MACHVAIA DON'T LIVE IN ISOLATION. Although the ones I know seldom vote, they do the same everyday things most Americans are inclined to do: work, shop, cook, sleep, watch television, answer the phone, and follow the changing trends and fashions. As Machvaia lose the backing of the extended family and the support of the group, they compare themselves more often to Americans, particularly the "rich" and middle-class. For those I know, Aid to Dependent Children is no longer a free money windfall. Now, contact with that agency and their impossible-to-read list of rules and forms is considered tragically demeaning.

Most Machvaia adults still find the money to manage the essentials, food, housing, and the gifts, clothes, *dahro*, weddings, and so forth, and continue, in a less ostentatious fashion, to celebrate at parties and rituals. But the size of parties has shrunk from hundreds in a rented hall—often this was the Proud Bird in Los Angeles where walls could be folded back to increase the available space—to relatives and friends in the home. Once, the people were either getting ready for an occasion, a wedding, *slava*, baptism, etc., or reviewing the last one attended. Northern California afforded the possibility of one a week; in Los Angeles, where most Machvaia live, life was one continuous party. But earning a living is the current priority. Guests now tend to arrive at the end of their working days, and the hour for lighting the *slava* candle and taking the bride through the gate has moved from noon to late afternoon. The people have less time for each other, and less time to get together.

In 2000, Pretty Bobbie complained:

These feasts are very expensive. They used to have more.
But we don't have the money. The whole cycle is fading out.
Because we're not so close, not so much clans anymore.
Now we're thinking like individuals. Don't see each other
so much. Used to be everything was public and anyone
could attend. Now, you have to call up before coming over.
Have to be invited. Same at halls. If you're not called, you
don't go. Just like Americans. What they're doing now is
keeping to themselves. They still have *vitchera* and the next
day [*slava*] they light the candle and cook. We still have
holidays, Easter, Christmas, all the holidays. But we're
slowing down.

## Going American

Banton (1981:32–37) sees ethnic change and assimilation as a process in which cultural differences are reduced. Faced with alternatives, he finds this is often the result of the choices of individuals, rather than the group as a whole. In *Anthropology of Experience*,

Bruner (1986:12) writes that people are active agents in the historical process.

> They construct their own world . . . Selves, social organizations, and cultures are not given but are problematic and always in production. Cultural change, cultural continuity, and cultural transmission all occur simultaneously in the experience and expressions of social life.

Lola was usually loath to talk about the old days. For years, whenever I asked her about her childhood, she would hurriedly assure me she was "modern and up to date. You know I was born here." If I persisted, she would state, eyebrows flying up emphatically, "I told you that before. I'm American, not old fashioned." Despite the difficulties and the costs, the families with which I had the closest connections were not adverse to change. Indeed, I was told that despite the many Machvaia institutions of separation, even isolation, they liked and admired Americans.

The people now say they are "going American," a complaint I first heard when Machvaia girls began to run away. Loss of respect etiquette is deplored; during this past century, both men and women have become more careless about respect avoidance. Going American apparently has costs; many young people have difficulty starting a family; they marry, divorce, remarry—like the rest of America—and find it challenging to earn a living. As fortune telling becomes problematical, more wage earning is expected of both men and women. But the modes of preparing the young for their new financial responsibilities seem, as yet, to be invented.

Drinking, once considered a good luck activity that "makes us strong," has become more occasional as the people took heed of the link between heavy alcohol consumption and the health of the liver. With diabetes on the rise, donuts and half-and-half have largely disappeared from in-home hospitality. Formerly all Machvaia in good standing were welcome, and the front door of the house was never locked. But now no one drops in without calling ahead or is likely to show up at an event without a phone invitation. Hospitality service is no longer instantaneous like it was when I visited Lola. Nor is it unlimited. Now, when I arrive, the Machvanka of the house joins me for a few conversational minutes before instructing the children to bring me a glass and a cold bottle of water from the refrigerator. If it is afternoon, my host family takes me to a local restaurant.

Once, the purity-minded housewife was thrilled with the possibilities of America, the bleach, the paper towels, Lysol, the continual raft of new, and more potent, cleaning agents advertised on radio and television. Once, to avoid pollution dangers, the people carried their bedding in the trunk of the car when they traveled, and, if they flew, they took their sheets and a pillow with them in a suitcase. Lola explained about arranging marriage in the old days, when what mattered was simplistically apparent:

> If you're looking for a girl for your son to marry, you ask her for a glass of water. And if she serves you a clean glass with clean hands, then you think she's good.

In the past, upper and lower body items were washed separately; men's, women's, and children's. Forty years ago, to maintain their ritual goodness, Machvanki hand-washed all their giant tablecloths in the kitchen sink and complained about the difficulty wringing, rinsing, and getting them dry. Now, disposable tablecloths or plastic place mats are preferred and the giant tablecloth goes, by itself, into the household's one automatic washer. Once, water bills were enormous. During a water shortage in San Francisco, I remember that Bibi's $400 water bill—Bibi and her maid were always cleaning—involved a sizable fine and a plumber from Pacific Gas & Electric to check for a leak.

WHEN I BEGAN MY STUDIES, the families I visited spoke Romani at home; Romani was a child's first language. English was supplemented with occasional Romani. The television was often on in Katy's storefront, but largely as a background noise; no one seemed to pay it much attention. Now, television may be a grandchild's all-day entertainment. One young man I know even taught himself to read before he was six by faithfully watching Sesame Street. Television and education, Bellah writes (2006:322), are America's chief agencies of socialization.

Robert Bellah finds the cultural power of American English overwhelming, the major factor in acculturation; when language goes, he affirms, so does, in any deep sense, cultural difference (320). Currently, most Machvaia children know very little Romani. Instead, they speak standard and fluent English.

The cultural power of American public school education, however, is negligible; the vast majority of children never finish grade school, least of all high school. The Machvaia household is seldom organized around the needs of a child to get up early, go to school, and find the time for homework. Some Machvaia children are home-schooled with the help of computer lessons. Others, as it was decades back, learn to read and write in a piecemeal fashion, a little time spent with a client here, with an uncle there.

GINA IS ONE OF MY FAVORITE YOUNG WOMEN. Gina is smart, forward thinking, and had hoped to stay in the same middle-class neighborhood where her three children might go through the school system without interruption. "I am not going to move around. This is where I plan to raise my children."

But in such refined suburban circumstances, Gina couldn't advertise her means of employment with a sign. Whenever the opportunity arose, she had to drive hours to tell fortunes with a friend or with her mother. Gina is enterprising. She talks about how Martha Stewart—she saw her on television—started with one cake and went on to make millions. Gina entered a Pillsbury pie contest with a version of pineapple Gypsy strudel (*gushvada*). She even got a business license to cook candy and cakes, to sell at coffee shops and cafes. As she points out, "Fortune telling is up and down. Sometimes you get customer, sometimes not. But everybody eats all the time."

Gina also briefly tried advertising online to market a pricey flower creation she makes: Gemstone roses. But her mother got sick and for months the family was out of town, at the bedside, and the funeral, the *pomani*. On their return, the local school tried private tutoring, but the children were so far behind that they soon dropped out entirely. The fact that the household was in the depressive mourning state likely added to the learning problem. Her means to income gone and no longer able, in any case, to afford her rented house in the suburbs, the family began to travel.

NOW THE PEOPLE LIVE IN CITIES where "everything costs money," where landlords refuse to rent to giant extended families and, encouraged by state aid for the elderly and to families with small children, household size has shrunk. In the past century, the number of offspring has declined from eleven or twelve, to two or three. At one time health was closely tied to Machvaia virtue, and *nasvalimos* (sickness) was believed to be the inevitable result of shame commission and/or association with Outsiders. Now, without the least hesitation or moral stigma, any sign of illness is immediately brought to the attention of Outsider medical doctors. Now, as children defy their elders and do whatever they please, the shame that devolves on those who fail to live in a family right (*vorta*) and raise their children in keeping with custom, no longer has the impact it did.

As seems the invariable case with change, whatever is gained is often, simultaneously, a loss of another kind. As the nuclear family unit gets more emphasis, extended family living has suffered. Grandparents, uncles, and aunts are no longer invariably consulted during crises; nor are they obliged to help. As the influence of elders (and ancestors) erodes, the expansive power, the security of harmonious in-group feeling is less apparent, as is the expectation and excitement surrounding public events. Human relationships, the bonding, blissful moments they spent together were once what the people lived for. Now earning a living is given priority over parties. Once, the people knew who they were, what they were born to do, and they were proud to be Machvaia. Now they aren't entirely sure of what that means.

## Employment

By tradition and according to the ideal, a Machvano's role is to protect and the woman's to provide. But the role of Machvano as an Aly Khan playboy-prince is dated. Most young Machvaia husbands and fathers are required to help with household expenses; they sell used cars, boats, trailers. Sales are the Machvano's forté. Some, I hear, sell real estate. For those whose wives still tell fortunes, the husbands run errands and care for the children.

These days, it usually takes both partners, working together, to raise a family. However, owing to centuries of job insecurity and trying to deal with hostile laws and customs, as well as the challenge of changing economic environments and the uncertainties involved in finding and claiming clients, it can be supposed that the Machvaia lifestyle must always have been equal opportunity in some fashion.

In America, the men's means of employment (playing the stock market, buying and selling real estate and cars, fixing fenders, collecting scrap metal— activities that rank in status from higher to lower) were considered essential to survival, but without the virtue of honor or respect. Earned money involves Outsiders and threatens the loss of a man's ascendant status. Unlike visiting and enjoying Machvaia hospitality, attending *krisa*, or entertaining, all culture-bound activities that relate to the welfare of the community, the business of earning money lacks the refinement of fellowship, generosity, mutual aid, spiritual import, and "good times."

In 1972, when we both were living in Seattle, Lola stunned me by interpreting one of her dreams in which I approached her carrying a cardboard piled with shit on my head as "Good. That's good. Shit means money." Working for money, in the Machvaia view, is a necessary, but essentially profane and not particularly admirable, odor-free pursuit.

Money was once considered the obsession of Outsiders, and the people now complain that they are becoming more and more like the Outsiders. When the people were traveling, Bibi told me, everything, or nearly everything, could be traded—a service for food and water—or it was free. Perhaps reflecting their life experience in America, the Machvaia expressed profound delight with the scene in the movie *Cabaret* in which Liza Minelli and Joel Grey sing and dance to a cynical background patter of "Money, money, money." Now that Machvaia are "going American," the lack of *žao* (empathy) and interconnectedness found in daily contact with Americans leaves much to be desired.

ACCORDING TO BELLAH, television and education, America's chief factors of socialization, follow the narrative lines of state and market institutions. Somewhat bleakly, he writes: "Its only standard is money, and the only thing more sacred than money is more money." He notes that "a dominant element of the common cul-

210

ture is . . . utilitarian individualism, . . . moderated by expressive individualism (322–323) and that this destroys the sense of community and solidarity, as well as the sacredness of the individual (329)."

In truth, working an American-style job usually interferes with matters Machvaia deem of critical importance.

Chally explained the problem:

Most American people that have a job are all tied up. They go to jobs, come home at six or seven, and, the next day, they go back to work. Even the high executives, the people like Bill Gates, they have enough money to buy a country. But Bill Gates has to go to his office and see what's happening there. And he's hardly ever home.

Now, take the Gypsies. They'll work, the car business, doing fenders, telling fortunes, whatever it is they do. But it's always a job that doesn't tie them down. So if something comes along during the week, say a party, someone is sick, someone needs something, and, okay, he's ready to go. In a way it is kind of embarrassing to work. The idea is to keep control, to go to work or not go to work. It's the freedom they want. That's all they are after. [The centuries that Roma were slaves in Romania may have something to do with their anti-authoritarian bias and their prejudice against working for Outsiders.]

Of course who knows what will happen in the future? The young people are so widespread [no longer living in tight-knit extended family situations] and there are so many [the fortune telling population has increased and available territory is limited] that they cause a lot of problems. They get modernized and don't go for the old rules. They flirt around and do a lot of things that were unheard of in the old days. Even myself, at my age, seventy-seven, I can't expect the young to put up with what I did when I was young.

Then, Old Chally sadly admitted that the young with money have too easy a life and they drink too much, adding, "So I see, not too far in the future, the culture slips away."

## Pinky and Sunshine, 2001

I met Pinky in the early Seventies when she and her father King
came to Seattle to pick up Katy. Pinky and I share a novel history:
when she was a teenager and I was in my forties, we were arrested
for telling fortunes—our first time telling fortunes!—at a fair, which,
as we found out later, was in another Machvaia family's territory.

For some time after Katy and King divorced, I would see Pinky
at the public events and learned she, too, had divorced her husband.
In the summer of 2001, I stopped by her house, a three-bedroom on
a busy street. It was easy to find: a "Psychic" sign with their telephone
number hung in the window next to their front door. During my two-
hour visit, as we talked and drank coffee, the phone rang thirteen
times, customers calling who were told by Sunshine, Pinky's tall
eighteen-year-old daughter, to "call back later." When I mentioned
that business seemed to be excellent and that thirteen was more rings
for a similar period than at any of the other houses I'd been in of
late, Pinky was quite pleased. Thirteen is a lucky number for Gypsies.

During my visit, Pinky and Sunshine were eager to discuss
Christianity, their newfound faith.

> *Pinky:* We turned very much Christian. We pray to the Lord.
> We turned pretty much to reading the Bible. And now I
> know why. Cause God always holds you accountable. And if
> you never read it, then you can figure you're a Gypsy, and
> you always got a way out. You could always say, I didn't know!

> *Sunshine:* But we like to know. We want to know and do the
> right way. We go to a little church near the ocean.

> *Djuhli* (that's me): Do you want to marry a Christian man,
> Sunshine?

> *Sunshine:* Yah. I would want a Christian man. I want
> somebody who knows the Lord and is close to the Lord.
> Because I want my life to be right. Someone to be very
> spiritual. I want things to work out right and have the Lord in
> our lives—if we don't, where is it gonna lead us? But you
> know, everything's a gamble. You don't know what's gonna
> happen. Even with the Christian ones.

**212**

*Pinky:* There was one she was interested in. But we couldn't trust him. And if we can't trust now, we can't trust later. He called a lot of girls and said he liked them just to get some money. It's okay to be his friend. But . . .

*Sunshine:* The problem is the Christians are already married or very young. And even Christians, to tell you the truth, there are a few who are no good. They act innocent and good, but they cheat on their wives. That's why we prefer the American church to the Gypsy church. Because I know what they're about. You go to church for one thing, to praise the Lord.

Also, the Americans in the church they attend may not know that Pinky and Sunshine tell fortunes, which is categorized as the Devil's work and forbidden by Pentecostal Christian rules.

At that moment, Pinky's son who is maybe sixteen leaves with two young men in their car to look for work—they buy and sell used cars. She explains that he doesn't drive yet and tells him to avoid the pool hall.

TWO YEARS LATER, when I drive by Pinky's *ofisa*, the sign is gone. I ask how she is making a living, and she affirms Machvaia belief in unlimited good by answering, "the Lord will provide." Sunshine now has a baby, and Pinky says "God is sending this boy big bundles of love. He don't have a father. So God is making everybody love him." Pinky's son is married, and Pinky is now a Prayer Warrior. They go to either the local Gypsy church or the American "Christian" church. As a family, she claims, they have never been happier. She loves the Christians: "You know they care for you with all their hearts." The church has provided her with a community who "help each other," a vast community. "When I go online, I know people (Gypsies) in Germany, London, all over."

The Evangelical movement is widespread in Europe. Magdalena Slavkova (2007:223) studies Gypsies in Bulgaria and attributes their attraction to Evangelical Christianity as owing much to the unemployment resulting from the collapse of the old system of socialism. Pinky, on the other hand, chose to downgrade economically in order to join the State-side Gypsy Christian movement.

Slavkova lists other reasons for the movement's allure that seem more in keeping with Pinky's situation. "The possibility to serve God in their own churches, and to have pastors chosen from their community . . . a chance to feel like a special and chosen people, united emotionally by the belief of their own salvation in the name of Jesus Christ . . . The everyday terms of address of 'brothers and sisters' [and] an active social relationship, based on tolerance, understanding and mutual assistance."

## Mrs. Bridges

Recently, I was at a *pomana*, a memorial feast for the Dead One, with Fatima, Lola's lovely daughter-in-law, the wife of Boyd. When we began talking about the Gypsy Pentecostal Christians, I said I was sorry to learn that Katy, formerly my favorite "religious specialist" regarding matters of ritual and belief, had become a Pentecostal. I knew this because at the last *pomana* we attended, Katy insisted we leave the minute the incense was lighted that welcomes the ancestors to the table. Instead we went to the restaurant next door for dinner, and I regretted missing most of the ritual. Katy's third husband Chally isn't Christian nor likely to become one. But Katy still flies north to spend months with her half-Kalderasha children, and they are now Pentecostal Christians. In fact, Katy's children tell me most of the Kalderasha they know are Pentecostal Christians. Why, I asked Fatima, have some of the Machvaia, Katy and Pinky included, abandoned their tradition of ritual and belief—a tradition I spent a good many years studying!—to become Born-Again.

As Fatima said in 2003:

They must have just found God. Gypsies believe in God, but they must have just found him close. I always felt He was close. That's because of Mrs. Bridges.

At that time [1930s–1940s], when I was little, the women did their business elsewhere, in downtown storefronts, and we lived all together, several Gypsy families, house to house. And we were always having parties. My father didn't drink, but he would bring in barrels of beer to the front yard. And keep it coming. At that time, the Gypsies had a lot of respect and they were proud of who they were. Other people didn't think much of them. But they themselves were very proud. And they didn't marry out of the race and they didn't let anybody in, no American friends. That's why Mrs. Bridges was so special. She'd pick up everybody. She had one of those big cars, a Bonnie and Clyde car, and she'd stop, and we'd come a-running, pack into the car like sardines; all she'd do was blow her horn.

Our parents were so happy. 'Go! Go! Go! Quick! Quick! Quick!' They didn't want us to learn about God. They wanted us to get the hell out of there.

Her Mission was on Fifth Street, and you know what Fifth Street was—nothing but the hobos and drunkards, the worst part of Los Angeles. They probably rented that place for nothing. After awhile, I think she gave up on us. We all knew what we were going to do when we grew up. But we loved her. She had the love of every Gypsy child that she ever knew. We loved her. She glowed, she was radiant with light! Oh my goodness!

The other Mission lady was Mrs. Nelson. She was rather stern. Nobody really liked her. She would get mad no matter what we did and we were all dirty, dirty clothes, dirty hair. My mother would open my braids just once a week, for a bath. My hair was thick, thick hair, and it was long and full of tangles. When they washed my hair and combed it, it took two people and their arms would hurt. It was the worst day of my life when Saturday came. But Mrs. Bridges was a saint. She gave up her life for the Gypsies. She was a missionary in the true sense of the word. Even when she didn't have a church—I guess the Mission gave up on Gypsies—we would go to see her in her little room. We loved her that much, that we wanted to be with her and have her tell us her stories.

After that, Mrs. Bridges was just around the corner. She had one little room, a little gas hot-plate where she would make us little kids cocoa, and she would give us graham crackers. She had a board where she would put the dolls and tell us stories. We learned all about Jesus, Moses, all of them.

And we'd have to sing. And pray. And we'd have to say we'd repent our sins. And we did all that. But to us that didn't mean anything. We went for the cocoa and the cookies. And to be together with our friends.

After I married and moved away, I didn't see her any more. But I heard that she went to the people's houses that she used to teach when they were children. They were always glad to see her. And they would give her a room [to teach in] and she would teach their children. They would call everybody on the telephone and bring all the children together. And I heard that the Gypsies went together and bought her a car—cause she wasn't getting paid nothing any more. And when she died, they paid for her funeral.

We loved Mrs. Bridges.

## Recycling

But when I told Fatima that the Born-Again Christian Gypsies believe only those who have been baptized by the immersion Pentecostal method will go to heaven, she tucked a straying strand of hair into her bun, and a shadow of irritation flickered across her normally serene face.

That's ridiculous. You know all Gypsies go to heaven. Well, maybe that's not it exactly. There's a heaven and a hell, and I don't expect everybody gets to heaven on the first try. When God sees we're not good enough, instead of throwing us to hell, He throws us back here for another life. Anyhow, how do we know there is a hell? I believe He keeps sending us back until we get to be goody-goody. And then He takes us up to Him. He recycles. But if we are so bad He can't think we can ever improve, He sends us to hell. That's what I believe. It makes sense. I never done anything real bad in my life. I think I'm a pretty goody-goody person. You hear a lot about old souls these days. Old souls are people who keep getting recycled.

Now write that down. You have to get it right in your book.

I understand the Pentecostals sing beautiful hymns at their Sunday service, and at the Roma Pentecostal church Pinky goes to, they are encouraged on special occasions to dance. A church with singing and dancing has important elements of tradition and could provide a seductive chapter in the future history of the Church of Cheese. When the older generation dies out, will everyone Machvaia, like so many of the other Roma, become Born-Agains?

I call Fatima to ask her. She admits "the whole world is changing." Sometimes the Christians come to their parties; sometimes they don't. How many Machvaia are Christians? "Some."

She admits she seldom fasts any more and "many of the people stopped making *slava*." (Her family, indeed, has stopped.) People don't travel for rituals like they did. People are "too modern, too much for themselves, and not as generous," meaning they are not throwing money away with stylish aplomb—this, I remember with a pang, was always Lola's preference! "Before," she says, "life was beautiful, easy, and now it's hectic."

But she still keeps her kitchen and her cooking *vorta* (right and pure). When they stay overnight in a motel, although her husband Boyd doesn't worry about the practices of the hotel laundry or his bedding's contact with previous tenants, she invariably puts her own pillowcase, or a blouse, over her hotel pillow.

Despite the tendency toward going American, Fatima assured me that the Machvaia will always be together—sharing and together. She, too, can't imagine a time when Machvaia might fail to be generous. But, as she admitted, she didn't really know much about what the young Machvaia people were doing. Neither, unfortunately, do I.

## It's John Travolta's Fault

In 2000, Luludji, a rather conservative Machvanka whose *ofisa* is a few blocks from where I once lived in Pacific Heights shared her thoughts with me: John Travolta, she had decided, ruined the Machvaia.

A month ago, Kenny and I were talking about that, about how everyone copied John Travolta, everybody started

217

changing. Everybody went to pot. Free to be was the word. And now it's like, this is what I'm going to do and I don't care who's involved or who gets hurt. There's no more elderly to punish them. There's no more fear [of elders, ancestors, ghosts, bad luck], no more. In my day, you wasn't so afraid of God because, being All-Goodness, you know he would forgive. But parents, the grandparents don't forgive, and now who cares? Now who's going to point the finger on who? [The finger of shame signifying disapproval and creating the gossip that stains reputation.]

That old tradition way is gone. And the California Gypsies are the last to change. The New York Gypsies were first. Then the down-South were next. We didn't used to talk to people from New York—it was like saying people from the ghetto came. In New York, you get a little bit of everything, all mixed up [in terms of intermarriage of *vitsi* and custom]. But California was last.

*Conclusion*

# PO DROM IN AMERICA

## How It Began

On the whole, the United States, already a varietal mix, has been a relatively benign environment for the various groups popularly called Gypsies. In some contrast to the average Kalderasha *vitsa* of, according to Gropper (1998: 230), three hundred, the Machvaia population grew to about 5,000. Most aren't visible in the ethnic sense and, even today, the Machvaia in America can, if they like, successfully hide their identity. But, when the Machvaia first arrived with their horses, their wagons, and their tents, they were easily recognized as Gypsies. On occasion they were stopped, penalized, harassed.

Normally, Lola didn't like to talk about the old days. But, as I began to travel to California to meet more Machvaia—sometimes I was gone for months—to encourage me to spend more time in Seattle, she began to entice me with stories about *po drom* (on the road), when the people were still traveling. One afternoon, over coffee, she recalled the time her mother-in-law and her sister-in-law were strip-searched by Nevada police and ordered to dance in the nude on a table.

> *Lola:* My mother-in-law didn't like it and she didn't want to stand there like that. She turned around and stuck her *bul* (backside) in their faces. 'Here's so you can see through and through.' I think they could have sued the police But we didn't know about that then.

**219**

I was appalled, but the way Lola told this story made it clear that, from her standpoint, the shame had the reverse effect. The polluting effect of males viewing a female's genitals was an event considered "the worst," and, combined with the women's curses—in Romani, of course—might well render the men impotent, debilitated by disease, and possibly result in their untimely deaths. But maybe not, Lola shrugged, since the police weren't Roma by blood.

I SUSPECT I LEARNED VERY LITTLE about incidents of Outsider cruelty when the people were traveling, in part because my Gypsy friends didn't want to upset me, but also because Machvaia believe that recounting the bad luck of past sorrows tends to make them recur. Move on, Lola would say, and forget. In 1995, however, I was visiting Boyd's family and he bravely recounted an experience his people had *po drom* (on the road), offering, at the story's end, a whitewash of explanation.

*Boyd:* Our history is sad. My grandfather Atarino was crossing a ranch and the rancher warned him to leave. So the wagons traveled all day and camped. But that was still the rancher's property. So the rancher's men strung up the Gypsy men and whipped them. They would have killed them if the Gypsy women hadn't stopped them.

The reason was probably that they thought the Gypsies were squatters and wanted land. Used to be that people owned land after cultivating it for awhile.

At the turn of the 20th century, when the people were fresh from Serbia, they sold horses, worked odd jobs, told fortunes, and begged for the necessities. Lola was sent to the farmer's door to ask for food because, as she explained, "I was littlest and prettiest." Bibi admitted, "It was a hard life. A very hard life."

Lola's father died when Lola was still small and Stanya, her mother, was left with a wagonload of children. For a time, they joined Stanya's brother, Zhurka. Stanya had many offers of marriage from men, Lola said, who were already married. Eventually she remarried, but the marriage didn't last. Stanya's adult sons refused to share Stanya's money.

BIBI WAS STILL A LITTLE GIRL when her family "got" Lola as *bori.* "Nonnie was seven when I was nine. Prahli was younger. My father [Atarino] fixed my hair and did the cooking."

Atarino's family made their living by splitting up. His eldest son Bahto and the women, Atarino's wife and the daughters-in-law, traveled by train half the year, following the fairs and telling fortunes, "like a circus . . . six months traveling and six months camping. In contrast, Atarino and the children didn't move much. "All summer," Bibi said, "we didn't see them."

In the fall, the family assembled in Pueblo or Colorado Springs, and "it would take us months to get there." The winters were cold. On nice winter days, they washed clothes, cleared the wagons out, and Bibi's father traded horses.

> *Bibi:* To keep the tent warm, we had hay under the tent and an old stove with a hole in it. Then, one dollar was a fortune, and no one needed money. We got food from the farmers. You could just put a horse out in a field and let him eat. We bought oil for the lanterns, five cents a can. Everything else was trade. Or free.

The trip from New York to California by wagon took six to seven months. Rural America, dotted with fields and farms, seemed vast and perhaps not that different from the Serbian province the newcomers had left. *Po drom* was a time of scary ghosts and fears— Lola allowed that ghosts were fears, but Bibi didn't think so: "Ghosts are ghosts!" It was a time when elders were obeyed without question, in part because the country, language, and the customs were strange, traveling slow and difficult, destinations uncertain, and a family had to stick together. It was a time of bravura myths and legends, of memorable dancing and musical exploits, of heroic fables and extraordinary accomplishments—Madame Butterfly's, for example, whose name was suggested by the capacious skirts she held above her head and fluttered when she danced. Back then, good luck implied the happiness of endless possibilities and unlimited resources and, failing to find these boons, the people promptly went *po drom* to look for luck. Then, whenever they met other Roma on the road, the people explained they were from Machva, Serbia; they identified themselves as the people of Machva. The Machvaia.

A new *vitsa* (named lineage group) was born through the people's Serbian connection, the back velar accent of their Romanes, their similar food preferences, the familiarity of expectations regarding respect behaviors, belief systems and the custom of *slava*; these influenced Machvaia marital choices and the people's future. (Interestingly, by the time I began fieldwork in Seattle, many of the other American Roma, including those not from Serbia, seem also to have adopted the *slava*.)

THE FIRST ROM FROM MACHVA was Zhurka Adamovich; his descendants are known as Adams. Zhurka's brother was Georgi; his lineage is also known as Adams, or Adamovich, the most common surname in Serbia. Zhurka's sister Maria married Elia and that lineage became the Lees. Zhurka's sister's daughter Lola married Bahto who was the son of Zhurka's first cousin, Atarino Pavlovich; this lineage is known as Pavlovich or Williams. Atarino's nephew, the hot-tempered Rožarko, married to the white-skinned Turkish Gypsy Nata, started the Todorovich lineage. Atarino's wife had three brothers, Ĵivko, Yotsa Pete, and Tukano; they followed her to America and became the second Adams *vitsa*. Mitza of Serbia married Iesho Merino; he was from an Italian carnival family who traveled the world. Iesho married his three sons to Zhurka's granddaughters, a lineage now known as the Merinos. There are several lineages called Yovanovich and one has more of a history in New York than California. Raiko Yovanovitch was the eldest of a number of brothers in a lineage sometimes called Raikershti, suggesting Raiko may have been a Serbian Kalderasha Rom. Zhurka's nieces married two of Raiko's sons and among their California descendants are Madame Butterfly and her money-lucky younger cousin, 1-2-3. A pair of brothers, Three-Fingered Ĵivko, and Tété Yovanovich, arrived with their Serbian Gypsy wives, soon followed by cousins Dushano John and his brother Aratso. (When we met in the Seventies, Ĵivko's wife, Old Loli, was, the people said, older than one hundred.) After Dushano John's wife left him, he married Atarino's daughter, Kata; that lineage is called the Johns. More recent additions, the ones of which I am aware, are the Los Angeles

Stevens—the second marriage of Big George Adams, Zhurka's notable grandson, was to a Stevens—and a San Diego Marx family. A *vitsa*, as Sutherland notes (182) is primarily a unit of identification, and five generations of marriage in America to mostly Roma of Serbian background has created the *vitsa* Machvaia. (See Sutherland: 1975 for more about *vitsi*.)

BY THE LATE EIGHTIES, Katy had married again. A considerable catch, good-natured Chally was heir to a lucrative California fortune-telling territory and a house in San Jose with a tiny orchard. Single women in his age group wanted him. Happy Katy got him.

Chally admitted he had never met Zhurka. But Chally wanted me to know that more than a hundred years ago, "Zhurka was already advanced. He had foresight and did a great many great things. My wife is related to Zhurka." He was very proud of this last.

Learning I intended to write a book about his people, Chally wanted to impress me, his new wife's friend, with the importance of his *vitsa*. Machvaia, he said, are pretty much close knit. They speak different, different words, different pronunciations, and "we don't mix much with the other Gypsies." He pointed out the Machvaia tendency to "Irish skin," as the people put it. His grandmother, Mitza Adamovich, had green eyes and red hair. Many Kalderasha were now rich and comfortably off. But Machvaia, he said, had been rich for most of the last century. Chally gave examples:

> Lažo Lee. Lažo's mother had a big family of sons. They owned a saloon—most of the old-timers were booze people. And when the train depot wanted that property, they bought it—like it or not, you had to sell to them. So Lažo had a lump sum of money. In those days, $100, 000 was big money.
>
> Dushano John was rich, too; he was known as Dushano Barvalo, big, rich, and important. He saved—he was smart that way. It is a known fact that the IRS got him; they knew he was Barvalo.

I have heard this story differently. Barbara Miller, who I addressed as Bibio, says Dushano's wife, not he, made, saved, and handled the money, that Dushano couldn't read and had no idea what was written in his savings account. When the IRS asked to see his bank book, he didn't hesitate and gave it to them. Bibio didn't remember how much time Dushano spent in jail.

Presuming the past was instrumental to the present, I spent many hours in Bibi's storefront, learning about the days of old. Like Chally, Bibi was concerned with impressing me with the superior rank of the Machvaia *vitsa*.

Zhurka knew my father's mother in Serbia. She was a big shot. Grandmother Puda had a *cafana*—that's like a coffee house here. In the Old Country, [the Serbs give a dowry of] property, cows, pigs, when you marry your daughter. Puda had three daughters. She advertised for a groom and people came to spend money at her *cafana*. The restaurant had tables inside and outside. The [prospective suitors] would stay several weeks and she'd make money. My grandfather was dead and she did all this by herself.

Grandmother Puda was friends to kings and queens. When the Queen was having a party, she would send her carriage for my grandmother so she could entertain the people by giving them their fortune. Then the Serbs began to fight the Turks, and my grandmother wanted her son to [avoid conscription]. She told Atarino to go with Zhurka to America. My grandmother was also a little embarrassed that Atarino had married my mother, Seka. She was plain and lower class. So Puda sent him away.

My parents had four children already when they came to this country [and four more children later]. My father was a no-name in Serbia. He built his name here.

When his sons grew up, my father, Atarino, went back to Serbia for brides. That was the last time he saw his mother.

## Zhurka

According to those who remember, Zhurka arrived in America sometime before the turn of the 20th century. Then he went back to sell his farms in Serbia and told his friends and relatives about the opportunity for "good living" in America, how there weren't too many Gypsies, how the natives were rich and generous.

ON HIS SECOND TRIP TO AMERICA, Zhurka returned with his parents, a son Marko, a daughter, his wife. According to Lola:

> Zhurka gave my parents money for the boat and they all came together. My mother said he was right; America was rich. The place she left was pretty poor.

Lola, Zhurka's niece, recalled her uncle as "smart, dark, heavy set, and brave." She had this to say in 1970:

> He was really good at business. Full of ideas for making money. I remember when he set up a Gypsy Village at the Chicago World's Fair—I think that's what it was. His wife Mileva played a Gypsy Queen with a throne and a crown, and handed out hat pins as souvenirs. The daughter-in-law and my mother danced—Gypsy dancing. Then, everyone went to booths and told some fortunes.
>
> The village lasted a month. Zhurka made money, lots of money. With the money, he bought a block of apartments in Sacramento. Before that, he bought land in Chicago, a wheat farm in North Dakota, property in San Pablo. He stayed in California most of his life. Had a grocery store, a butcher shop, a cleaners, and Americans worked for him. He was Ashundo Rom. Big. He never got in trouble with nobody, he always was a business man. Good tempered. He didn't dance. But his son did.

But even the best and luckiest families can feel the sting of ill fortune. When Zhurka's daughter died, Zhurka was left with one child who didn't take after his father.

*Bibi:* Marko was a drinker, an eater, and he wasn't much for business. He had a walnut farm in Los Angeles, but his wife made all the money. What was she like? Really pretty, and a redhead. But Šrecha had a hot temper and couldn't get along with her mother-in-law. [Šrecha's mother-in-law was Marko's stepmother. Marko's mother had died and Zhurka remarried.] Marko sided with his wife. [At that time, as in Hindu custom, a son who sided with his wife rather than his mother brought shame to the family.] Zhurka disowned him.

My father and Zhurka were close friends. Before he died [because he now had no Machvaia son to depend on], Zhurka asked my father to take care of his funeral arrangements.

Marko and Šrecha are buried in a large multi-plex mausoleum in the Machvaia area of a Sacramento cemetery, at some distance from Zurka's little house. Zhurka's mausoleum, I note, was recently furnished with a television set. I think of it as an alternate reality, the Land of the Dead Ones. The Machvaia graveyard is a land visited Easter, Memorial Day, all holidays, as often possible.

BY THE MID-TWENTIES, Machvaia families had cars and began setting up fortune telling offices in cities and towns. By the Thirties, looking for business and staying long enough to test the income-making possibilities of an area, most families were developing a seasonal territory. Summer months, the north California Machvaia met on the shores of the Sacramento River to pitch tents, party, celebrate Saint George's *slava* or Saint Anne's, arrange marriages, and exchange gossip. This summer recreation of the earlier traveling days continued until World War II, about which time two teenaged sisters drowned in the Sacramento River, and the river became bad luck.

In 1994, Rose, had more to say about *po drom*:

> My mother says that in those days, when you arrived at someone's tent, you'd give the woman all your money. No banks, no safety deposits. People carried everything they had with them and the woman of the house could always be trusted. In those days, people shared and helped, gave whatever was needed, the shirt off the back if you asked for it. And there was real trust. Real respect.

Now, since the young people went to school and we stayed in one place for awhile, we got to know Americans. We got American friends and we changed. No trust like there once was between Gypsies. No more Ashundo Rom. That was a Rom with a good name, a nice family, keep out of trouble with the other [Roma] people. A classy man who could keep his family in line. A well-liked man with a good reputation.

Rose went on to explain about reputation. It seems that an Ashundo Rom is a man who has been married only once and to someone of the Machvaia kind; a man who has no one in his family or bloodline who ever tried running away, *nashlimos*, to America; no one in his family was ever arrested by the American (Outsider) police; this is a man who has lived in harmony with all the other Roma in the same *vitsa*, i.e., he lacks jealous enemies who might start defaming rumors.

Becoming Ashundo was, of course, a much better possibility when traveling was slow and difficult, communication by phone problematical, immigrant families small, their reputation stories still in Serbia, and those met and feted on the road might never be seen again.

*Rose:* Now, when something [bad] happens, nobody can hide the shame. People will call on the phone, send telegrams, email. The daughter-in-law goes home to her family and tells all your family secrets. Some way, the word gets out. Used to be a family could keep a secret and cover up. Now, we know everyone has someone in his family who is doing things they shouldn't. Some kind of hanky-panky. No more perfect reputations. No more perfect families. No more Ashundo Rom. Maybe Zhurka was the last Ashundo Rom.

Once, the Machvaia were high class and lucky, the most beautiful, pure, and respected of all the Roma. Parties were what the people lived for and no one, Gypsy or not, could drink, dance, sing, or show the Saints a better time. Once, the Old Ones were obeyed without question; They knew everything important and, transitioning into Dead Ones, became a first-line defense for the living. When Out-siders were still Outsiders, the Machvaia were mostly kinsmen, cousins, and they stuck together like glue. Water and grass for the horses were easily found, alms freely given, food freely shared, and generosity the norm. Money, although handy on occasion, was crit-ically rated as another *dihli* (crazy) Outsider obsession.

But that was another time.

# BIBLIOGRAPHY

Banton, Michael. "The Direction and Speed of Ethnic Change." In *Ethnic Change*, edited by Charles F. Keyes. 31–52. Seattle: U of Washington Press, 1981.

Bellah, Robert. "Is There a Common American Culture." In *The Robert Bellah Reader*, edited by Robert N. Bellah & Steven M. Tipton. 319–332. Durham: Duke University, 2006.

Brown, Steven & Lawrence M. Parsons." The Neuroscience of Dance." In *Scientific American*. 78–83. July 2008.

Bruner, Edward M. "Experience and its expressions." In *The Anthropology of Experience*, edited by E.M.Bruner & V.W. Turner. 3–30. Urbana, Ill: U of Illinois Press, 1986.

Cartwright, Garth. *Princes Amongst Men: Journeys with Gypsy Musicians.* London: Serpent's Tail, 2005.

Das, Veena. "On the Categorization of Space in Hindu Ritual" In *Text and Context: The Social Anthropology of Tradition*, edited by Ravinda K. Jain. 9–27. Philadelphia: Institute for the Study of Human Issues, 1977.

David, Kenneth A. "Until marriage do us part: a cultural account of Jaffna Tamil categories for kinsmen." *Man*, n.s., 8: 521–535. 1973

Douglas, Mary. *Purity and Danger.* London: Routledge and Kegan Paul, 1966.

Ehrenreich, Barbara. *Dancing in the Streets: A History of Collective Joy.* NY; Henry Holt & Co, 2006.

Fraser, Angus. *The Gypsies.* Oxford: Blackwell, 1992.

Freeman, Walter. "A Neurobiological Role of Music in Social Bonding." In *The Origins of Music*, edited by Nils L. Wallin, Björn Merker, and Steven Brown. 411–424. Cambridge, Mass.: MIT Press, 2000.

Gheorghe, Nicolae & Thomas Acton. "Citizens of the world and nowhere: Minority, Ethnic and human rights for the Roma for the last hurrah of the nation-state." In *Between past and future— the Roma of Central and Eastern Europe*, edited by Will Guy. 54–70. Great Britain: University of Hertfordshire Press, 2001.

Gjerdman, Olof & Erik Ljungberg. *The Language of the Swedish Coppersmith Gipsy Johan Dimitri Taikon.*Uppsala: A-B Lundequistska, 1963.

Goffman, Ernest. *Interaction Ritual: Essays on Face-to-Face Behavior.* New York: Pantheon, 1967.

———— *Stigma; notes on the management of spoiled identity.* Englewood Cliffs, N.J.: Prentice Hall, 1963.

Gresham, David, Bharti Morar, Peter A. Underhill, Giuseppe Passarino, Alice A. Lin, Cheryl Wise, Dora Angelicheva, Francesc Calafell, Peter J. Oefner, Peidong Shen, Ivailo Tournev, Rosario de Pablo, Vaidutis Kučinskas, Anna Perez-Lezaun, Elena Marushiakova, Vesselin Popov, Luba Kalaydjieva. "Origins and Divergence of the Roma (Gypsies)." *American J. of Human Genetics* 69: 1314–1331. 2001.

Gropper, Rena Cotton. "Sex Dichotomy Among the Kalderaš Gypsies" In *Gypsies: An Interdisciplinary Reader*, edited by Diane Tong. 219–232. NY: Garland Publishing, 1998.

———— *Gypsies In The City*. Princeton: The Darwin Press, 1975.

———— "Urban Nomads—the Gypsies of New York City," In *Transactions of the New York Academy of Sciences*. Series II: 29: 1050–1056. 1967.

Halpern, Joel M. & Barbara Kerewsky Halpern. *A Serbian Village in Historical Perspective.* New York: Holt, Rinehart & Winston, 1972.

Hancock, Ian. *We Are The Romani People.* Hertfordshire: U of Hertfordshire Press, 2002.

———— "The schooling of Romani Americans: an overview." Keynote paper read before the Second International Conference on the Psycholinguistic and Sociolinguistic Problems of Roma Children's Education in Europe, Varna, Bulgaria, 1999.

Harper, Edward B. "Fear and the Status of Women." In *Southwestern Journal of Anthropology* 25: 81–95. 1969.

Hughes-Freeland, Felicia. "Introduction" In *Ritual, Performance, Media,* edited by F. Hughes-Freeland. ASA Monographs 35: 1–28. London: Routledge, 1998.

Inden, Ronald B. *Marriage and Rank in Bengali Culture: A history of caste and clan in Middle Period Bengal.* Berkeley: U of California Press, 1976.

Ioviță, Radu P. and Theodore G. Shurr. "Reconstructing the Origins and Migrations of Diasporic Populations; The Case of the European Gypsies." *American Anthropologist,* v 106, no.2: 267–81. 2004.

Keyes, Charles F. "The Dialectics of Ethnic Change." In *Ethnic Change,* edited by Charles Keyes. 3–30. Seattle: U of Washington Press, 1981.

Khare, Ravindra S. *The Hindu Hearth and Home.* Durham, N Carolina: Academic Press, 1975.

Kolenda, Pauline M. "Religious Anxiety and Hindu Fate." *Journal of Asian Studies* 23: 71–81. 1964.

Kovats, Martin. "The emergence of European Roma policy." In *Between past and future: the Roma of Central and Eastern Europe,* edited by Will Guy. 93–116. Hertfordshire; U of Hertfordshire Press, 2001.

Lacková, Ilona. *A false dawn: My life as a Gypsy woman in Slovania.* Recorded, translated from Romani and edited by Milena Hübschmannová. Translated from Czech by Carleton Bulkin. Centre de recherches tsiganes: University of Hertfordshire Press, 1999.

Langer, Suzanne. *Feeling and Form: A Theory of Art.* London: Routledge and Kegan Paul, 1953.

Leblon, Bernard. *Musiques Tsiganes et Flamenco.* Paris: L'Harmattan, 1990.

Lee, Ronald. "The Gypsies in Canada." *JGLS*, 5th series, v. 47: 12–20. 1968.

Marriott, McKim. "Hindu Transactions: Diversity Without Dualism." In *Transaction and Meaning: Directions in the Anthropology of Exchange and Symbolic Behavior,* edited by Bruce Kapferer. 109–142. Philadelphia: Institute for the Study of Human Issues, 1976.

Marriott, McKim & Ronald B. Inden. "Toward an Ethnosociology of South Asian Caste Systems." In *The New Wind: Changing Identities in South Asia,* edited by Kenneth David. 227–238. The Hague: Mouton Publishers, 1977.

———— Caste systems. *Encyclopaedia Britannica.* Vol. 3, 1974.

———— Towards an ethnosociology of Hindu caste systems. 9th International Congress of Anthropological and Theological Sciences, Chicago. Paper no. 2206, 1973.

Matras, Yaron. *Romani: A linguistic introduction.* Cambridge: Cambridge U Press, 2002.

Mauss, Marcel. *The Gift: The Form and Reason for Exchange in Archaic Societies,* trans W. D. Halls, NY: Norton, 1990. From earlier *Essai sur le Don,* Presses Universitaires de France, 1950.

Maximoff, Mateo "Coutumes des Tsiganes Kalderash." In *Etudes Tsiganes* 6 (1) July-September 10–17, 1960.

Meyrowitz, Joshua. "Redefining the Situation: Extending dramaturgy into a theory of social change and media effects." In *Beyond Goffman: studies on communication, institution, and social interaction,* edited by Stephen H. Riggins. 64–97. Berlin: Mouton de Gruyter, 1990.

Miller, Carol. "Luck: How Machvaia Make It and Keep It." In *Journal of the Gypsy Lore Society* 5, v7, #1: 1–26. 1997.

— "American Rom and the ideology of defilement." In *Gypsies, Tinkers, and other Travellers,* edited by Farnham Rehfisch. 41–54. London: Academic Press, 1975.

Myers, John. "The 'Greek' Nomads in South Wales." In *JGLS* Third Series 22, #3: 84–100. 1943.

Nettl, Bruno. "An Ethnomusicologist Contemplates Universals in Musical Sound and Musical Culture." In *The Origins of Music,* edited by Nils L. Wallin, Björn Merker, and Steven Brown. 463–472. Cambridge: MIT Press, 2000.

Nicholas, Ralph W. & Ronald Inden. "The defining features of kinship in Bengali culture." Mimeographed, 1970.

O'Flaherty, Wendy Doniger. "Introduction." In *Karma and Rebirth in Classical Indian Tradition,* edited by O'Flaherty. ix–xxv. Berkeley: University of California Press, 1980a.

———— "Karma and Rebirth in the Vedas and Puranas." In *Karma and Rebirth in Classical Indian Tradition,* edited by O'Flaherty. ix–xxv. Berkeley: U of California Press, 1980b.

Ortner, Sherry B. & Harriet Whitehead. "Introduction: Accounting for Sexual Meanings" In *Sexual Meanings*, edited by Ortner and Whitehead. 1–27. Cambridge: Cambridge University Press, 1981.

Petrović, Dr. Alexander. "*BaX thai BibaX* (Good and Bad Luck)." *JGLS*; 3rd series. v XIX: 34–42. 1940.

———— "The Celebration of Christmas, New Year, and Easter Among the Serbian Gypsies." *JGLS*; 3rd series, v XVII: 67–74. 1938.

Poueyto, Jean-Luc. "The Here and Beyond in the Manush World-view" in *Ethnic Identities In Dynamic Perspective*, edited by Sheila Salo & Csaba Prónai. 19–23. Budapest: Gondolat, 2003.

Salo, Matt & Sheila. "Gypsy Immigration to the United States" In *Papers from the Sixth and Seventh Annual Meetings, Gypsy Lore Society*, North American Chapter, #3, edited by Joanne Grumet. 85–96. New York, 1986.

Sampson, John. *The Dialect of the gypsies of Wales, being the older form of British Romani preserved in the speech of the clan of Abram Wood.* Oxford; Clarendan, 1926.

Schieffelin, Edward L. "Problematizing performance" In *Ritual, Performance, Media*, edited by Felicia Hughes-Freeland, ASA Monograph 35. 194–207. London: Routledge, 1998.

Simić, Andrei. "Winners and Losers: Aging Yugoslavs in a Changing World" In *Life's Career—Aging: Cultural Variations on Growing Old*, edited by Barbara G. Myerhoff & Andrei Simić. 77–105. Beverly Hills: Sage Publications, 1978.

Slavkova, Magdalena. "Evangelical Gypsies in Bulgaria: Way of life and performance of identity" In *Romani Studies* 5th Series v.XVI #2: 205–46. 2007.

Spencer, Paul. *Society and the Dance: The social anthropology of process and performance*, edited by Paul Spencer. Cambridge: Cambridge University Press, 1985.

Spiro, Melford. *Anthropological Other or Burmese Brother?* New Brunswick(USA): Transaction Publishers, 1992.

Sutherland, Anne. *Gypsies, the Hidden Americans.* NY: The Free Press, 1975.

Sway, Marlene. *Familiar Strangers: Gypsy Life in America.* Chicago: U. of Illinois Press, 1988.

Thomas, Paul. *Hindu Religion, Customs, and Manners.* Bombay: D. B. Taraporevela Sons & Co.(n.d.)

Tillhagen, Carl-Herman. "Funeral and Death Customs of the Swedish Gypsies" In *JGLS* XXXI 1–2, (1952): 29–54.

Tong, Diane. *Gypsy Folktales.* San Diego: Harcourt Brace Jovanovich, 1989.

Turner, Victor W. *The Anthropology of Performance.* NY: PAJ Publications, 1986.

——— "Death and the Dead in the Pilgrimage Process." In *Religious Encounters with Death: insights from the history and anthropology of religions,* edited by Frank Reynolds & Earle H. Waugh. 24–39. University Park: Pennsylvania State University Press, 1977.

——— *The Ritual Process.* London: Routledge Kegan and Paul, 1969.

Vishnevsky, Victor. *Memories of a Gypsy.* Maryland: Salo Press, 2006.

Wadley, Susan S. *Struggling with destiny in Karimpur,1925–1984.* Berkeley: U of California Press, 1994.

Weyrauch, Walter O. & Maureen Anne Bell. "Autonomous Lawmaking" In *Gypsy Law: Romani Legal Traditions and Culture,* edited by W.O. Weyrauch. 11–87. Berkeley: U of California Press, 2001.

Williams, Patrick. *Gypsy World: The Silence of the Living and the Voices of the Dead,* translated by Catherine Tihanyi. Chicago: The U of Chicago Press, 2003.

——— Review of "Musiques Tsiganes et Flamenco" by Bernard Leblon. JGLS 5, v 2, no 1:85–89. 1992.

Yoors, Jan. *The Gypsies.* NY: Simon and Schuster, 1967.

# GLOSSARY

*R*omani vocabulary and pronunciation.

In the preceding text, many places and personal names have been changed, except for those of the dead. In choosing new Gypsy names, I have stayed within the realm of possibility; Mileva (Mee-lay-vah), Duda (Doo-dah), Zhurka (Zhoor-kah), Duiyo (Doo-ee-yo) and spelled according to sound—as best I could. American-style names are spelled accordingly, Katy, Boyd, Robert, Ephram.

e or é=say, i=see, a=saw, o=sew, u=sue, g=go, ie=ever, ž=azure,

X=loch as in Scottish pronunciation.
r is a French flap.
R, as Rom, Roma, romani, a post-velar sounded/aspirated roll at the back of the throat.
romani terms ending in av=Ow!

abéav—wedding, wedding ritual
baro, i—big, masculine, feminine
baX—good luck
bori, boria—daughter-in-law, daughters-in-law
capella—chapel for Dead One
chivri, chivro—godparent, fem, masc.
dahro—gift
devlesko, godly, 'up'

235

diklo—scarf
djuhli—American woman
gadzé—all non-Gypsy people
gindo, ginduria—thought, intent, (singular, plural).
gushvada—strudel
kris, krisa—law and court, (singular, plural).
latcho, latchi—good, masculine, feminine
marimé—defiled, impure
muli, mulo, mulé—dead woman, dead man, many Dead Ones.
ofisa, ofisuria—fortune telling office (singular, plural)
patchiv, patchiva—respect or party honoring a special
    person, many parties of honor
pomana, i—funeral commemoration (singular, plural)
sarma—stuffed cabbage rolls
sevahpo—favor, help, holy gift
slava, slavi, slavaria—saint-day (singular, plural), slava
    celebrants
vitsa, vitsi—named lineage group (singular, plural)
vužo—clean, pure
žaléa—grief